Legitimate and Illegitimate Discrimination:

New Issues in Migration

Legitimate and Illegitimate Discrimination:
New Issues in Migration

EDITED BY

Howard Adelman

York Lanes Press, Inc.
Toronto

Canadian Cataloguing in Publication Data

Main entry under title:

Legitimate and illegitimate discrimination: new issues in migration

Includes bibliographical references and index.
ISBN 1–55014–238–0

1. Refugees — Government policy.
2. Emigration and immigration — Government policy
I. Adelman, Howard, 1938–   .

JV6346.R4L44 1944   325'.21   C95–930249–2

Published by
York Lanes Press, Inc.
Suite 351, York Lanes
York University
4700 Keele Street
North York ON M3J 1P3
Canada

Printed in Canada by University of Toronto Press Inc.

Contents

Introduction

Howard Adelman

This volume is concerned with legitimacy. In general, governments are considered legitimate if they effectively control the states and territories that they govern, and are recognized by other states as doing so. Democratic governments are considered legitimate only if they are selected by and are responsive to their constituents and operate according to due process and the law of the land. Increasingly democratic governments are no longer willing to recognize other governments as legitimate if they achieve power through conquest (e.g., Iraq's invasion of Kuwait) or through the overthrow of a democratically-elected government (e.g., the military overthrow of President Jean-Bertrand Aristide of Haiti in September 1991), or, in some cases, even when the state exercises authority and rule over a specified territory of the state occupied by a concentrated minority-nationality that is unwilling to be subject to the sovereign will of the majority population.

This volume, which reflects situations in 1991, contends that these traditional concepts of legitimacy (effective control, rule by consent of the governed, acceptance by concentrated minorities) are not a democratic state's only criteria of legitimacy. Whether that government interferes with its members' freedom to leave also reflects on its democratic legitimacy. This now seems uncontroversial, although it was not always so. When liberal theory was formulated, theorists contended that individuals had only a conditional right of expatriation—members were allowed to leave if the state did not require their services for defence or if they surrendered any claims to property. In the twentieth century, Communist regimes sometimes allowed expatriation only if individuals repaid costs the state incurred in their health care and education. However, the right to leave is now accepted as a universal criterion for determining the legitimacy of a democratic state.

Three corollaries of the principle of freedom to leave are also valid. If the members of a state are forced to flee, the legitimacy of that government is questionable. If members cannot leave, the government is not democratically legitimate. If members must leave, the government is also not democratically legitimate.

The controversial additional principle concerns the right to enter, not the right to leave. If individuals cannot enter another state when circumstances in their state of habitual residence have forced their exodus, the democratic legitimacy of the government that is denying them entry is also questionable. The claim that legitimacy of democratic states also depends on the freedom of refugees to enter, to work and possibly become members of that state, are controversial principles for determining legitimacy. Like the principle of freedom to leave, the right of entry for refugees concerns migration. Unlike the principle of the freedom to leave, or any other principle concerning the legitimacy of a democratic government, legitimacy in this case depends on the treatment of nonmembers. The right of refugees to enter is the major principle that we will explore.

Generally, the view is widespread that all states, including democratic ones, have the right to exclude nonmembers at will. More importantly, it is generally considered a sovereign state's prerogative to decide who to accept or reject as new members. This volume challenges those widespread beliefs. While limiting access and determining who may or may not become members remains a legitimate prerogative of a sovereign democratic state, the criteria, rules and processes for doing so must be compatible with their character as democratic states. Democratic states cannot use undemocratic methods to limit access or determine the selection procedures for admitting new members, temporary visitors or workers. The authority to admit new members or temporary residents is *not* an absolute but a restricted authority for a democratic state. Furthermore, and even more controversially, democratic states have an obligation to admit genuine refugees as members.

Though we will touch on the rules for entry of visitors, students and temporary workers, this volume concentrates on providing guidelines for *immigration* procedures in democratic states. These guidelines will not be deduced from first principles in a Rawlsian way from the principles of entry to membership in a perfectly just democratic society. These papers are concerned with rules establishing legitimacy rather than the moral and theoretical justification of those rules, whether that justification is based on natural law theory, theories of sovereign power, theories of consent, justice or republican political theory. Rainer Bauböck's theoretical essay is intended to clarify those principles of legitimacy but not their justification.

Membership in any prosperous Western democratic society is a scarce commodity in this overcrowded world. We are not concerned with the first principles of distributive justice for allocating such a scarce resource among the many who would like to gain access to it. We want to argue that, in order to be legitimate, a democratic state must provide access to membership and do so in a way that is compatible with democratic norms. By surveying, analyzing and critiquing the norms prevalent in a variety of states, we hope to clarify the principles delimiting legitimate and illegitimate immigration criteria.

We will note the rules legitimating migration in the Third World as well as in developed states. Furthermore, we are concerned with contemporary rules legitimating immigration, as well as with the way those rules have changed (or resisted change) over time. In the United States and Australia racism was once accepted as a legitimate basis for selecting immigrants. Racism may continue to be the basis for preventing Haitians from seeking refugee asylum in the United States, but it is no longer considered legitimate. Keeping out those Haitians who are illegal economic migrants is legitimate. Determining whether the Haitians are, in fact, economic migrants or refugees is another question. The United States court has already ruled that such a determination cannot be avoided by interdicting vessels at sea and sending the passengers back to Haiti. Such actions are both illegitimate and illegal. Thus, the process for determining exclusion becomes as important as the exclusion itself.

While some principles of immigration have been discarded as illegitimate in Western states, principles of control that were previously almost unknown in colonial Africa have become commonplace in postindependence Africa. Once there was little impediment to human mobility between and among the colonies. In colonial Africa, as Essuman-Johnson makes clear in his paper, emigration from (not immigration into) a colony was once seen as the problem. Through immigration, a host colony gained a reservoir of labour and skills, as well as an additional source of tax revenue, while a sending colony lost these assets. The question then was whether certain types of emigration could be considered illegitimate. The situation has been radically altered. Now obstacles to human movement are widespread even when people of the same tribe or family reside on both sides of the border of states that began to emerge into independence in the sixties and seventies. The migration of Hutu into Rwanda and Tanzania is a case in point.

With the development of the postcolonial state, issues of national identity and sovereignty required legal norms to determine who was a citizen and who was an alien, and, hence, who was or was not entitled to the benefits of membership in the state. The issue was not so much who could legitimately enter as who could legitimately stay. The results were often mass expulsion orders of what are now considered foreign nationals, even though many of them were settled for a considerable time in the newly independent country.

Such rules then translated themselves into entry and stay rules that generally followed the patterns of Western developed nation-states. Non-members (such as tourists, visiting relatives, temporary workers or managers and professionals assigned to a country for a limited period) are subjected to entry controls. They have no automatic right of entry and must request permission to enter or stay beyond a specified period. Others are denied entry because of a number of ostensibly legitimate reasons—they pose a health risk to society, they have a criminal record or membership in an illegal organization or because they cannot prove that they will be able to support themselves when living in the host society. These were the same rationales used to justify mass expulsions of undesirable aliens, particularly when economic downturns made a reservoir of labour redundant.

Refugees were another matter. The principle of legitimacy for determining refugee status could once be summed up by the dictum that my enemy's enemy is my friend. Anti-Communists who managed to flee the countries behind the once-mighty Iron Curtain were granted virtually automatic entry into Western states. Anti-colonial freedom fighters who fled from states still under colonial rule were granted virtually automatic asylum in the first countries to achieve independence. But the principle began to be applied to those who were in conflict with the postcolonial independence regime itself, particularly if the rulers of that state were regarded with displeasure by the rulers of the host state. Sometimes those fleeing were former rulers themselves, ousted by coups or discarded for corrupt practices.

More recently, attempts have been made to apply more universalistic criteria, either those defined by the Convention or those implied by more extended definitions, such as the definition used by the Organization of African Unity (OAU). But neither formulation includes environmental refugees, those who are forced to migrate because of natural or man-made environmental disasters. They are initially assisted by the local population and ignored by the government. Eventually compassion fatigue sets in and local hospitality wanes. For example, the Sahel cattle herdsmen who fled into Ghana were first assisted by the local citizens and ignored by government officials, then subsequently regarded as illegal aliens whose herds were thought to endanger the health of Ghanaian cattle. The Sahel herdsmen were eventually expelled. The danger of expulsion now haunts the much larger groups who have fled areas of conflict as Western aid becomes more restricted and as the West turns its concentration on Eastern Europe, as Gaim Kibreab points out.

Thus, the development of the nation-state and its concomitant bureaucracies has meant the initiation of membership controls in border areas where local and regional values and norms were once predominant, especially among relations within the same kinship group on both sides of a border. In other words, legitimacy is not a matter that can be abstracted from the geography of a region, its history or local kinship structures that straddle the borders of states. In some cases a state in which historical tradition predominates may be on one side of a border, while a state dominated by a central governing structure may be on the other side. The former may regard migration into the other state as legitimate and normal, while the latter host state may regard the same migratory movement as illegitimate, particularly if the numbers are numerous. Sometimes, as Anthony Ayok-Chol shows, some of those considered illegitimate migrants have been settled in the host state for a long time and achieved leadership positions in the local villages; others were in fact citizens of the state, but were regarded as aliens because they lacked adequate documentation.

Religion has also played a part in defining values and norms for appropriate behaviour to strangers, especially to those in need. In all three Western religions, persecution and flight are central themes. Jesus was persecuted and died for his beliefs. The Jews' flight from slavery in Egypt is a hallmark of Jewish memory. Muhammad was a refugee, a *hijra*, who fled from Mecca to Medina. As Grant Farr points out, the Afghan refugees, who make up almost one-third of the world's refugee population, are referred to as *Muharajin*. Thus, Muslim refugees are not only a group with legitimate rights to be helped but are to be esteemed as following in the footsteps of Muhammad.

These norms are not unlike the norms developed by Western states and adopted by international agencies for universal application for the treatment of refugees who flee because they have a well-founded fear of persecution. But religious norms have a wider scope. The religious norms, in contrast to the norms incorporated by the International Convention, deal with refugees who flee from situations of conflict and cross international borders, as well as those internally displaced by such conflicts. There are large gaps between the obligations imposed by religious norms and the institutional mechanisms to be applied to these irregular movements. Furthermore, it is often very difficult to distinguish between these movements and economic migration. The facilities for dealing with these irregular movements are often jeopardized by massive movements of returning guest workers. For example, Pakistanis who returned from working in the Gulf, just before the Gulf War, resented having to compete for jobs with "refugees" from neighbouring Afghanistan. The absence of an international protocol or regime that can help governments to differentiate between legitimate and illegitimate action in such situations means that such governments are influenced primarily by the passions and interests of their domestic constituencies, especially during a crisis. Though legitimacy depends on a government responding to its constituents, it also depends on due process and the rule of law, both of which are liable to be sacrificed when dealing with foreigners on one's own territory in a time of crisis. The lack of such normative guidelines may be because we do not have a conceptual base for institutionalizing assistance to migrants fleeing civil strife, which, in turn, presents serious obstacles to the proper treatment of such migrants. It also exacerbates the number of refugees who are thrown into an illegal status in countries that offer no protective regime whatsoever.

Gaim Kibreab provides a striking example where there is an international set of norms, but where there is also a broader regional norm that appears to be more generous and humane, although it is inoperative and ineffective. He suggests that the failure to distinguish between refugees who flee persecution and those who flee other life-threatening situations, such as environmental disasters, threatens the regime constructed to protect even the narrowest class of refugees. When mass asylum goes beyond the capacity or ability of local states to cope or the willingness of the international community to provide aid, then protection for those who flee persecution is threatened. Distinctions among and between different groups of migrants are not only necessary to provide the appropriate protection and assistance to other types of migrants, but to protect the regime carefully constructed over the years to protect Convention refugees.

Using the research of and analyses of our various contributors, in the opening chapter I construct a schema for determining which actions of states are or are not legitimate in controlling and regulating immigration. In other words, this study has been used to determine the various forms of legitimate and illegitimate migration and to elucidate norms that are appropriate for states to adopt if they are to be considered legitimate democratic states in dealing with migration flows. This schema can provide a guide for and, in turn, can be tested in reading the subsequent chapters.

PART ONE

Theory

1

Legitimate Immigration Control[1]

Rainer Bauböck

Most debates about immigration control among scientific scholars, as well as political practitioners, focus on the question of how liberal or restrictive regulations should be towards specific groups, and which instruments are needed to make policies more efficient. They rarely consider whether selecting immigrants and limiting immigration are acceptable as legitimate prerogatives of receiving states. After all, isn't the right to decide on the admission of aliens one of the hallmarks of sovereignty?

If might makes right, this is certainly true. All states do claim a right to control immigration. Most of them also try to enforce it—although they often experience difficulties in doing so. However, *democratic legitimacy* requires that the exercise of state power must be compatible with whatever rights individuals and social groups are assumed to enjoy in a democracy. The question then is whether, under contemporary conditions, a general *right* to immigration has become an essential condition for a free and democratic society.

In the following analysis I will explore the general structure of arguments for immigration control. My purpose is to check their compatibility with democratic norms. If all of them fail this test, that would lend strong support to the cosmopolitan idea of universal freedom of movement unrestricted by state borders. Although I want to present an argument that could legitimate immigration control, this will not make the idea of open borders less attractive but will rather serve as a guideline towards a gradual realization of that target. Answers can be different depending on whether we look at the issue factually or normatively. The following will be mostly a normative discussion of immigration control, not a comparative and historical exami-

3

nation of state policies in this area.[2] I hold that the idea of *democratic* citizenship contains a normative thrust that can be explained as *equality* in internal distributions of rights and *universality* in the inclusion of all social groups who can raise legitimate claims to social membership.[3]

There are two different levels at which normative debates can be carried on, which I will call *legitimation* and *justification*.[4] Legitimation of immigration control implies an argument that exclusive distribution of a social good is compatible with generally accepted norms and/or positive laws in a society. While legitimation confronts social actions or relations with norms of existing social institutions, justification relates them to theories about what norms ought to be adopted to achieve some moral goal. And while justification has to resolve contradiction and restore consistency, the task of analysing legitimation is to highlight and interpret contradictions. These can be either contradictions between conflicting norms, which will find their expression in policy dilemmas, or they can be contradictions between norms and their implementation in laws and policies. In the latter the analysis will develop into a critique of the ideological use of norms in politics. In this paper I will be more concerned with legitimation, i.e., with examining arguments for immigration control in the light of norms that apply to Western states' present political systems.

Communities and Citizenship

Arguments in favour of immigration control commonly presuppose: 1) the existence of a community whose common interests are (can be) represented by controlling immigration; 2) internal distributions of one or more social goods that would be affected negatively by uncontrolled immigration.

It is far from self-evident that both conditions are met by modern Western nation-states. We should not accept out of hand dominant interpretations of the type of community these states represent, nor should we assume as self-evident that the internal distribution of social goods must be protected by immigration control. If all such arguments can be rejected it seems clear that the individual liberty of free migration should have priority over claims of receiving states to be entitled to immigration control. But what is a community? Can modern nation-states and complex societies still be regarded as communities? Let me start with a very cautious and minimalist definition of community that combines both elements of our initial presuppositions for legitimate immigration control. I shall call a community *any group of persons within which there is a (re)distribution of some social good for which criteria of membership are essential to legitimate inclusion and exclusion.*[5]

Communities can be dissolved in two ways. One is by abandoning membership criteria for the distribution of a social good, i.e., through the elimination of external boundaries. The second is by changing the character of a social good and its distribution in such a way that membership becomes irrelevant. Recognizing a certain right, which had previously been exclusive to a political community, as a universal human right would be an example of the first method of dissolution. Abolishing a right to a certain share in a social good and leaving its further distribution to voluntary exchange and gifts could serve as an illustration for the second method.

If we look at territorial societies we will have to consider whether they can actually be regarded as communities. Capitalist markets are distributive systems that do not operate via membership requirements even when their range is factually limited to one particular country,[6] so it is not obvious that Western nation-states form *economic* communities. On the other hand these states do form *political* communities by restricting rights of participation in collective decision making to those who are recognized as members.

Complex societies are characterized by complex patterns of communities. There are many different kinds of communities within most past and all present states. Some of them extend beyond territorial borders as well as beyond boundaries of membership in the larger society. Nation-states themselves can be regarded as communities in some aspects, whereas they have lost their communitarian features in others. But surely modern nation-states must be regarded as communities of citizenship? I think this is evident only if we conceive of citizenship as nothing more than a legal expression of nationality. I would like to propose an alternative definition of citizenship as *a set of rights that is institutionalized within a political community and distributed to its members, and whose legitimation refers to norms of equality and universality in this distribution.*

My hypothesis is that citizenship conceived as a bundle of rights (rather than as national membership) is a social good with high internal complexity. Some elements of this bundle are limited to territorial or national membership of states, whereas other rights of citizenship have become extended to nonmembers outside and can no longer be regarded as exclusive social goods. Internally, territorial and national memberships are no longer congruent sets. Some rights of citizenship have been distributed to all those living or working in the territory of a state. Others, like voting rights, have generally remained tied to what I will call nominal citizenship.

I shall argue later on that the distribution of citizenship as a social good can legitimate immigration control. Citizenship is a heterogeneous and complex good with different ranges of distribution for its different rights. For each element of citizenship, we will have to decide whether control of immigration is legitimate because the right is or must remain exclusive or, alternatively, whether control has become illegitimate because the relevant right is either no longer or should be no longer exclusive.

Distributions of Social Goods and Immigration Control

Many different social goods have been used to legitimate immigration control by those who say that their internal distributions must be maintained. In present and past policies, among the most important of these goods have been the following: racial homogeneity, common culture, internal and external security, limited natural resources and economic welfare. I cannot deal adequately with each of these in this paper, but I will try to make some general as well as some specific remarks about each of them before suggesting an alternative perspective.

Protecting some of these goods seems to require selection rather than control in terms of overall numbers. If racial or cultural homogeneity is to be protected, those who possess the same genetic or cultural traits as the receiving society's population should be welcome because their participation in the distribution of the social good does not diminish it but contributes to its production or maintenance. On the other hand, ecological strains caused by overpopulation and limited natural resources generally require limiting numbers rather than selecting immigrants (except when different categories of immigrants can be expected to use these resources very differently). Economic welfare and security concerns would lead to a combination of both forms of immigration control. Immigrants could be selected according to their special skills or their net contributions to the economy or have their criminal and political records taken into account. But simultaneously there might be concerns that beyond a certain threshold the sheer number of immigrants diminishes security and economic welfare.

A second distinction closely related to the one between quantitative limitation and qualitative selection is between territorial and internal exclusion. The logic of protecting internal distributions requires excluding those who are not recognized as actual or potential members of communities. Denying access to a territory is one way of enforcing such exclusion.  This is especially relevant where territory is among the key social goods distributed to members only. In industrial societies this is not the case, but territorial exclusion can be a way of protecting distributive institutions that operate on a territorial basis and transfer goods to everybody within a territory. The other possibility is internal exclusion, i.e., the segregation of a community and its distributive systems from others who live in the same territory and society. For example, this is how communities of faith operate within modern societies. Lateral segregation between cultural and religious groups, and hierarchical segregation between the genders, estates or castes, were general features of premodern states. These distinctions have been gradually removed rather than vanishing completely in modern society. In the public sphere internal exclusion is most problematic when it is based on

[handwritten: democracies do not condemn internal exclusion - Aparth.]

ascriptive membership and effected by the state itself. Apartheid has become the contemporary catchword for the most infamous example of such policies. However, with regard to immigrants many forms of internal exclusion are still widely practiced and accepted as legitimate in Western states. These include legal discrimination of aliens, public disregard for their particular cultures, and a lack of policies to combat social segregation in areas such as housing and employment. It seems that such internal exclusion compensates to some extent for the relative openness of state territories. The emphasis on territorial or internal exclusion will generally *[handwritten: ✳]* correlate with the demand for limitation or selection of immigrants.

The argument for racial homogeneity has become discredited, although it should be remembered that it was still employed even by liberal Western states after World War II, e.g., in the White Australia Policy until 1972 or in the U.S. policy of excluding Chinese and Japanese immigrants from access to citizenship and, more indirectly, in national quota regulations of immigration control until 1965. Today it is frequently revived in a slightly more subtle form with the same practical effect. According to the old racism, humanity could be divided into distinct biological groups, which could be ranked according to their inherent superiority or inferiority. The new racism replaces these biological hierarchies with cultural ones, but retains the biological element by assuming that xenophobia and "genetic nepotism" are innate, genetically determined behavioural patterns. Therefore, immigration policies should limit inflows of groups perceived as aliens in order to prevent violent internal conflicts.

Even if there were a universal human disposition to act aggressively towards aliens, this would not answer the decisive questions. Who is regarded as an alien in which context, and what are the norms for regulating behaviour in such encounters? The definitions of these boundaries and norms are doubtless cultural ones and they seem to be almost infinitely variable across different societies. The modern nationalist imperative that cultural and political boundaries should coincide[7] has meant that political and cultural exclusions have reinforced each other. In this context an alien is not only culturally different. Cultural boundaries identify the *Volk* as a sovereign political community. Modern racism has drawn the borderline between ethnic groups who were regarded as assimilable into a national culture and those who were not, but this need not be done by proclaiming the biological inferiority of certain races. The same result can be achieved by combining the hypothesis of the genetic determination of xenophobia with the idea that individuals socialized in certain cultures cannot adapt to liberal societies. *[handwritten: Key]*

[handwritten right margin: Assimilable]

When stripped of such racist overtones, culturalist arguments for immigration control or internal exclusion can certainly be respectable and should

[handwritten bottom: ✳ Territorial exclusion - North]
[handwritten bottom: ✳ Internal exclusion - S.E. Asia & Africa to some extent]

be taken seriously. A fairly uncontroversial example is the right of Native Americans in the United States and Canada to restrict immigration of other citizens onto their reserves. Both conditions for the legitimation of immigration control, which I postulated earlier, are clearly met in this case. Groups of Native Americans are seen, and see themselves, as distinctive cultural and ethnic communities, and over access to territory is essential to maintain their particular cultures.

The same can be said of other minorities whose survival as communities might be threatened by unselected immigration. This issue involves the difficult question of how to draw the boundaries between individual and collective rights internally, as well as externally. As long as a government represents a dominant culture, minorities can legitimately demand recognition of their collective rights and autonomy. In a democratic state this must be limited not only by parallel collective rights of other groups, but also by the right of individuals within each group to change their affiliation. If autonomy is granted to a territorial minority, it will turn into a locally dominant majority. To which extent can it now use its power to discriminate against individuals outside its ethnic community? Clearly, selecting immigrants into the area according to their ethnic background is a form of discrimination. If a minority—unlike Native Americans—cannot demand restrictions on immigration from within the state, should it then be allowed to curb inflows of culturally alien immigrants from abroad into its territory?

This issue has been hotly debated in the Canadian province of Quebec or in Belgium where the formally bilingual status of Brussels is under pressure because of large-scale immigration from outside. There are forms of preserving and developing local minority cultures that are compatible with the basic unitary structures of a democratic state. Among these is local linguistic plurality, or even minority hegemony, in public institutions such as schools and offices. Immigrants from other parts of the country, as well as from abroad, can be asked to comply with minority rights by learning the local language. Restrictions on internal migration are a more controversial matter because they sacrifice an important basic right of citizenship. Cultural selection of immigrants from abroad may therefore be seen as a more acceptable demand. It may be raised by minorities who are not in a position to deny members of the national majority admission as immigrants, but who can argue that their survival as cultural communities is at stake. However, the limits to such demands must become tighter the more successful a minority is in gaining access to state power, which is the decisive resource for its survival under modern conditions. By transforming itself from an ethnic group into a nationality, i.e., by gaining partial autonomy and constituting itself as a state within a state, a minority opens itself to all the claims immigrants can raise towards nation-states. In this article I am concerned with these latter claims rather than those towards cultural minorities.

Contemporary analyses of nationalism[8] have argued that the rise of the nation-state dramatically changes the distribution of one specific social good—standardized literary culture. Modern nation-states create a fairly homogeneous internal distribution of this social good and it is within that common body of knowledge that nationalist ideologies can flourish and become attractive but distorted interpretations of the social conditions of modernity. This seems to support the argument that in modern societies high cultures are indeed basic social goods whose distribution is organized within nation-states and can legitimately be protected by immigration control.

My main objection is that I doubt whether the mode of distribution of these national cultures creates communities with necessarily exclusive membership. Ethnic cultures, which are transmitted by socialization within the milieux of the family and small-scale village communities, are exclusive because their distributive range is inherently limited and their core institutions cannot be substituted by bureaucratic ones. In contrast, national culture can only be created and distributed within the institutions of a modern bureaucratic state, first of all within its educational system. In contrast to ethnic cultures, a national one is no longer self-reproducing. It becomes consciously manufactured and manipulated. The range of its distribution covers the entire population of a state. Rather than reflecting in its institutional design the exclusivity of the different cultures within society, it turns into a motor for assimilating them all into a single unified high culture that is distinctly different from the popular traditions.[9] If these institutions have successfully managed the transformation of locally established cultures into national ones, how can they be threatened by the arrival of individual immigrants of different cultural origins? There are no obvious external limits to membership in distributions of national cultures. Just as Western nation-states generally have assimilated their internal populations into a single or very few national cultures, traditional countries of immigration have been confident of their cultures' assimilative power towards immigrants from abroad.

However, many contemporary analyses maintain that this picture has changed. The idea of immigration countries as cultural melting-pots has been replaced with that of an ethnic revival and the emergence of multicultural societies. This is certainly not the result of immigration overwhelming the assimilative capacity of cultural institutions. Rather it appears that recently the internal drive towards cultural homogenization has become weaker and new forms of heterogeneity come to the fore. The ethnic mobilization of immigrants is an element highlighting (but not causing) this process. Western societies are still quite far from a general dissociation between state and culture, comparable to the separation between state and religion that marked the beginning of modernity. Rather than becoming a purely private matter, cultural difference is used as a political resource in the public sphere. There is an ongoing ideological battle about whether this increasing diversity of cultures within Western states should be fought or accepted as inevitable, or even beneficial. A nationalist revival that interprets the culture of dominant populations in ethnic terms is under way. This could well lead to demands for more cultural selectivity in immigration policies. I assume that democratic norms speak for tolerating diversity and for promoting equality, openness and social desegregation between all cultural groups in society. It might be difficult to follow all of these principles simultaneously, but none of them lends itself easily to the exclusion of immigrants on cultural grounds.[10]

Nevertheless, there may be special cases that justify not general exclusion but temporary priorities for immigrants with a certain cultural and ethnic background. Free immigration and automatic citizenship for immigrants from Eastern Europe with a German background is among the more controversial examples. There are two different arguments legitimating this policy. One refers to a special responsibility the German state carries for all the consequences of the Nazi crimes. When the postwar Stalinist regimes started to persecute and expel summarily ethnic Germans, the Federal Republic had to be a safe haven for these people who had nowhere else to go. The second argument is based on an ethnic definition of the German nation, which is still enshrined in the present constitution, although it emerged at a time when the only factor of unity among dozens of German states was a common high cultural language. I find the first argument perfectly legitimate, while the second one must be seen as dangerous for democracy. It might seem that both lead to the same policies. However, this is not true. Only the second argument also legitimates the German policy of legal discrimination against non-German immigrants and its tough conditions for naturalization. And only in this perspective can ethnic citizenship for German immigrants be regarded as a permanent national interest rather than as a temporary policy dictated by historical circumstances. Moreover, the first argument could also lead to a policy of preferential immigration for those groups who were the main victims of the Nazi regime, i.e., Jews and Gypsies.[11]

In addition to the racial and cultural arguments for immigration control, there is the security issue. It consists of two different elements. On the one hand, there are statements about specific characteristics of immigrants. On the other hand, security, just like natural resources, might be a scarce good that is diminished as the population density increases. As this second claim broadly overlaps with the issues of ecological and demographic stability, I will not deal with it separately here.

One characteristic of immigrants that is traditionally viewed as a risk to external security is that, as alien citizens, they may remain loyal to another state. This argument views immigrants, just because of their nominal citizenship, as representatives of states and governments and does not take into account the real motives for large-scale immigration, which are either apolitical or based on opposition to the ruling regime in the state they left. Of course, in a state of war there may be conflicting duties and loyalties, but such a scenario cannot serve as a guideline for legitimate immigration control in times of peace. Often the external security argument overlaps with the racist and culturalist one. Summary internment, even of naturalized immigrants of Japanese origin in the United States after the attack on Pearl Harbor, was based on openly racist ideas. Restrictive policies towards other immigrants were supported by the assumption that they had been socialized in a different political system and therefore could not be expected to respect the values and norms of the receiving society.[12] In the United States the dominant legal tradition is based on John Locke's view that citizenship is the result of an implicit social contract that is made explicit in the act of naturalization.[13] However, as the example illustrates, racist interpretations of cultural differences can nevertheless lead to a deterministic concept of political loyalty.

Concerns with internal security in international movements of persons are certainly legitimate with regard to persons engaging in internationally organized crime. Often there is an implicit assumption that criminals are overrepresented among migrants, either because of their alien descent or because of their specific biographical experience (such as having been uprooted and estranged in their homelands, or living in ghettos and slums in the immigration countries). However, many statistics show that criminal activity among labour immigrants of the first generation is significantly lower than among the native-born population of the same class and age groups when gender composition is controlled. Undoubtedly, open borders for tourism have contributed to the spread of certain criminal activities and they also open routes of escape for those perpetrating them. This phenomenon certainly cannot be reduced by special control and selection among those who are motivated by the quest for asylum, work or life with their families who have migrated before them.

The ecological issue is a fourth argument for immigration control. Each territory contains a certain amount of nonrenewable resources that are depleted with increased population. As a general argument, this seems a perfectly legitimate basis for quantitative limits on immigration. However, Western industrialized nations have generally declining birth rates and immigrants barely compensate for this decline. Secondly, if nonrenewable resources are diminished at ever-growing rates, this is not due to immigration but to technologies of production and consumption patterns that increase the per capita use of these resources. Thirdly, the development of large cities is the prime example of undesirable effects of free migration on ecological balance. However, quantitative limitation of immigration from abroad is certainly no remedy. Acute ecological crises in cities such as Mexico City, Cairo or even Tokyo have not been caused by *international* migration. Furthermore, state regulation of immigration usually does not control access into overcrowded big cities. Internal freedom of movement is a universal human right enshrined in international law, even for alien citizens, so how could a British immigration officer deny entry to an immigrant arriving in Dover or Heathrow by arguing that London is overpopulated?

Collective economic welfare is the last item on the list of social goods referred to in immigration control. I will not pretend to deal adequately with this complex and controversial issue here. Many books have been written about the beneficial or detrimental effects of large-scale migration of labour on national economies. Here I only want to point to a few conceptual problems in the premises of a welfarist legitimation of immigration control, which have been mentioned by other authors before. Welfarist arguments applied to nation-states assume a given population, the collective welfare of which is to be measured and maximized. Utilitarians, who represent a special type of welfarists, do this by maximizing either aggregate or average individual utilities within this collective.[14] But utilitarianism cannot argue that only utilities of these persons and no others should be included in the calculation. Either the existence of states and self-reproducing populations within these states are presupposed as a given empirical fact or these boundaries and their effects are ignored altogether. Henry Sidgwick and others have contrasted the national and the cosmopolitan perspectives as two different views whose merits cannot be decided a priori.[15] This is only a minor dilemma, as long as we are talking about separate populations in distant territories. Where there is no interaction between two societies, the proposal of counting utilities separately in each of them is the more convincing one, since counting them jointly might lead to the conclusion that redistribution would be needed to maximize common welfare. But how can that be done if there are no structures for interaction and there is no experience of community beyond the borders? International migration obviously intensifies this utilitarian dilemma considerably because it involves not only interaction but even exchange of populations. The general principle that each individual has to count as one and one only does not say anything about distinctions between nominal citizens, alien residents and potential immigrants outside borders. Even in the simple case of a one-way migration from one state to a second one, there are four different sets of populations that we could choose for welfarist calculations of migration effects in a national perspective: 1) the receiving country without immigrants; 2) the receiving country including immigrants; 3) the sending country without emigrants; and 4) the sending country including emigrants.

These four options depend on whether we focus on the sending country or the receiving country and whether we define membership in terms of residence or citizenship.[16] Finally, there is a fifth set that combines the populations of receiving and sending countries and includes migrants.[17] This would be the reference population in the cosmopolitan perspective. When we analyse empirical cases of migratory flows to ascertain whether immigration control could help to maximize common welfare, we can hardly expect all five approaches to lead to the same answer.

A liberal utilitarian who is not impressed by nationalist arguments will most probably choose the fifth option, but even within this perspective there might be contradictions that are hard to resolve. There will often be considerable losses of welfare in the country of emigration because, frequently, skilled workers and entrepreneurs are most inclined to leave when the doors are open. The question of whether welfare in the receiving country will grow with free immigration depends strongly on which measure we choose; aggregate welfare might increase while per capita welfare can decline. Moreover, there will be very different welfare effects for different social groups: employers of immigrant labour will generally profit the most; consumers might have the more modest and more widely distributed benefit of lower prices, but competing native workers and earlier immigrants will lose.[18] It is far from obvious that these differences should be eliminated by using aggregated or average utilities in measuring common welfare rather than giving greater weight to the interests of those who are more disadvantaged.[19] There seems to be less difficulty in estimating the utility of free migration for individual migrants. Indeed, if migration is voluntary, and if we assume rational behaviour of utility-maximizing persons, there must have been some expected gain that caused territorial movement. However, such expectations are often frustrated in actual migrations, and in the end migrants find themselves trapped in the country of immigration in a situation that would not have prompted them to come had they only known of it before. So paternalistic states might even argue that denying such imprudent migrants access (or exit) will maximize their own long-term utility.

All this leads to the conclusion that free migration between two states might, under certain conditions, be considered even detrimental to common welfare from the cosmopolitan perspective. As this view cannot legitimate immigration control by referring to national membership, it would require paternalistic restrictions of individual rights, i.e., a form of enlightened dictatorship, in these cases.

The polar opposite of the utilitarian perspective would be an entitlement theory of migration. If free migration were a universal right, or should be one according to some political philosophies, none of these welfarist arguments could be accepted as relevant. Actual migration flows would then primarily be determined by individual utilities of migrants exercising their rights. Utilities of employers in the country of destination or of family members in the country of origin would be relevant only because, and in so far as, they enter the individual migrant's perception of his or her own interests.

A second major difficulty the welfarist argument shares with the culturalist one is that it is questionable whether it actually refers to *communities*, i.e., social systems with internal distributions in which the membership criterion is relevant. I have already pointed out that in a perfect world of liberal economics, with open markets as the absolutely dominant system of economic distribution, nobody can claim to be a *member* of such a distributive system. This is why economic liberals must favour unlimited freedom of migration if they want to be consistent. However, in the real world there are systems of economic redistribution that do not function as open markets and require membership. The most important of these systems (but certainly not the only ones) are those run by states. Do states that operate substantial systems of redistribution and control over market interactions thereby create communities of economic welfare? Could immigration control not be legitimated by showing that under certain conditions uncontrolled immigration will diminish economic welfare within these communities? If the answer is yes, it is still only an answer to the factual question of whether such communities might have rational reasons for controlling immigration. It does not solve the problem with reference to which general norms such exclusivity of economic welfare could be accepted as legitimate.

However, my own answer would not be affirmative in the first place. How can we know that the social good, the internal distribution of which is to be protected by state control, is actually the collective welfare of those participating in the community? Is this not an ideological assumption? In such an argument, collective welfare would not function as a social good that can be distributed in similar ways as the others in our list, but would be a goal[20] for distributions. What are actually and observably distributed are legal regulations, money and social services. It would be much more promising to look at these social goods and the normative grounds for their distribution than to construct ideal states untainted by any interests of particular social groups that intervene into the economic process with the aim of complying perfectly to welfarist theories.

Can Equal Citizenship Legitimate Immigration Control?

A more sober assessment of existing welfare states will reach the conclusion that they merit their title, not because their political systems are geared towards maximizing collective welfare, but because they issue laws and distribute money and services with normative reference to welfare *rights*. Achieving minimal thresholds rather than maximal welfare characterizes these states.

Many of these welfare rights are corporate in nature; they are given to specific social groups that exercise some control within the political system over distributions based on their rights. However, some social rights are the equal rights of all citizens; these, such as primary education in public schools, are the most basic ones. Welfare states differ widely in the extent to which basic rights of social citizenship set constraints for market distributions, and in the extent to which social rights are formulated as corporate rather than citizen rights.[21]

T.H. Marshall has characterized the welfare state as a hyphenated society, i.e., as a capitalist-democratic-welfare state.[22] It is the democratic element among these three that provides legitimation of social citizenship and a normative guideline for policies to reduce market inequalities, as well as within corporate systems of redistribution. The central argument of this section is that free immigration can destabilize this hyphenated structure. Immigration control can be legitimated insofar as it protects the internal equality of social citizenship because, in a capitalist economy, social citizenship can only develop within this structure.[23] Two important qualifications have to be added. First, there has to be a separate justification for choosing the receiving country as the relevant community. This will be provided by exploring the bounded nature of communities of citizenship and the asymmetry of emigration and immigration rights. Secondly, choosing citizenship as the relevant social good implies strong constraints on state regulation with regard to the status of immigrants before as well as after they enter. Before I take up these points, I will explore the different distributive ranges and boundaries of all three elements of citizenship; the civil, the political and the social one (Marshall 1965).

Civil Rights. In Western political opinion after World War II, civil rights have been increasingly considered universal human rights rather than a matter that can be left to legislation by individual states. If we accept this point of view, basic civil rights cannot be restricted to members of a political community and, therefore, civil rights can hardly provide a reason for restricting immigration.

The boundaries that are required to maintain civil rights are ones of territory rather than membership. In the Lockean tradition of political thought, the origin and present legitimacy of states rest on their protection of the natural rights of life, liberty and possessions for individuals who cannot be sufficiently protected in a state of nature.[24] Courts, police and armies are those institutions that are said to protect these same rights within civil society. One of the necessary but insufficient conditions of civil peace is that the range of power of these institutions must be territorially delimited. With the sole exception of diplomatic personnel, anybody within a state can be subjected to the power of its police and its courts. *Democratic* legitimacy of this power requires that *all* those potentially subjected in this way will also enjoy identical civil rights. Any distinctions between members and nonmembers with regard to these rights would expose the power of these institutions as illegitimate.

The only way civil rights can become part of an argument for immigration control is via the issue of security, which we have already discussed. Bruce Ackerman has made an interesting statement about this. He argues for a *prima facie* right of immigration based on migrants' ability to participate in liberal discourses about the legitimation of power. The immigrant who is not admitted is entitled to an explanation. As a liberal dialogue must respect the neutrality principle, any answer referring to a moral distinction ("because you are not as good as I am") will not be permitted. However, in the receiving state a certain high number (Z) of immigrants might trigger a fascist takeover by indigenous political forces or a similar threat to public order. In this rationale, the Z + 1 immigrant may legitimately be denied access. According to Ackerman, "The only reason for restricting immigration is to protect the ongoing process of liberal conversation itself."[25] This argument introduces a concern for civil rights at the extreme limits of immigration capacities, but uses a fundamental political right as a legitimation for general freedom of movement.

Political Rights. In communitarian political philosophy an equally fundamental concept of political rights has been used to deny a *prima facie* right of immigration and to set limits much narrower than Ackerman does. Michael Walzer has argued that the ideas of democracy, equality and justice presuppose the existence of bounded cultural and political communities. States must operate like clubs or families rather than like open neighbourhoods when admitting aliens. While Ackerman looks for a maximum threshold of immigration below which there should be free entries, Walzer's approach defines a minimal obligation of mutual aid, which makes states open to the claims of needy immigrants.[26] In my view, Walzer's principles provide too little scope for immigration rights; on the other hand, Ackerman's do not distinguish between different needs and entitlements of those who want to immigrate. Under present conditions, the maintenance of citizenship legitimates neither entirely free movement between political communities nor unrestrained control of movement by states. My objections depend on two suppositions: first, we are not concerned with an ideal theory of perfect liberal citizenship, but with the application of norms that can be supported within existing political systems; second, the crucial test for citizenship is neither given membership in a community nor the general human ability to participate in political discourse but rather having a *position* in which one can claim equal rights.

In the real world, there is no doubt that political rights are not universal but attached to states conceived as communities. The right of membership is the most fundamental political right on which all others are built. States control it at two different points; at the point of access to the territory and in their rules for transferring and acquiring nominal citizenship.[27] Walzer argues strongly that immigrants "must be set on the road to citizenship."[28] This means minimizing or abandoning control over nominal citizenship because it creates two different classes of residents within the same political community. But how convincing is the argument that immigration control must then be even stronger in order to stabilize this community and its internal political rights?

Political rights are about participation in collective decisions. In autocratic polities the collective has no other boundaries than those set by the effectiveness of coercion. Decisions may concern anyone who is within the reach of power and can be made to obey an order. Democratic decisions, however, presuppose that at a given time a given number of persons is entitled to take part in the collective exercise of power. Ideally, the collective that determines the laws is the same collective subjected to those laws. This Aristotelian and Rousseauian image of democracy is far from reality; it also has its inherent contradictions. In representative democracy the ordinary citizen does not take part in legislation, but participates in deciding how the legislative body shall be composed. Representative democracy thus separates the rulers and the ruled. Its claim to be a form of democracy rests on two principles: the ruled must enjoy basic rights of citizenship; the rulers must legitimate their actions by referring to the articulated interests of the ruled. It is not the first of these two aspects that presupposes boundaries of the community but the second one.

The need for boundaries in order to organize democratic decision making does not automatically entail immigration control. To show this I will contrast a representative democracy that is open for free immigration and that gives immigrants full political rights with a situation of more extreme openness, which indeed would be incompatible with political democracy. Imagine a global democracy in which every household in the world has a terminal linked to a giant computer in the Centre for Computerized Legislation. People can vote on any issue that is put to them. Anyone can participate in collective decisions. Such a telecommunication democracy would mobilize only tiny percentages of the total enfranchised population for decisions on any particular issue. This type of political community would be extremely loose. Everybody would enjoy the same political rights, and, because of direct participation, these would be even more substantial compared to those of a representative democracy. But this system fails the test of democratic legitimation—the tie between those who participate in decisions and those who are affected by them will be much looser than it already is in representative democracy.

Free immigration would create a very different situation. Residence would still be a crucial requirement of membership and exclude the rest of the world from participation. Further, if we distinguish travellers from migrants, we will also exclude those who are present on a purely temporary basis and those whose only purpose is to participate in the political decisions of another country. Such a community would be a very open one indeed, but it would not have to shed those boundaries that are essential for building a viable democracy. And democracy itself, rather than a common national culture, would be the essential foundation of community. Of course, some minimal standards of common culture (beyond all the different cultures of communities within the wider society) would still be an essential requirement. But immigration societies could build such a common culture more easily when the objective is democratic participation in decision making by all groups of the resident population, rather than imposing the value systems of one dominant group on others.

Social Rights. Social rights are a different matter. They require a certain amount of closure. But we have to be clear about why that is so.[29] The logic of the argument for immigration control often goes as follows: firstly, the welfare state is misconceived by thinking of it as an egalitarian distribution of income and wealth. Secondly, internal exclusions are thought to be inadmissible, undesirable or unachievable. From these two premises the conclusion follows that free immigration would equally diminish everyone's share. Any group of people invited to a birthday party among whom a cake of a given size is to be divided will be interested in keeping the number of additional guests as small as possible. Immigrants are often seen in this way. They are attracted by the wealth of Western nations and if they are admitted, the generous nature of our social rights will mean that all end up having less than before. Even if this were a correct view of the welfare state, it would only provide an explanation for a conflict of interests, but not a principle of legitimation that could be applied universally. On the contrary, the same argument would speak for free immigration in order to achieve a more equal distribution of wealth internationally.

What is basically wrong with this line of reasoning is the idea that wealth and income in welfare states are public goods distributed for private consumption, rather than private goods that are to some extent redistributed by public regulation. So as a next step, let us assume a revised model, in which there is an egalitarian distribution of private resources at some point in time. Freedom of transactions (exchanges, gifts and bequests) between individuals will mean that such a distribution will necessarily become more unequal over time. But citizens in this society might agree that inequalities resulting from certain risks should be avoided. For example, they may think that no one should become impoverished by necessary expensive medical treatment. If they are strongly convinced of this, they will decide to have a tax-financed national health service with free provision of medical care.

Now suppose that in a neighbouring society, citizens believe that private insurance is good enough to cover this risk and that anybody who has not taken out insurance should carry the full risk of potential poverty or inadequate treatment. If there is free migration between both societies and full citizenship entitlements for anybody in the respective territories, this creates a dilemma for the welfare state.[30] Its citizens are faced with the following options: they can decide to deny entry to those immigrants from the neighbouring state who are in bad health or who come for expensive medical treatment; they can let them in, but deny them medical treatment if they do not pay for it; they can increase their own taxes to pay for any costs of medical care for immigrants; or they can decide to abolish the whole system as unworkable and incompatible with their belief in free migration. The citizens of the country with free-market health care do not face these difficult choices. As everybody has to pay full costs, anybody can come and use their health care institutions. Bottlenecks in provision caused by an inflow of immigrants will presumably be removed through rising prices and/or expanding supply.

So the real issue is whether citizens have a political right to decide on redistributive policies of the type discussed[31] and whether their collective right to introduce a social right can supersede an individual right of free movement. My own answer would be affirmative because individual political rights have to correspond to substantial collective rights of self-determination. There is not much point in political participation if the collective cannot even make a decision to redistribute private resources to some extent because this either collides directly with property rights or indirectly with a right of free movement.[32]

In a final step of the argument we have to realize that many of the assumptions we have made still do not fit the true case of immigration into welfare states. First, as pointed out before, citizens themselves do not decide on redistribution, but let their representatives decide for them. Secondly, immigrants are not only beneficiaries but also contributors to those funds that are redistributed in welfare policies. Usually the balance between contributions and payments is strongly positive during the first phases of labour migration.[33] Therefore, the case of underinsured citizens of the United States who try to come to Canada for medical treatment is a special one that cannot be accepted as a general model for the effect of free immigration on welfare states.

There are two different distributions that we have to examine in our discussion of social rights. One is the distribution of material benefits, which is the content of the right, e.g., free medical care or public education; the second one is the distribution of the right itself. Of course, the two can be linked, as in the case just analysed. An equal and universal distribution of a social right may be jeopardized because there are not enough resources to finance equal benefits for everybody. But both distributions can operate separately as well. It may be impossible to introduce or maintain a social right, although there are plenty of resources and a political majority in favour of doing so. The obstacles may be powerful corporate interests and political actors who are able to prevent redistributive measures, but obstacles could also be embedded in an economic system that creates its own countervailing forces against too extensive redistribution.

This is what I want to argue. Free immigration can be a threat to social rights in a hyphenated society, not because it diminishes scarce resources, but because it can undermine state regulation of markets. When there are no limits to the supply of labour or the demand for housing, policy efforts to guarantee a minimum standard of wages, working and living conditions can easily be thwarted. Social rights in a capitalist economy presuppose, on the one hand, a certain amount of success in economic growth and profits, and, on the other hand, the capacity and willingness of political authorities and voluntary associations, such as trade unions, to constrain the operation of free markets. Democratic citizenship is incompatible with strong internal restrictions on labour supply, except with regard to specific groups, such as seniors, children or pregnant women. Where this has been respected, the stabilization of social rights has depended upon constraints on the labour supply from outside. If immigration were exclusively regulated by the internal demand for additional labour, the effect would not be a redistribution of social rights and their benefits so that a cake of a given size is divided into smaller shares. It would lead to a shrinking of the cake itself, or, to be more precise, to a diminishing of the *availability* of resources for redistribution.[34]

One could argue that numbers of immigrants among the workforce do not threaten social rights; rather, the threat comes from undesirable jobs that are designed to be filled by immigrants. Still, when internal demand and external supply of labour are rising simultaneously, regulation of both jobs and labour supply will be necessary. What this implies for immigration control is a quantitative limit to access.

Some readers could object that social rights are not that important as long as free immigration can be justified because it improves the situation of immigrants who have stronger needs than the better-off workers of the receiving society.[35] My point is that social rights link up with political citizenship. The first linkage has already emerged from the discussion of the health care models. Substantial political rights must include the right to make a collective decision about the redistribution of private resources. The second linkage, which completes this argument, is that in a hyphenated society substantial political rights also depend on making such decisions.

Limited working hours, health and accident insurance, minimum wages, child-care facilities—all these and many other features of the welfare state are essential requirements for a broad participation in political life. Citizens in the ancient republics of Greece and Rome understood perfectly well that independence from the need to work was essential for their type of political democracy. In a capitalist society this has become an unrealistic idea for the great majority of the population. A minimum of independence from work, achieved through work and social rights tied to work, family and citizenship, has become the more modest contemporary precondition for political participation. There can be no stable and inclusive democracy in a capitalist economy without substantial social rights. This is the harsh lesson of many attempts at democratization in the so-called Third World and in Eastern Europe today. It also helps to explain why residual welfare states, such as the United States, have developed into rather unrepresentative democracies. Abandoning social rights for the benefit of a broader redistribution of those benefits, which can be gained by participating in metropolitan labour markets, could also mean falling back into an even less representative form of democracy than exists presently in Western states.

Three Worlds of Citizenship. We can sum up the argument by imagining three artificial worlds. The first would be a global system of minimal states[36] protecting only civil rights. Minimal states require territorial institutions, but no formation of community. While civil rights would be essentially the same everywhere, their protection would be organized by local administrations. Such a political system would be perfectly compatible with global free markets (for goods, money and labour). In such a world there might be many communities that could restrict immigration to protect their specific internal distributions, but states would not be regarded as such communities. The territorial nature of states would, therefore, not imply legitimating general restrictions on the movements of individuals.

The second world is one in which citizenship becomes democratic by adding political rights to civil ones. Now state institutions must not only be territorial but also correspond to a delimited membership for those involved in collective decision making. In nonnomadic societies the basic requirement for membership will be residence. We can imagine this world as one of open neighbourhoods that decide on their own local affairs. Anybody is free to move into the neighbourhood and everybody living there is entitled to participate in the decision making. What is the status of those who just walk through the area? When they try to mug somebody on the street, they will be arrested by the local police. When they are mugged themselves, they will be protected by the police. But they will be legitimately excluded from the neighbourhood assembly, which is open only to residents. The civil cum political rights model of democracy is compatible with general freedom of movement for all those who do not enter the political community, plus a more specific freedom of immigration leading to future residence.

In the third world, social rights are added to civil and political ones. If the economy is a capitalist one, social rights will be indispensable for guaranteeing a minimal level of universal participation. The main instrument to create and maintain social rights will be the regulation of labour markets and employment relations by the state. In this world, neighbourhoods could only remain as open as before if social rights were the same everywhere. Once there are substantially different levels of social protection and redistribution, immigrants will be attracted. Immigrants might also be needed for economic growth, but beyond a certain level, immigration will undermine the internal capacity for political regulation of the economy. Membership in the distribution of social rights will not only be determined by a residence criterion. The number of additional members admitted from outside will also have to be limited.

If we wanted to develop a realistic model of the present situation, rather than a normative frame of democratic citizenship, we would have to construct a fourth world in which cultural rights are added to the list. As already discussed in the previous section, one could then conclude that this additional element requires *selection* rather than limitation, i.e., an even stronger criterion of communal membership than mere restrictions on the numbers of immigrants.

Table 1: Elements of Citizenship and Boundaries of Membership

Citizenship rights	Type of state created by accumulated rights	Boundaries of membership
civil rights	minimal state boundaries	none, but territorial of institutions
political rights	formalistic democracy	determination by criterion of residence
social rights	"hyphenated society" capitalist-democratic-welfare-state	quantitative limitation of access
cultural rights	nationalist welfare state	qualitative selection in admissions

In this section I have provided an argument for immigration control that involves an indirect threat to democratic citizenship and political participation when social rights based on the regulation of markets cannot be maintained. This is a danger that is very different from Bruce Ackerman's scenario of free immigration that leads to a fascist coup, but I think it is a more real and permanent feature of our societies. Those who argue for free immigration have to face its consequences for the distribution of citizenship. Those who think that democracy is worth being developed beyond its contemporary forms, even as long as its minor present achievements are not spread evenly across the globe, will be able to formulate an argument for immigration control on these grounds.

Asymmetry of Emigration Rights and Immigration Rights

One of the most common arguments against immigration control is that it seems contradictory to grant unconditional emigration rights, but to restrict rights of immigration. Why should only the right of emigration be considered part of a universal package of civil rights, whereas immigration is subjected to the constraints of state regulation? Does not emigration also affect social redistribution in the sending countries, just as immigration does in the receiving ones? How can we say that social citizenship might legitimate immigration control without conceding that it also legitimates emigration control? I will try to examine both of these objections.[37] To answer the first question one could look for specific properties and effects of emigration rights that are different from those of immigration rights. There are two theories that could explain such a difference.

A.O. Hirschman has argued that the *exit option* is one way of improving social institutions and their activities. The other one is *voice*, i.e., the internal reaction of members of an institution, or consumers of its output, against a deterioration of quality.[38] Exit rights are an institutional safeguard against a natural tendency towards slackness. Such improvements cannot be ascribed to entries in the same way. It is stimulating to regard democracy as a bundle of such institutional safeguards within the political system that maximizes the possibilities for improvement by institutionalizing both the right of emigration and rights of participation as elements of citizenship.

A second argument for emigration rights that cannot be applied to immigration rights is not concerned with efficiency but with the properties of institutions. Robert Nozick (and others before him) have pointed out that emigration rights can be employed as a test and as a minimal safeguard for *voluntary* membership in institutions and communities.[39] But this is a necessary rather than a sufficient condition for voluntariness. Communities without emigration rights can be called unfree ones. However, not all communities with emigration rights can be said to be free just because of this single feature. Freedom also consists in participation and *voice*. Furthermore, voluntariness and freedom need not be the same and there are even reasons for not accepting the claim that unrestrained emigration makes for voluntary membership. My right to renounce membership in a chess club is proof that I adhere to it voluntarily, whereas my right to leave the country where I was born and raised does not indicate exactly the same situation. There are at least three differences involved. The first is that with regard to the club, one can point to an actual admission procedure in which no force was employed, whereas there is no such event in the case of native-born citizens. The second difference is that most people don't invest all their fortunes and life projects into a leisure club, while many of them do this with regard to the country where they live. The third is that there are many other clubs that I can join almost at will, while it is much harder to find other countries that will admit me as an immigrant.[40]

So the right of immigration could serve as an even stronger indicator of voluntary membership, provided it comes in addition to the right of emigration and not in its place. Imagine a religious order that gives everybody who has spoken an oath of allegiance a right to join, but denies exit rights thereafter. In a way this membership is also voluntary, but clearly in a different way than that in the chess club, which runs a more selective admission procedure, but which you can quit at any time.[41] For our present argument, it is not important to substantiate Nozick's claim that emigration rights are somehow more fundamental in all contexts (and not only in those of movements between states). It is sufficient to say that both explain very different concepts of freedom and that the first does not entail the second.

But could there not be an argument that emigration rights do imply immigration rights because without the second the first will be meaningless as rights? What is the use of my right to leave if I have nowhere to go? Can I be said to enjoy any right at all in this case? There is a ring of truth in this question, but the answer will again have to point out less apparent distinctions. Emigration rights are necessarily particular to the community one leaves behind; they have to be guaranteed and institutionalized within this community because no one else can give that right to leave. As far as immigration rights are logically implied by emigration rights, they are not particular to any community. What is necessary to a right of emigration is that there be some place in the world to which a person can go, rather than a right to choose a particular destination. My right of emigration, therefore, does not in itself give me a claim to be admitted into any specific community. In the general case, asymmetry can be justified by the simple fact that in movements of persons there is always one starting point, but there are usually many possible destinations. This situation would be very different if there were just two countries or communities. Then and only then would rights of emigration and immigration have to be exactly symmetrical if the right of emigration is to be more than an empty promise.[42] However, a weaker version of the argument for symmetry can be maintained even for less specific cases. It is clearly not enough for a substantial right of emigration that somewhere out there are other countries or communities. At least one of them must be *accessible* for *actual emigrants*. From this we could deduce that the right of emigration puts a duty on potential communities of immigration not to deny entry to those for whom this particular community is the only one they can actually go to. This is a substantial conclusion because it makes no reference to the motives of emigration. What it implies is far from trivial: if the right of emigration is to be considered a universal human right, there must be at least one other country for each person that would be willing to admit him or her whenever and for whatever reasons he or she decides to immigrate. The only permissible exceptions to this right of immigration would be those that also justify general restrictions on the right of emigration. (No country can be obliged to admit a notorious criminal on the run from the authorities of his home country.) The obvious difficulty in putting this principle into practice is to decide *which* country would be obligated.

The same kind of asymmetry arises—and could be challenged—between criteria for rejecting applicants for immigration and criteria for expelling residents from the territory of a state. There are good arguments for demanding stronger protection against expulsions than what exists pres-entry even in democratic states—for nominal citizens, resident aliens and even for those who have entered illegally but have managed to settle in the receiving society.[43] However, it is difficult to maintain that by not expelling illegal immigrants a country of immigration incurs an *obligation* to admit all future immigrants who circumvent legal regulations. The argument for symmetry is much stronger with regard to rejections in legal applications. But even here one could say that a criminal record (measured by the standards of a democratic polity) could be legitimate grounds for rejecting such an applicant while the same criminal record does not automatically warrant expelling him or her. This asymmetry can be defended on the grounds that membership in residential communities gives rise to a strong claim of being allowed to stay (and to reintegrate after a prison sentence), which the applicant from outside lacks. The limits to this argument are that an immigrant may have even stronger claims to be admitted if his country threatens him with punishment that violates human rights, such as torture or the death penalty.

Expulsions are one form of involuntary emigration. The general point made above that universal emigration rights presuppose that for every emigrant there is at least one community willing to accept him or her must be seen as one among several conditions for permissible expulsions. The whole list would probably read as follows:

- Only *individual* acts that *break the law* of a country can lead to expulsions.
- Expulsions are not permitted when a person has acquired an *entitlement of residence*.
- A strong rule of *nonrefoulement* must be respected in all cases, i.e., persons cannot be expelled if they run the risk of being persecuted, tortured or treated inhumanely in the country to which they will be sent.
- Nobody can be expelled who would thereby become a *stateless person or a refugee in orbit*, i.e., who would not be legally admitted as a regular resident in another country.

While the priority of emigration rights over immigration rights can be explained in a theory of citizenship, cosmopolitan welfarism might recommend the inverse asymmetry, i.e., control over emigration but a right to free immigration. Collective welfare in the sending countries is negatively affected by what is commonly called the brain drain. Doubtless, immigration control is completely ineffective in stopping this movement of skilled and qualified immigrants because such people are actually given priority in most immigration regulations. Emigration control (e.g., by imposing a tax on "human capital export," as the Ceausescu regime used to do) can be much more successful. Free immigration of those who have been allowed to leave would, on the other hand, probably maximize collective welfare in a liberal market economy when measured by aggregate utilities. In fact, not only emigration countries but also states of destination have engaged in policies of controlling outward movements of undesirable immigrants. A recent example is the carriers liability regulations in most Western countries, which impose heavy fines on airlines that bring in refugees without the required travel documents. This is an attempt to shift the point and the agencies of control away from the authorities of the receiving countries to private institutions and to sending states. It illustrates that general restrictions on emigration serve dictatorial purposes, even when they are imposed by democratic states. The only way of stopping undesirable emigration is by offering incentives to stay, but leaving the decision to the individuals concerned. This conclusion depends on seeing human rights and citizenship rights as having priority over collective welfare.

This leads us to the second question posed at the beginning of this section. It was formulated forcefully by Robert Nozick in a statement not meant to attack emigration rights but the civic duty to pay taxes and contribute otherwise to the internal social redistribution necessary to create social rights. "What rationale yields the result that the person be permitted to emigrate, yet forbidden to stay and opt out of the compulsory scheme of social provision? If providing for the needy is of overriding importance, this does militate against allowing internal opting out; but it also speaks against allowing external emigration."[44]

Rationales for the right of emigration and the duty of internal social contribution are clearly different, but that does not imply that they are incompatible. Reconciling them generally requires no more than a lexical ordering in cases where there could be conflicting claims.[45] Nozick seems to assume that they must be contradictory because both have a different logic. What appears as a contradiction can in most cases be resolved by formulating constraints. The crucial distortion in Nozick's presentation of the argument for social rights is that he assumes that they are of *overriding* importance for their defenders without specifying which other rights they are meant to override in which theory.

Hard cases arise only when rights are ranked equally or when there is no prior agreement about their ranking.[46] There are three types of possible solutions. The first is to decide which right should be generally given priority in cases where conflicting rights can be applied. The second is a solution of mutual constraints, in which the overlapping area is divided between conflicting rights using a criterion that determines the proximity of a case to the space covered by one of the rights. The third solution is defining the overlapping area as one in which neither right of the original set applies, but for which a new right must be defined. It is obvious that

Solution 2 presents most problems because it entails a case by case judgement, whereas in solutions 1 and 3, cases can be decided immediately once it has determined which category they fall into.

Diagram 1: Solutions for Conflicts Between Unranked Rights

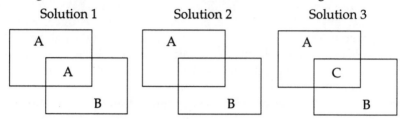

In the conflict discussed by Nozick I would propose Solution 1 for general cases: the right of emigration works as a constraint on the duty of contribution. Nobody willing to emigrate can be forced to stay because his or her resources are needed for internal redistribution. This implies that the right of emigration is the more fundamental one. We could interpret this as a lexical priority of liberty. Only after everybody who wants to emigrate has had a chance to do so can we determine the set of remaining persons who are then obliged to contribute.

There can be also constraining rules in the opposite direction, as long as these do not effectively undermine the right of emigration and do not impose unfair charges on those willing to leave. Somebody who has not paid his or her taxes may be required to do so before leaving the country. But no emigrant can be asked to pay back the costs of his or her education when education is free for all citizens. This would be unfair because it creates a fundamental inequality between would-be emigrants and other citizens. The basic rule is simply that potential emigrants must be treated as equal citizens up to the point of emigration (and in some respects even beyond this point until they renounce their citizenship). As long as the constraints of internal contributions on the right of emigration do not create a special situation for potential emigrants, we are still within a Solution 1 situation.

There may be, however, other kinds of constraints that lead to one of the other two solutions. Let us concede that a right of emigration may be restricted or even denied for certain categories of citizens if other and more weighty interests of the emigration society are at stake. Take as an example a state that has committed itself to total nuclear disarmament. Should it not deny emigration rights to its experts on nuclear technology when they want to go to another country that demands their skills? Which of the three solutions best represents this argument? We have in fact not argued for restricting the right of emigration by a duty of internal contributions to social welfare, but introduced a new and different criterion for specific cases. This combines solutions 1 and 3. I cannot think of any formulation of the conflict between a right of emigration and social rights plus the duty of internal contributions they entail, which would suggest a Solution 2 situation. Therefore, I am inclined to think that what Nozick views as a contradiction or inconsistency is not even a problem from which particularly hard cases will emerge.

Diagram 2: A Solution for a Tripartite Conflict of Rights

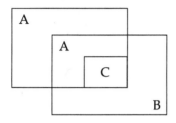

A. Right of emigration

B. Social rights of internal redistribution

C. Special rights of state of emigration

The general priority of the right of emigration does open a legitimate possibility of evasion from duties of internal contribution. But if there is no other way to avoid this duty, this may raise the costs of evasion to a high level for many potential emigrants. Leaving one's country is not an easy decision and for most people the costs of paying their contributions is probably much smaller than the costs of emigration. Even if some emigrants can evade internal contributions without costs because they are no longer interested in the benefits of membership, in most cases they will not be able to evade paying similar contributions in the country of destination. Once there is no longer a Lockean state of nature, emigration does not lead to opting out of compulsory contribution for social provisions, but only shifts contributions to a different community. Where there is a possibility of special exemption from such obligations for immigrants, this appears to be unfair, as are tax havens for foreign owners of capital. Exempting immigrants from internal contributions is just as unfair as charging emigrants additional fees above the general level of internal contributions. The former discrimination is simply the inverse form of the latter.

Having explained the general reasons for the asymmetry of emigration and immigration rights, we can now conclude by looking at the different effects both kinds of rights have for the boundaries of political communities. I want to propose three hypotheses:

(1) *Free immigration is an expression of the fusion of separate communities into a single one.*

Once migration between territorial states is no longer controlled, immigration rights turn into freedom of movement. Within a space of unlimited freedom of movement, the boundaries between separate political communities can only be stabilized if those moving around are excluded from political participation. If they are included because democratic citizenship demands universality of representation among the resident population, a fusion of communities takes place. After the Maastricht summit, the European Community states appear to be at some point between separate nation-states and fusion. There is not yet a plan to give full parliamentarian voting rights to EC citizens within all EC states. Freedom of movement is a general right that includes "third country aliens." This will be one of the effects of the Schengen treaty, which aims to abolish border controls between the territories of signatory states. But control of aliens at the external borders of "Schengenland" will be stricter than now and, for these aliens, rights of movement will remain separated from political rights. Unless they naturalize, they will not be accepted as members of the future United States of Europe.

(2) Extended immigration rights are an indication that a community expands beyond its borders and potentially includes other groups of persons.

Immigration rights are different from freedom of movement in that they are perfectly compatible with a general control of borders. An immigration right is either an exemption from that control or more usually a right to be admitted after control. By entitling a certain category of persons to immigrate, a political community accepts a special responsibility towards this group. This responsibility must be interpreted as an expression of actual or potential membership. The right of remigration of nominal citizens (or immigration for those born abroad), which is accepted as a principle of international law, is only the most obvious case. I want to argue that a broader concept of citizenship focusing on extended distributions of rights implies additional entry rights for those immigrants who can base their claims on need or on a special relation to the receiving society. These are primarily refugees and family members of resident aliens. But it could also be argued that immigration rights should be extended in long-term chain migrations, which have created strong links between societies.

As Walzer points out, refugees differ from other kinds of immigrants because what they look for is not work or land but membership in a community.[47] A refugee is someone who has been forcefully deprived of this membership (directly by expulsion and violence or indirectly by being deprived of the means for survival within the community). So must we not say that granting asylum is an expression of accepting someone as a member? And if the right of asylum does—as it should—entail a right of immigration, does this not in a way extend the boundaries of membership beyond both nationality and territory?

This is even clearer in the case of family reunification for resident aliens. There is a double right involved in this: the right of family members abroad to join their relatives, which is formulated as a universal human right (it is implied in Article 8 of the European Convention on Human Rights) and the right of resident immigrants to have their relatives admitted to rejoin them. The latter right is obviously based on residential membership in the society of immigration rather than on universal human needs. That is why this right is often subjected to constraints that indirectly express differences in membership (such as required periods of residence and waiting times before the right can be enjoyed).

(3) Free emigration has neither effect; it does not redefine the boundaries and the membership of a community, but it expresses a basic form of internal liberty.

If emigration rights were restricted to certain categories of persons, as immigration rights are, they could not be regarded as an element of equal citizenship. Emigration rights must be broadly identical with free emigration (except for those marginal cases that I have already discussed). In the usual terminology this is a negative liberty rather than a positive claim-right.

Equality in the distribution of rights is the central characteristic of democratic citizenship. The right of emigration and rights of immigration have different ranges in present political systems. Although many present restrictions on immigration cannot be legitimated with reference to democratic norms, the general difference between these ranges can be. This should help to understand the seemingly paradoxical result of my analysis:

- Equal citizenship demands that specific rights of immigration can and must reach beyond established state borders, but it does not imply that they can be made universal as long as there are separate political communities.
- The right of emigration has become a universal human right, but its effect is not to stretch or merge communities. Equality of exit rights is nothing more or less than a necessary condition for a minimum of liberty inside each political community.

Conclusion

My intention in this paper has not been to vindicate present immigration controls by Western welfare states. Rather, I have looked for new ground from where these policies could be consistently criticized. Consistency of critique requires confronting difficult normative issues involved in immigration policies. The ground I have discovered seems to be a middle one between the conventional perspectives of national communitarianism and cosmopolitan liberalism. I have refused to accept a priori assumptions implied in both approaches. The national view starts from a self-evident right of states to deny entry to any alien person, which is only afterwards mitigated by the introduction of certain human rights. The cosmopolitan view argues for a *prima facie* right of immigration, where the burden of proof of exhausted integration capacities lies with the receiving state.

My strategy has been to start from the communitarian point of view but to dismiss its central claim that state authorities who reject an immigrant represent the interests of a closed political community. Instead, I have suggested a definition of community that is relative to distributions of social goods. This allows me to ask two critical questions about the structure of communities: first, whether internal distributions actually refer to congruent sets of participants; second, which general norms can endorse the closure of a specific distribution towards outsiders?

In applying this analysis to immigration control I have rejected most of the conventional reasons (the racist, culturalist, security, ecologic and welfarist arguments), either because exclusion has become normatively indefensible or because distributions are actually no longer based on membership criteria. Instead I have suggested that the civil, political and social rights of citizenship are social goods whose intrinsic properties *could* provide a legitimation for protecting their distributions. However, if the concept of citizenship is not restricted to the frame of national membership, we can see that its different elements create distributions of different range. While the civil element has become universal (normatively rather than actually), the political element indeed requires bounded communities. Nevertheless, these boundaries are those of residential societies and do not imply the exclusion of immigrants who can become residents. It is the social rather than the political element, which under certain conditions, requires immigration control. These conditions are those of a hyphenated society, i.e., one in which representative democracy includes welfare rights that operate within capitalist markets.

I have finally addressed one of the main arguments for the cosmopolitan view, which is that there should be a symmetry of emigration and immigration rights. My conclusion is that this suggestion can be supported for some specific cases, but not as a general one in a world that consists of individuals and communities, and where migrations have a determinate starting point but more than one destination.

What implications would this analysis have for evaluating immigration policies? An existing flow of migration can be patterned in two different ways: qualitatively, i.e., via selection, and quantitatively, i.e., via fixing numbers for admission during a time period. The perspective I have chosen would imply that quantitative limitations must be nondiscriminatory, i.e., refrain from excluding immigrants because of criteria that violate a right of equal respect and concern.[48] But this view also implies a principle of selection, namely giving entitlements and priority to those immigrants whose claims can be defended on the basis of human or citizen rights. Compared with the racist and culturalist principles, this mode of selection has a different function with regard to the distribution of citizenship as a social good. It is not a method of distinguishing populations who by their personal characteristics are either qualified or unqualified to share in its distribution. Rather, selection is determined by their specific circumstances. Preference for those immigrants who have the strongest needs and claims enhances internal political and social citizenship, not by adding human resources for its reproduction, but by confirming its basic standards. These are participatory memberships in a political community respecting civil liberties, and social memberships entailing rights to a minimum of material security, education and leisure.

Only after all these constraints on immigration regulation have been implemented can quantitative control legitimately refer to considerations about costs and benefits for the receiving society as a community of welfare rights. From this follow two important conclusions: first, the essential precondition for free migration between states is the extension of social rights beyond nation-state borders; and secondly, once social rights have become effectively equalized within a transnational space, there is no more legitimation for restricting immigration. This is true regardless of whether equalization takes place as an adjustment towards higher or towards lower standards. A dismantling of welfare rights creates a world in which immigration control becomes harder to defend. An enrichment of universal citizenship with social rights would create a very different world, but one with similar consequences for immigration rights.

Immigrants who are entitled to come might create costs to the society, but the point of giving them a right of entry is that these costs can only be reduced by means other than limiting their entries. Immigrants who do not enjoy entry rights might create two different kinds of costs to the receiving community: costs of admission and costs of deterrence. In many cases costs of admission will actually be benefits because most industrial states need significant immigration to keep their economies going, which again is one of the preconditions for establishing and maintaining social rights. Above certain thresholds of immigration, benefits might turn into costs that will presumably rise with the number of immigrants. This provides an incentive to introduce quota regulations. However, these imply costs of enforcement, i.e., costs of deterring additional immigrants beyond the legal contingent. Costs for maintaining border controls, checking the identity of immigrants, introducing employer sanctions, etc., are not only to be measured in monetary terms. They are also costs with regard to civil liberties for the receiving society as a whole. While I have argued that certain forms of immigration control can be legitimated by democratic principles, it could nevertheless turn out that such regulations are not feasible because deterrence is either ineffective, or its costs will be too high in a democratic state.

This dilemma indicates that behind the analysis of legitimation, there still lurk some difficult questions of efficiency. However, in contrast to the present immigration policy debate, I would insist that the former have to be answered first before the latter can be dealt with. It is the general logic of political argument that demands this. If we started with questions of efficiency, we would also hardly understand the predicament of the present situation. It is true that modern technologies of information and transportation have greatly facilitated long-distance migration, but technologies of social control have developed simultaneously. Contemporary Western states don't lack the *capability* of restricting immigration flows, but they are caught in a legitimation trap. If they try to implement all available means, they will thereby undermine their own stability. Guaranteeing a basic amount of negative freedom and of positive rights is an essential requirement for stability of these regimes and there are many vested interests in society to prevent their overthrow. This is where normative analysis and the analysis of norms could meet. While the latter is a task for comparative and historical research, I hope to have convinced readers that even if the former must primarily be a theoretical exercise, it is not necessarily empty moralizing disconnected from social reality.

But I have also tried to go further than that by suggesting that democratic citizenship implies much stronger constraints on immigration control than those that exist in present policies. That raises the stakes for debates about efficiency. These constraints would considerably reduce the margins within which policies can try to be efficient. Some might think that all I have done is to provide conditions for the legitimation of policies that cannot be successful under those very conditions anyway. There is, however, a more optimistic interpretation as well. What immigration policies should do is to try and minimize the sum of costs of deterrence plus costs of admission. This will include silent toleration of a certain excess of immigration beyond the legal quota. If this illegal contingent grows too large and costs of admission rise dramatically, a combined policy of *regularization* (legalizing past immigration) and *regulation* (new attempts of enforcing controls for the future) will become inevitable. Sudden moves towards abandoning all immigration control risk provoking catastrophic situations that will probably lead to backlashes and even more restrictive forms of national closure. A gradual reduction of the controlled segment within migration flows and a continuous expansion of the flows that are either unregulated or regulated via specific entitlements could be the only feasible way to come closer to the cosmopolitan utopia, which is, after all, the more attractive one.

This optimistic outlook is seen from a manageable situation in which immigration pressure and absorption capacities are not too far apart. There is, however, a catastrophic scenario as well. Suppose the optimal level of immigration is very low, the immigration potential very high, and costs of admission increase very fast with every immigrant above the optimum. In this case both costs of admission and costs of deterrence might each exceed the acceptable threshold in a democratic society. This indicates not only a crisis but an acute normative dilemma as well. There are then two contradictory conclusions about what a receiving society should do. The costs of admission argument would imply that we have to cut off all further immigration beyond that threshold, i.e., pay any price in terms of deterrence. But the costs of deterrence argument suggests the exactly opposite policy: once you are no longer able to stem the tide by permissible means, you have to open the floodgates. There are quite a number of countries today facing this dilemma. I do not think that any Western industrialized state is presently among them.

Notes

1. A first version of this article, which included two additional sections on problems of policy implementation, was presented at a Viennese conference on "Mass Migration in Europe" in March 1992, jointly organized by the Institute for Advanced Studies (Vienna), the International Institute for Applied System Analysis (Laxenburg, Austria) and the Institute for Future Research (Stockholm). I am indebted to many colleagues for useful comments, most of all to Howard Adelman, whose suggestions and critical remarks went far beyond what editors normally do to help authors revise their papers.

2. For the latter aspect, consult Hammar (1985).

3. Bauböck, "Migration and Citizenship," 27-48.

4. A similar idea has been expressed by Joseph Carens, who distinguishes a foundationalist approach in normative political analysis from a contextualist one (Carens 1988b).

5. Some readers may find the lack of subjective criteria irritating. What about belonging, the sense of community, communal identity and identification, which figure prominently in distinctions between *Gemeinschaft* and *Gesellschaft*? I do not want to suggest that these are irrelevant criteria. My objectivist definition only tries to avoid assumptions about their causal impact on the formation of communities. A community need not be preceded by a sense of community. Instead of being a precondition, "belonging" could either be regarded as a social good that is distributed to members only, or as a byproduct of communal distributions of other goods.

6. This seems to me the essential meaning of the notion of a free market. Precapitalist markets were generally not free in this sense. The roles of individual actors were largely prescribed by their membership in different ethnic, religious and status groups.

7. Gellner, *Nations and Nationalism.*

8. Gellner, *Nations and Nationalism;* Anderson, *Imagined Communities: On the Origins and Spread of Nationalism;* Hobsbawm, *Nations and Nationalism Since 1780.*

9. Gellner, *Nations and Nationalism.*

10. Howard Adelman has made the point to me that such norms might support that "immigrants should be selected who agree to respect cultural diversity and support principles of tolerance" (private communication). This sounds fair, but surely cannot be determined on the basis of immigrants' cultural origins. A professed nationalist or religious zealot might be denied entry because his individual record substantiates the expectation that he will not respect these norms. But predictions of individual behaviour, based on assumed character- istics of a cultural collective, should never be accepted as legitimate grounds for discrimination.

11. Wilpert, "Migration and Ethnicity in a Non-Immigration Country: Foreigners in a United Germany," 49-62.

12. Some illustrative examples from the history of U.S. immigration are given by Zolberg (1987:277ff.).

13. Schuck and Smith, *Citizenship Without Consent: Illegal Aliens in the American Polity.*

14. For theoretical critiques of utilitarian and more generally of welfarist theories of justice, see Rawls (1973) and Dworkin (1981).

15. Sidgwick's view, which seems to be the conventional wisdom of his age, is that from the point of the receiving society, free migration is desirable because it maximizes economic benefits in the long run just as free trade does. On the other hand, he fears that this would lead to a declining sense of national identity, which is indispensable for the internal cohesion of political communities (Sidgwick 1897:308ff.).

16. "It can be seen that one of the reasons why it is so difficult to achieve agreement on estimated costs and benefits of immigration is that a proper calculation should take into account the country of origin as well as the country of destination. Moreover, it is by no means clear to which of these collectivities one should attribute the costs and benefits experienced by the migrants them- selves" (Zolberg 1987:265).

17. This set must include immigrants because they are obviously members of one or both societies regardless of whether we choose residence or citizenship as the membership criterion.

18. Lichtenberg, "Mexican Migration and U.S. Policy: A Guide for the Perplexed."

19. Rawls's difference principle would be a nonwelfarist argument for radically different weights (Rawls 1973).

20. Or, in Robert Nozick's terms, as an end-state principle (Nozick 1974:153ff.).

21. Esping-Andersen, *The Three Worlds of Welfare Capitalism.*

22. Marshall, *The Right to Welfare and Other Essays.*

23. I have dealt with this question more extensively in another recent paper (Bauböck 1992).

24. Locke, *The Second Treatise of Government.*

25. Ackerman, *Social Justice in the Liberal State*, 95.

26. Walzer, *Spheres of Justice: A Defence of Pluralism*, 31-63.

27. Hammar, *Democracy and the Nation-State: Aliens, Denizens and Citizens in a World of International Migration.*

28. Walzer, *Spheres of Justice*, 60.

29. The influential contribution that Gary Freeman (1986) made on this topic is not clear enough in that respect.

30. This hypothetical situation is modelled according to Joseph Carens's discussion of potential U.S. immigration to Canada because of the latter's national health service (Carens 1988a and 1992).

31. Libertarians of Robert Nozick's kind would say no.

32. I would propose a right of immigration at least for those whose basic human right to life would be threatened by refusing them medical treatment. This is similar to the argument for open borders for refugees. But certainly a welfare state that provides needy aliens with free medical care under this rule would be entitled to try and reclaim its cost from the sending country. If immigrants have already been admitted for another reason (e.g., as refugees, labour migrants or for family reunification) they should receive health care under the same regulations as all other citizens.

33. I do not think that this is a relevant fact for deciding whether immigrants should enjoy the same social rights as nominal citizens.

34. For theories of distributive justice, it would be an interesting task to examine the special properties of distributions in which not only individual shares but also the total sum of resources shrink as additional recipients are included.

35. In fact many empirical analyses show that existing systems of social redistribution benefit the middle classes more than those at the bottom of the income scale. Some theoretical explanations for this effect are explored by Nozick (1974:274f.). But, as I have pointed out before, it is a misconception to think of social rights only as a way of redistributing economic wealth.

36. The description of this world is broadly identical with Robert Nozick's framework for utopia (Nozick 1974:307-334). However, Nozick does not conclude that there would be a right of free movement between states. This seems to be due to his starting point, which is John Locke's version of the social contract. As

Nozick assumes that the minimal state arises from individuals contracting to form protective associations (Nozick 1974:10-26), a membership criterion is already introduced at the very beginning of the hypothetical history of the minimal state, even though it would be neither necessary nor legitimate in the end.

37. Aristide Zolberg points out that this asymmetry also involves on between individual and collective rights: "Whereas free exit is a concomitant of the priority accorded in liberal theory to the rights of individuals—regardless of the impact the exercise of these rights might have on the collectivity o f origin— when it comes to entry, priority is accorded to the national interest of the collectivities of destination" (Zolberg 1987:270).

38. Hirschman, *Exit, Voice and Loyalty*.

39. Nozick, *Anarchy, State, and Utopia*, 299.

40. All these reasons can also be brought forward against Michael Walzer's analogy between states and clubs with regard to admission policies (Walzer 1983:40f.).

41. From these considerations we could generate a scale of voluntariness consisting of different combinations of exit, entry and participation rights. The notion of perfect freedom should probably be reserved for the combination of all three.

42. In his argument for a liberal admission policy, Bruce Ackerman assumes that there are only two countries, the East and the West. This is a crucial simplification and it may have influenced his conclusion that there is a *prima facie* right of immigration (Ackerman 1980:93).

43. Carens, "Aliens and Citizens: The Case for Open Borders."

44. Nozick, *Anarchy, State, and Utopia*, 173.

45. Rawls, *A Theory of Justice*.

46. On hard cases and how to resolve them, see Dworkin (1977:81ff.).

47. Walzer, *Spheres of Justice*, 48f.

48. Dworkin, "What is Equality? Part 1: Equality of Welfare," 180ff.

References

Ackerman, Bruce. *Social Justice in the Liberal State*. New Haven and London: Yale University Press, 1980.

Anderson, Benedict. *Imagined Communities: On the Origins and Spread of Nationalism*. London: Verso, 1983.

Bauböck, Rainer. "Migration and Citizenship." In *New Community* (Fall 1991):27-48.

_____. "Entitlement and Regulation: Immigration Control in Welfare States." In *Transitions*, edited by Hedwig Rudolph. Wissenschaftszentrum Berlin. Forthcoming.

Carens, Joseph. "Aliens and Citizens: The Case for Open Borders." *The Review of Politics* 49, no. 2 (1987).

_____. "Immigration and the Welfare State." In *Democracy and the Welfare State*, edited by Amy Gutman, 207-230. New Jersey: Princeton University Press, 1988a.

_____. "Nationalism and the Exclusion of Immigrants: Lessons from Australian Immigration Policy." In *Open Borders? Closed Societies: The Ethical and Political Issues*, edited by Mark Gibney, 41-60. Westport: Greenwood Press, 1988b.

_____. "Migration and Morality: A Liberal Egalitarian Perspective." In *Free Movement*, edited by Brian Barry and Robert Goodin, 25-47. London: Harvester, 1992.

Dworkin, Ronald. *Taking Rights Seriously*. Cambridge, MA: Harvard University Press, 1977.

_____. "What Is Equality? Part 1: Equality of Welfare." In *Philosophy and Public Affairs* 10, no. 3 (1981).

Elster, Jon. "Local Justice." In *Archives européennes de sociologie* 31, no. 1 (1990):117-140.

Esping-Andersen, Gosta. *The Three Worlds of Welfare Capitalism*. Oxford and Cambridge: Polity Press, 1990.

Fullinwider, Robert K. "Citizenship and Welfare." In *Democracy and the Welfare State*, edited by Amy Gutman, 261-278. Princeton: Princeton University Press, 1988.

Gellner, Ernest. *Nations and Nationalism*. Cambridge: Cambridge University Press, 1983.

Hammar, Tomas, ed. *European Immigration Policy: A Comparative Study*. Cambridge: Cambridge University Press, 1985.

_____. *Democracy and the Nation-State: Aliens, Denizens and Citizens in a World of International Migration*. Avebury: Aldershot, 1990.

Hirschman, A.O. *Exit, Voice and Loyalty*. Cambridge, MA: Harvard University Press, 1970.

Hobsbawm, Eric. *Nations and Nationalism Since 1780*. Cambridge: Cambridge University Press, 1990.

Lichtenberg, Judith. "Mexican Migration and U.S. Policy: A Guide for the Perplexed." In *The Border That Joins: Mexican Migrants and U.S. Responsibility*, edited by P.G. Brown and H. Shue. New Jersey: Rowman and Littlefield, 1983.

Locke, John. *The Second Treatise of Government*. New York: Macmillan, 1689/1965.

Marshall, T.H. "Citizenship and Social Class." In *Citizenship and Social Development: Essays by T. H. Marshall*, 71-134. New York: Anchor Books, 1948/65.

_____. *The Right to Welfare and Other Essays*. London: Heinemann Educational Books, 1981.

Nozick, Robert. *Anarchy, State, and Utopia*. Oxford: Blackwell, 1974.

Rawls, John. *A Theory of Justice*. Oxford: Oxford University Press, 1973.

Schuck, Peter H., and Roger M. Smith. *Citizenship Without Consent: Illegal Aliens in the American Polity*. New Haven and London: Yale University Press, 1985.

Sidgwick, Henry. *The Elements of Politics*. 2d ed. London: Macmillan, 1897.

Walzer, Michael. *Spheres of Justice: A Defence of Pluralism.* New York: Basic Books, 1983.

Wilpert, Czarina. "Migration and Ethnicity in a Non-Immigration Country: Foreigners in a United Germany." In *New Community* 18, no. 1 (1991):49-62.

Zolberg, Aristide. "Keeping Them Out: Ethical Dilemmas of Immigration Policy." In *International Ethics in the Nuclear Age*, edited by Robert J. Myers, 261-297. Boston: University Press of America, 1987.

2

The Concept of Legitimacy Applied to Immigration

Howard Adelman

This chapter attempts to construct a schema for differentiating between legitimate and illegitimate actions by democratic states to control and regulate immigration.

At the base of the schema is the civil society, in which individuals are free to act and move without the state's permission or authority. This area of free action includes the selling of labour, the purchasing of goods, and engaging in exchange and commerce. Those sales and exchanges may be regulated by social norms and state laws, but participation in them (except where public safety is at stake) does not require state permission.

The dilemma is whether nonmembers of a state may participate in the economic sector of the state's civil society without the state's permission. They are clearly permitted to do so as consumers, but are they as purchasers of land and shares in vital industries, as workers, producers or sellers of products and services? Is it legitimate to import foreign labour to work on farms, in industries or in domestic occupations? The international consensus among democratic states is that the importation of foreign labour not only can be regulated to discriminate between the legitimate and the illegitimate, but should be regulated to prevent exploitation of foreign labourers.

Generally, the importation of temporary workers is regarded as exceptional for some areas (the farm sector) and in some circumstances. Then, it is only for short periods and with clear protection of wages and hours of work. When workers are needed for longer periods, it is preferable to give them an option to migrate, bring their families, take up permanent residence and eventually obtain full membership in their adopted states. When contract workers are employed for one or two year periods, their wages and work hours should be regulated and a compensation package should be provided to the sending countries to assist in reintegration when these workers return home. It is clear that the international community lacks a Convention and Protocol to govern the importation and use of temporary labour to define and delimit what treatment is considered legitimate and what is illegitimate.

With respect to services and the products themselves (and the movement of individuals necessary to sell those products), the *de jure* right of people to sell their wares is accepted; it is the de facto exercise of those rights that are limited, but these limitations are in the process of being dismantled, at least within large regions, as the concept of free trade takes hold. This is also true of most restrictions on the purchase of farm land or the purchase of shares in the energy industry.

In the realm of rights within the civil society (as distinct from the arena of needs concerned with capital, labour, commerce and consumption) there are parallels between the needs and rights aspects. In consumption and human rights, there are no limits placed on nonmembers of the state to differentiate them from members. Citizens and noncitizens in the civil society have their human rights protected. Refugee claimants, in particular, have the right to counsel to press their claims, in addition to other rights normally accorded members of the civil society, regardless of whether they are citizens or not. Similarly, in the economic as well as the rights areas of the civil society, protection is accorded to both economic migrants and refugees.

Ownership of property or shares by foreigners may be regulated, as well as the selling of labour, goods or services. In the rights area, there are strict regulations about entry regarding who can or cannot access any rights claim system, such as a claim for refugee status. For those claiming such status, there are further restrictions. For example, individuals who are already pursuing a refugee claim elsewhere may not be permitted entry into the system.

Thus, if the civil society forms the base of the schema, the political state is the crown because the state sets the rules governing access and use of the civil society. But the state also has its own agenda. Individuals have obligations to the state of which they are members, and the state has a responsibility to protect them. One aspect of the state's responsibility is the controlled entry of migrants.

The welfare system and nationality are two other dimensions to the schema in addition to the civil society and the state. Access to membership in the nation that constitutes the state's majority population is the most difficult area in which to assess legitimacy issues. We will return to this most complex of issues.

The welfare system is more easily understood and grasped. A state may be obligated to provide certain forms of welfare—minimum wages, limited hours and other forms of basic guaranteed conditions. However, temporary workers do not have the same welfare protection as members of that society, such as rights to pensions, the same minimum wages, etc. Membership in the welfare society of a state gives individuals, whether they are citizens or not, equal access to the welfare benefits of that society, such as equal access to education, unemployment insurance or the health care system. Welfare for temporary workers may be restricted to what is guaranteed by the insurance provided or as a consequence of the work performed.

The basic schematic framework for determining legitimacy can be laid out as follows:

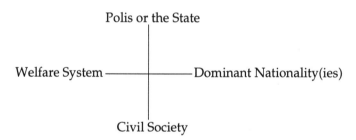

Polis or the State

Welfare System ———————— Dominant Nationality(ies)

Civil Society

A state is expected to fulfil various types of obligations for different groups of migrants. The most straightforward obligations *appear* to be those for Convention refugees. A state that is a signatory to the Convention is obliged not to return refugees to countries from which they fled in fear of persecution. It is also obligated to give them protection, either on a temporary basis or a permanent one by giving them the right to become members of that state. It sounds clear and simple, but is it? Two different obligations are spelled out. One is a negative obligation—what a state must not do. The other is a positive obligation—what a state must do.

The problem is that states engage in many activities to avoid the positive obligations so that they will not be in situations where they are in breach of their negative ones. There may be a corollary to the Kibreab rule (the more refugees a state has, the fewer it is willing to receive)—the more refugees a state has that it cannot return, the more likely it is to engage in activities to prevent more refugees from arriving who might seek asylum and whom they would be obligated not to return. To prevent the arrival of those without documents or with false documents, states use visa controls and

Kibreab rule

Adelman rule

carrier sanctions. They go even further. For those who do arrive, states adopt principles—such as "country of first asylum" or "safe first country"—to avoid responsibility for deciding which refugees are Convention refugees and which are not. Using these principles, they send potential refugee claimants back to another country that they might have traversed en route where they can make their asylum claims. Clearly, even the norms governing Convention refugees are inadequate as they are currently conceived and articulated.

However, most problems do not arise over the small group of Convention refugee claimants who actually reach a country's border. Problems are least likely to arise when individuals are clearly being persecuted and need asylum, and the receiving society is sensitive to their plight and identifies with the refugees. Serious problems arise when large numbers of non-Convention refugees flee for their survival because economic conditions in the sending countries have deteriorated as a result of man-made or natural disasters.

States do not have an obligation to take in economic or environmental "refugees." However, they do have an obligation to provide temporary sustenance, so that these types of refugees do not have to flee in the first place. And providing such sustenance cannot be simply a matter of charity. It must be an obligation entered into in advance to provide assistance in cases of emergency. Burden-sharing should be an obligation in an international welfare system to ensure conditions for the minimal survival of all humans. An international insurance fund must be created to cover such disasters.

What about those who flee en masse from political conflict? The numbers overwhelm the possibility of any individual refugee determination system. In any case, most of those who flee are not refugees who have a well-founded fear of persecution because of who they are or because of the organizations to which they belong. They fear being caught in the crossfire of competing political factions. Are they legitimate migrants? What policies must states adopt towards these humanitarian refugees from conflicts if the states are to be considered legitimately democratic?

They cannot send them back to where their lives will be at risk. On the other hand, states have no obligation to offer them permanent membership as if they were Convention refugees, at least not at first. However, if the conflict continues for several years, then temporary asylum should be converted automatically to an option to establish permanent status. A limbo status should have a time limit. During the interim period, the welfare, education and health needs of those in limbo should be met.

Are there limits to such obligations? What if the cost of providing for the welfare needs of these temporary residents means that the facilities and

[handwritten: African ports use this argument but are more such schemes!]

[handwritten: Q]

support for those of a country's own citizens are at risk? What happens if the *[handwritten: Q]* health, education and welfare conditions of one's own citizens deteriorate? What happens if one country alone carries the major burden, not only in terms of numbers, but in costs and sacrifices for helping the refugees? Is there no limit to this obligation to provide temporary protection? *[handwritten: Q]*

What has been suggested above are a number of metaguidelines for determining which actions are considered illegitimate in dealing with migrants. Note that the question of legitimacy and illegitimacy has clearly shifted from the migrants to the actions of government. For people in desperate situations, issues of legitimacy are beside the point. For established governments they are not. We need guidelines for articulating what are and what are not legitimate actions for a government when faced with such situations. And to arrive at these guidelines, we need a conceptual framework to devise principles. *[handwritten: Key]*

One metaprinciple states that the principles of legitimacy vary with different groups of migrants. Thus, economic migrants require one set of *[handwritten: (1)]* responses, while Convention refugees require another. The groups may overlap. As suggested earlier, economic migrants, who are imported as temporary workers but who are allowed to remain for long periods, have the same rights as Convention refugees have acquired in practice—the right to become full members of the host state. *[handwritten: This option does not exist in Af.]*

A second metaprinciple states that the principles of legitimate activity vary with the type of action expected of the host state as well as with the group being hosted. Thus, legitimacy of a state requires that the state not *[handwritten: a(2)]* allow its members to exploit temporary workers in the number of hours they work, the working conditions and other terms of employment. But if those temporary workers came under a short-term contract and were not allowed to extend their stay, then the host state has no obligation to permit them to apply for membership in the host society. But Convention refugees have such rights. If a state's activities are to be considered legitimate, its *[handwritten: Extended too far!]* obligations are not limited to *nonrefoulement* and simple obeisance to Article 33 of the Convention. States are obliged to follow all the articles and all subsequent practices that have emerged over time and through developments in case-law to protect Convention refugees. These include providing an opportunity for Convention refugees to become citizens of the state and to participate in the society during the interim period, short of assuming the full rights and obligations of citizens.

A third metaprinciple states that what is considered legitimate and illegitimate state activity in the treatment of migrants varies with the share of the burden borne by that state. Thus, the impact of the burden on the host *[handwritten: (3)]* society is not the only factor. The ability and willingness of other states to share the burden can set limits on one's obligations to Convention refugees, even if one's country is a country of first asylum. For example, if a group is clearly being persecuted and, in an "ethnic cleansing" operation, driven across the border, then the receiving state—if it has already taken in refugees that constitute 10 percent of its own population, if other countries have not agreed to resettle some of these refugees, and the refugees have no kin relationship with the state's members—then it may be fully legitimate to close the borders to any further new arrivals in such circumstances.

The last point leads to the fourth metaprinciple. The state's obligation varies with the kinship links between the migrants and the host population. This might at first seem discriminatory or even racist. Nevertheless, any study of actions that are considered legitimate or illegitimate by states responding to mass migrations recognizes that the extent of responsibility varies when the population at risk has some sort of shared identity— ethnicity, language, religion, ideology—with the host society.

Thus, in deriving guidelines for determining legitimate and illegitimate state responses towards migrants, four aspects must be taken into account when assessing which actions are legitimate and which are not: 1) the type of migrant group, 2) the type of obligation expected to be assumed by the host, 3) the burden of the obligation on the host relative to other states and 4) the identity relationship of the migratory group to the host society. Even though all four aspects for determining obligations must be considered when assessing the legitimacy or illegitimacy of a state's actions, the norms and rules applicable in each of the aspects can be articulated separately. Furthermore, each aspect has four different dimensions that correspond to the basic schema of the political state, civil society, welfare system and dominant nationality set out earlier.

There are four types of migrant groups that relate to the four basic dimensions of the schema above. The first group consists of refugees, both Convention refugees who flee because they fear persecution and humanitarian refugees who flee because the state is unwilling and/or unable to provide protection. The state is responsible for the security of its citizens. If it doesn't, won't or can't fulfil that function, or if it is the source of insecurity because it engages in persecution, then refugees are the result. States committed to accepting and fulfilling those obligations must pick up the slack and provide protection for those who flee. This means that the sovereignty of a state is no longer considered unboundaried when outsiders can claim the protection of this type of state.

The obligation to assume responsibility for refugees is not unboundaried. The share of the burden, the obligation assumed (whether the protection is temporary or that of permanent membership) and the identification of a state's own population with the refugees will all affect the limits of that obligation. It should, however, be noted that Western states that currently carry Convention refugee responsibilities have come nowhere near the limit to such an obligation. States that are (or aspire to be) legitimate democratic states are obliged to assume a proportionate share of responsibility for hosting humanitarian refugees in flight—either for a temporary period or for long-term membership and citizenship if the conflict is expected to be of some duration, and the hopes of the refugees' return seems slight—provided, of course, that the burden is shared somewhat.

The second group consists of temporary and short-term migrants— foreign students, business people, tourists and temporary skilled workers or labourers. A state is obligated to admit them, allow their free movement and protect their full civil rights, as long as they pose no threat to the state, its welfare system or the identity of its dominant nationality. With respect to the third and perhaps the only controversial point, it is quite justifiable to reject applications of neo-Nazis who, under the system of guaranteed civil liberties, want to spread hate propaganda against a particular group. If the national identity is tied to protecting everyone's liberties, then the liberty of those who would undermine such principles can itself be limited, including the liberty to enter one's country and spread hate propaganda. It is not necessary to establish that such individuals or groups threaten the security of anyone, merely that their behaviour offends fundamental principles of liberty per se.

As indicated earlier, there are boundary conditions on entry itself. It is illegitimate to import short-term labour if domestic labour is available to fulfil the tasks or if the importation of labour is simply a device to depress wage levels of the local population.

The third group of migrants consists of fellow nationals (not fellow citizens) or groups lacking a state guaranteed to protect that national group. If Hungarians are forced to flee Romania, then Hungary can be expected to resettle those in flight, even if the rest of the world assumes some share of the financial burden in the resettlement. Germany did this for East Germans; Israel assumed the obligation for Ethiopian and Soviet Jews. Croats can flee to Croatia and Serbs to Serbia in their ethnic battle. But what happens to the Muslims of Bosnia-Herzegovina? Who assumes responsibility for them? What about the Gypsies or Kurds who still lack states that can provide protection?

In cases where nationals lack a state of their own, the principle of burden-sharing becomes operative in its fullest sense. Aside from the obligations of other states to prevent such catastrophes and, as I have argued elsewhere, to intervene in such situations under certain circumstances, all states that claim to be democratic are obliged to assume a proportionate share of the burden for these humanitarian refugees.

The final group, and generally the smallest, are those who ask for temporary admission because they need access to a state's health or educational system. A state must have either excess and/or a specialized capacity to handle such cases as well as a willingness to permit noncitizens to access the system.

The primary beneficiaries are generally those who need specialized health or educational services unavailable in their home states and who can afford the full costs or are assisted by governments. They are most often the wealthy of other states. Unless providing such services to temporary migrants means that the host state will not be able to service its own citizens, then it is perfectly legitimate to allow temporary migration for this purpose. The most publicized situations are of those in medical and financial need who are offered such services, such as victims of the Chernobyl disaster or children who need open-heart surgery when their home states lack the skilled professionals and the infrastructure to perform such complex operations. Switzerland, for example, has established a specialized niche in assisting refugees who need long-term care.

A schema of types of migrants can be superimposed onto the primary scheme.

Types of Migrants

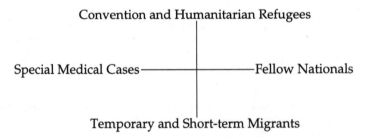

Convention and Humanitarian Refugees

Special Medical Cases ———————————— Fellow Nationals

Temporary and Short-term Migrants

If we now examine the types of obligations involved, we see that they fall into four categories that can be superimposed on the basic schema: 1) physical protection and *nonrefoulement*, 2) rights protection, 3) membership and 4) equality of access.

The first category above, the complementary positive and negative obligations of physical protection and *nonrefoulement*, were discussed earlier and are obligations extended to all refugees, even if the degree or the nature of that obligation varied with different types of refugees. Thus, the obligation not to return refugees to situations where their lives might be at risk is absolute and has the force of international agreements behind it for Convention refugees, whereas the obligation is only a moral one for humanitarian refugees. The obligation to provide membership is only *automatically* extended to refugees who are members of the dominant nationality, but comes into effect for other refugees and even guest workers after they have become permanently settled.

Also, as mentioned earlier, states have obligations to ensure that all temporary visitors and short-term workers have full human rights protection, and that such protection is not just restricted to its own citizens, nationals or refugees. While human rights obligations are universal and extended to anyone on a state's territory, welfare obligations are restricted and extended only to citizens, individuals who have been accepted for the citizenship track and special cases, such as the health care cases mentioned earlier, whom the state has admitted specifically for that purpose.

The United States appears to go further in accepting the obligation to educate the children of illegal aliens. This has been interpreted by American courts as a true obligation and not just an act of charity. Similarly, Canadian provinces provide welfare and legal aid to refugee claimants and not just those who have successfully proven that they are refugees. What is the rationale for extending the benefits of the health, education and welfare system to those who are not citizens and are not on the citizenship track?

The first thing to point out is that these people do not have equal access to the health, education and welfare (HEW) system, and equality of access is the hallmark of an obligation. The state may and does assume obligations to the *children* of illegal aliens because they are considered innocent victims whose futures should not be jeopardized because the American authorities were unable to enforce border controls. Furthermore, some of those children are American citizens, having been born in the United States. Thus, the consequences of educating one sibling and not another or denying education to large groups of children of illegal migrants would be far more destructive than extending that aspect of the health, education and welfare (HEW) system to them.

In the case of refugee claimants, there is a different problem. If a state assumes the obligations to protect refugees, then anyone *claiming* to be a refugee needs a minimal level of protection in order to survive and have the necessary resources, such as access to legal counsel, in order to establish the validity of his or her claim. Extending one aspect of the HEW obligations to refugee claimants is a direct byproduct of the essential obligation to them. However, there is no obligation to allow refugee claimants access to higher education or to specialized health care services. Obligations may be and are extended if they follow of necessity from the central obligation or if the consequences of denying access would be incompatible with the values of the society.

We thus have four types of obligations superimposed on the schema:

Types of Obligations

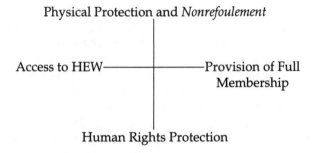

Physical Protection and *Nonrefoulement*

Access to HEW————————————Provision of Full
Membership

Human Rights Protection

In addition to considering the type of group and the variable types of obligations, another consideration is the share of the burden borne by a state given the specific group and the type of obligation involved. Burden-sharing has an equivocal meaning. It refers to the amount of assistance offered, the proportion of those in need who are assisted, the categories of people offered assistance, as well as the ratio of assistance relative to that provided by other states. Furthermore, the depiction of this principle as one of burden-sharing is also rather misleading since burden-sharing primarily suggests relativity with respect to the burden borne by other states. Yet, the degree of burden is, in fact, always determined by internal factors. These four factors are capacity, excess capacity, identity and international contracts.

A state has the obligation to provide food, shelter and emergency medical aid if migrants are hungry, homeless or suffering physical harm. No one on a state's territory should be allowed to go hungry or homeless as long as the state has the resources to provide for basic necessities. On the other hand, the burden borne by a state for treating certain medical conditions or providing access to schools would depend on excess capacity. For example, if the baby boom had progressed through a school system leaving excess capacity—facilities and surplus teachers up to a certain grade level—then the state can be expected to assume more of a burden in providing education up to that grade level for the children of illegal migrants.

Now it might appear that basic capacity and excess capacity are really the same thing, only that in the case of food, health and shelter all Western societies have excess capacity. The difference is that, in the area of basic needs, capacity is assumed unless a state can demonstrate that providing food, shelter or emergency medical care to refugees or irregular migrants would jeopardize the lives of its own citizens. In the case of the HEW system, there is no assumption of an obligation unless excess capacity can be demonstrated; that is, where it can be shown that the services offered would incur only marginal costs to the state.

A state's self-identity is the third factor in determining the extent of the burden related to a specific obligation towards a specific group of migrants. A state that bases its sense of self and ethics of obligation on premodern terms—such as on the requirements of religion in the case of Iran, which defines itself as an Islamic state—would assume its burden towards all followers of its religion. A state that defines itself in modern terms as a nation-state (England, France) or a new nation-state (America, Australia, Canada) or a pan-nationalist state (Italy, Germany, some Arab states) or a national liberation state (many African states, for example, that have the function of forging national identities) would have very different burdens from one another.

This third factor results in a positive obligation to others; but a state also has the obligation to protect its own citizens, collectively as well as individually. The extent of the burden is limited to the point at which an influx is *Rule* perceived as endangering the security of a state's citizens (for example, when those fleeing want to use the territory of the host state as a base for fighting a guerrilla war) or the national identity (when the incoming group is so large relative to the host population that the latter's self-identity is endangered). The latter points directly raise the issue of identity, the fourth factor in addition to the migrant group, the type of obligation and the burden that the society is asked to bear in assessing the legitimacy of exclusion and acceptance rules for entry.

There are four types of identity factors: family, language, class and ideology. Ethnicity, the most widely recognized identity factor, is (as we shall try to show) a composite and not a basic category. Race is not a legitimate category at all.

Family is the most critical ingredient of identity and has always posed a thorn to consensual theorists of membership who assume a radical individualism as the basis of their doctrine. Immediate family members—parents, spouses and children—have effectively been given virtually the same rights as the original migrating family member. A row in the press generally provokes widespread sympathetic support for the spouse, child or parent who is denied entry. The state is generally held to have an obligation towards the child, the spouse or the parent of an immediate family member with residence status in the country, which seems to be a logical consequence of its obligation towards individuals already resident in the country. After all, this is similar to the state's responsibilities towards its own citizens, where the state renders rights and protection to its citizens' minor children who are born and living abroad, presumably on the premise that a child is bound by the parent's membership until the child is of age to make her or his own choice. The only exception seems to be with respect to the welfare system in which migrating parents are required to reside in the state for a certain period before they are eligible to receive state pensions. This exception, in fact, confirms the principle of obligation while allowing a reasonable period for its application lest immediate family members gain access to social service benefits without making any commitment whatsoever to the new country.

Ethnicity is but an extension of the family category. The right of return based on line of descent is rooted in this factor. This right is given to Germans, Italians and Greeks. Israel provides an automatic right of return to Jews who usually don't speak Hebrew, who may have no ethnic characteristics in common (Ethiopian Jews) and may be secular or even antireligious with no knowledge of Judaism. (Many, if not most, Jewish migrants from the Soviet Union fall into this category.) But they are allowed entry because they identify with dominant nationality in at least one key aspect. This example also indicates that ethnicity alone is not the critical factor, for the national identity may not be based simply on ethnic characteristics. Furthermore, the ethnicity is often as not really a linguistic identification, at least in the first instance.

Nevertheless, it is considered legitimate to discriminate in favour of migrants who speak the same language, even when there is no common ethnicity. This is not simply because the costs of resettlement are reduced and access to the labour market is eased, but because those who speak the same language are considered already partially acculturated to the national identity. In the case of Convention refugees, however, language is irrelevant. Conversely, such discrimination becomes particularly important if the national group speaking the language is part of a diminishing minority, at least in relative terms.

Unlike language, class would seem to be irrelevant as a factor in legitimizing migration. In fact, it is perhaps the most critical factor other than family membership. In the group of temporary visitors—tourists, visitors or temporary workers—the middle or upper classes predominate with the exception of physical labourers who are imported for the harvest season or for construction projects. When domestic service workers are allowed entry, particularly when they are given the opportunity to become members of the society after fulfilling their contracts, generally the educational requirements for their entry are high enough to ensure that they come from a middle-class background. Radical egalitarians usually denounce such requirements as illegitimate discrimination against "lower" classes, but since these migrants are allowed in based on the host society's self-interest, and since the success of these societies depends on a continual upgrading of its workforce's skills, then discriminating in favour of a better class of migrant is indeed legitimate, which includes giving priority to investors who bring in capital that will create jobs for local citizens. Such preferential treatment is misrepresented when it is depicted as putting citizenship up for sale.

Using class as a factor is illegitimate only in the treatment of Convention refugees. But even in this group there is generally a very high proportion of educated individuals, especially relative to their numbers in the states from which they flee, for who else would have the funds, contacts and knowledge to seek refuge? Besides, such groups are often prime targets of persecution.

Class is *not* a factor when dealing with mass movements of persecuted minorities to countries of first asylum because the kinship factor across border areas is more important. Generally, however, those given entry permits in cases of mass movements—such as those who fled Hungary in 1956, Czechoslovakia in 1968, the Ugandan Asians kicked out by Idi Amin—were overwhelmingly members of the middle class.

Ideology is the last legitimate discriminatory factor, particularly for humanitarian refugees. The refugees' religious or political convictions are relevant criteria for those receiving them. Let me offer one odd example, a case where Canada allowed refugees to enter but never classified them as refugees for fear of insulting the United States. Canada permitted over 100,000 Americans to enter the country during the Vietnam War. This number was over and above the normal intakes, and Canada did not require those individuals and families to apply to immigrate from abroad. Draft dodgers, deserters and families that did not want their children to serve in the Vietnam War were not taken in as part of the immigration quota or in accordance with regular immigration criteria. On the other hand, they were not designated as refugees. Nevertheless, they were allowed to stay and become Canadians as if they were refugees, partly because Canada did not support the Vietnam War and because Canada gained immigrants who had a great deal in common with Canadians. But the main reasons had to do with the Canadian national identity, at least in English Canada, which was largely founded by Americans who were then British subjects and who were not sympathetic to the War of Independence. Ease of entry was also a way of asserting Canadian superiority when citizens of a country, that advertised itself as the best country in the world, chose to come north. In other words, they were allowed entry because they fitted in with the ideology that helped forge the Canadian identity.

Usually the ideological factors are far less subtle. The West gave preferential treatment to the those fleeing Communist regimes. Iran provides sanctuary to fellow members of their religion who fled Communists in Afghanistan or Saddam Hussein's tyranny in Iraq.

What I have tried to show is that the elements legitimating entry are far more complex, even with respect to admission to membership than the usual reductionist efforts to mediate between *jus soli* (place of birth) and *jus sanguinis* (line of descent). Membership rights, the ultimate permit to enter a society, are rooted in far more factors than these ascriptive issues or even simple consensual premises, for many involved and overlapping obligations and preferences determine who is and who is not given priority for entry. These obligations and preferences are not reducible to a form of social contract between the state and the individual, or an obligation based on descent or place of birth. For example, most states do not consider that children born of visitors have an automatic right to become citizens, though some traditional immigration countries generally accord that right. But such rights are products of the particular histories of those societies rather than a legitimating basis for entry to membership.

References

Adelman, Howard. "Humanitarian Intervention: The Case of the Kurds." In *International Journal of Refugee Law* 4, no. 1 (April 1992).

_____. "The Ethics of Humanitarian Intervention: The Case of the Kurdish Refugees." In *Public Affairs Quarterly: Special Issue on Refugees* 6, Issue 1 (January 1992).

PART TWO

Case Studies in
The Developing World

3

The African Refugee Regime with Emphasis on Northeastern Africa: The Emerging Issues

Gaim Kibreab

Introduction

This paper raises some critical issues in the African refugee regime. The economic, social and physical infrastructures of most of the African refugee-hosting countries are on the verge of collapse. These fragile infrastructures are further weakened by mass migration that may, in extreme cases, lead to disintegration of the delicate socio-economic fabric of the societies in question. In such situations mass migration may threaten the social, economic and political stability and security of the receiving societies. As Loescher observes, many host governments, especially the marginalized ones, are forced to "walk a tightrope in trying to balance economic, national security and humanitarian interests."[1] Hitherto the impact of mass migration between states has been palliated by international assistance, which has enabled many African governments to cope with the task of hosting refugees. In view of the dramatic changes at the end of the 1980s and the beginning of the 1990s, the strategic significance of many of the economically impoverished African states may be reduced in the post-Cold War period. This may in turn negatively affect the flow of refugee aid to such poor countries. If that happens, we may increasingly see humanitarian concerns (in the countries that are overwhelmed by the burden) being sacrificed in the interests of national security. In poor Third World countries nothing would be more threatening to the viability of asylum than the failure of the international donor community to adhere to the principle of burden-sharing as it is enshrined in the preambles of both the 1951 Convention and the Statute of the United Nations High Commissioner for Refugees (UNHCR).

One of the key elements that gave vitality and resilience to the African refugee regime has been international cooperation, i.e, mobilization of resources in the developed countries to finance operations of emergency relief and self-sufficiency programs. This does not, however, suggest that all the costs associated with hosting refugees are met by the contributions from donor countries. The host governments and societies, especially the poor, are the ones who bear the brunt of the burden because they have to share their natural resources with refugees.

The African refugee regime, especially in the poor countries, is already under heavy pressure. In Africa most self-sufficiency projects for refugees are based on agricultural production in which host governments allocate cultivable land and the UNHCR meets the costs of initial inputs and implements. The problem of land shortage has led to inappropriate land use practices in many countries. For example, land degradation in some of the refugee-receiving countries, like Somalia, Ethiopia, Sudan, Djibouti, Malawi and elsewhere, is becoming more critical with every passing year. This is caused by inappropriate land use practices, namely overcultivation without fallow periods or without use of yield-boosting or replenishing soil nutrients (fertilizers and organic manure, pesticides, insecticides, etc.), overgrazing due to shrinkage of grazing areas and increasing numbers of livestock and deforestation from excessive cutting of trees for fuel, construction materials, charcoal-making, clearance for cultivation, etc. The problem of environmental degradation is exacerbated by poverty in which the poorest section and the most marginalized groups, including refugees, cause heavy damage to the environment in the process of eking out a living. In these circumstances, poverty has become the cause and effect of environmental degradation.

In this context, the central question facing governments, agencies and academic analysts regarding the African refugee regime is whether or not the institution of asylum in such poor countries will withstand the onslaught of future developments engendered by demographic pressures, land shortages, poverty, environmental degradation and reduction of international assistance. The latter is expected as a result of increased demands and/or shifting of priorities in the international arena. The level of international assistance and environmental degradation are the two most critical key elements in determining, on the one hand, the magnitude of the caseload and on the other, the ability of the institution of asylum in such poor countries to cope with the ever-increasing categories of persons defined vaguely by the Organization of African Unity (OAU) Convention as refugees and by the various General Assembly resolutions and decisions of the Executive Committee of the High Commissioner for Refugees as "persons in refugee-like situation."

This paper will compare the problems in the institution of asylum in Western and African countries. It will argue that the institution of asylum is faced with serious problems not only in the Western countries. The deepening poverty in Africa is causing mass displacements within and between countries. The receiving countries are as poor as the sending countries; their ability to cope with large influxes without assistance from the donor countries is either extremely limited or nonexistent. In view of the denouement of the Cold War, which may lead to lessening of refugee aid to such poor countries, it will be argued that in the long term, the safety and durability of the institution of asylum is more questionable in poor Third World countries than in the affluent West.

One way of salvaging the institution of asylum in these poor countries may require a certain degree of streamlining to enable the poor host countries to distinguish the individuals in need of protection from the mass of persons who are lumped together as requiring assistance. To alleviate human suffering, it does not make sense to distinguish between the two categories, namely between those who flee because of actual or potential life-threatening political violence and those whose lives are threatened imminently by shortage of food and water. Both categories need food, shelter and water. This is not, however, the whole truth. The fact that both categories are destitute should not blur their differences. Those who flee because of life-threatening violence either because they were made targets or they were political activists do not only require food, water and shelter, but also protection against *nonrefoulement*.

This paper will argue that the major threat to individual protection in the African refugee regime is constituted in the OAU Convention, not only in the broad definition of the term "refugee," but particularly in the determination procedure of mass asylum. One way to overcome this shortcoming is through legitimate discrimination. If this is not done, illegitimate discrimination will be inevitable and the viability of the institution of asylum as it exists today will be threatened. It may sound paradoxical for the author to advocate individual status determination as opposed to mass determination when the latter largely seems to be favoured by African governments, donors and academic analysts. The OAU Convention has often been referred to as a model for the rest of the world;[2] this notwithstanding, it will be argued here that the major threat to the institution of asylum in the continent is enshrined in African practice based on this instrument. To see how this problem has arisen, it will be necessary to examine the origins of the institution of asylum in the international context.

Evolution of the International Refugee Regime

The evolution of the international refugee regime was marked by three major historical events, namely World War I, World War II and the processes of decolonization and nation building in the Third World countries. Organized response (albeit limited in scope and in terms of rights accorded to refugees) to the refugee problem dates back to immediate post-World War I when nearly 9.5 million refugees were produced as a result of the war.[3] Many more were also internally displaced. The League of Nations appointed Fridtjof Nansen as High Commissioner on behalf of the League in connection with the problems of Russian refugees in Europe in 1921. He was entrusted with the responsibility of supervising the resettlement or repatriation of Russians, Greeks, Turks and Bulgarians.[4]

This was undertaken as a temporary measure that was expected to end with the assimilation of the Russians, but new tensions and political crises in Central and Eastern Europe generated new waves of refugees. In 1933 the League appointed another High Commissioner "for refugees coming out of Germany."[5] These interventions were rudimentary, but they nevertheless laid the foundation for future institutions. The most effective institution of asylum was developed in the aftermath of World War II and with the onset of the Cold War hostilities. During that time refugees came from the totalitarian states. The largest numbers came from Hungary in 1956 and Czechoslovakia in 1968. The latter turned into a major refugee-producing country after the defeat of the Prague Spring uprising.

The 1951 Convention, with its temporal and geographic limitation, was designed to serve in the immediate post-World War II period. The definition of the term "refugee," adopted in the Statute of UNHCR and the Convention suggests that the major concern of the states that ratified the Convention pertained only to the refugees that were created during World War II. Even though World War II caused large and unprecedented population displacements, those who were displaced during the war and its aftermath were gradually absorbed into the national economies of the receiving countries, which were experiencing unprecedented rates of economic growth in the context of depleted population and high demand for labour. Their integration into the host societies was also facilitated by their cultural and racial backgrounds. Above all, however, the devastated post-war European economies' absorption capacity was facilitated by the financial and technical assistance provided by the United States of America in the form of the Marshall Plan, which was designed to facilitate quick economic recovery.[6] The solutions envisaged to the refugee problem by the 1951 Convention were therefore strongly influenced by the favourable socio-economic conditions that existed in the Western world immediately after the World War II.[7] On the basis of this instrument, Western practice, relating to solution of the refugee problem, is heavily biased in favour of permanent exile. As a result, international humanitarian intervention in the form of refugee assistance is focused on postflow activities. Preflow interventions are considered outside the purview of the international refugee regime because of the principle of state sovereignty. This approach has stretched the institution of asylum to near breaking point in some poor African host countries.[8]

The Refugee Definition

The refugee definition contained in the 1951 Convention is narrow. It underpins the presence of well-founded fear of persecution as a key element to refugee status.[9] The definition contains subjective and objective elements, i.e, "fear" and "well-foundedness" respectively.[10] However, meeting this criterion alone does not entitle a person to refugee status. It is a status available only to those who meet the above stated criterion and who are at the same time outside the country of their nationality.[11] The Convention also requires individual determination of refugee status because its major focus is the individual. As Zolberg et al. state:

> By capturing the classic types encompassed by the notion of refugee—that is, members or target groups and more active political dissenters—the convention's statute codified essential elements of the Western experience.... The selection of "persecution" as the key operational criterion was in keeping with the desire of the international community to make the status of refugee exceptional, so as to preclude overwhelming numbers.[12]

As we shall see later, those persons who are displaced within their own countries of origin due to "well-founded fear of persecution" do not fall within the realm of the refugee regime as defined by the 1951 Convention. Such persons are referred to as "internally displaced" persons, or for assistance purposes, as a category of "persons in refugee-like situation." Those who flee their countries of origin due to either man-made or natural disasters are not, according to the definition of the Convention, persons of concern to the UNHCR. They are considered as migrants falling outside the purview of the international refugee regime. The temporal and geographic limitations stipulated in the Convention[13] clearly show that the refugee problem and the activities of the organization entrusted with the responsibility to meet their needs were envisaged as temporary. They were intended to come to an end following the absorption or repatriation of the persons displaced during World War II and/or in its aftermath.

Contrary to what was envisaged by the states that ratified the Convention, the developments that have occurred during the last four decades show that violence unleashed by the two world wars was only one in the chain of recurrent waves of violence that cause population displacements. For example, in the colonial and semicolonial societies of Asia and Africa, the tensions, conflicts and frustrated expectations that accompanied decolonization and nation building generated mass exodus into countries where the 1951 Convention did not apply. The gap in the international organizational structure was soon felt and various UN General Assembly resolutions were passed requesting the UN High Commissioner to extend his "good offices" to meet the protection and material assistance needs of the new categories of refugees whose emergence was either not envisaged or excluded deliberately by the states that ratified the Convention. For example, in 1958 the General Assembly adopted resolution 1286 (XIII) requesting the High Commissioner to extend his "good office" to assist the Algerian refugees in Tunisia and Morocco.[14] During the repatriation of the same refugees, the General Assembly again passed resolutions 1500 (XV) and 1672 (XVI) requesting the High Commissioner to assist the returnees and the internally-displaced persons inside Algeria.[15] Since then several General Assembly resolutions have been passed extending the mandate of UNHCR on an ad hoc basis.

The temporal and geographic limitations were substantively eliminated with the adoption of the 1967 Protocol.[16] The coverage was widened to include territories that were excluded by the Convention. As a result of the "good offices" approach and the elimination of the temporal and geographic limitation, "The activities of UNHCR have developed well beyond the essentially promotional and diplomatic role envisaged for the office."[17]

The Definition of the Term "Refugee" in the OAU Convention

In view of the mass displacements that accompanied the anti-colonial struggles in Africa, notwithstanding the temporal and geographic elimination, the inadequacy of the narrow definition adopted by the 1951 Convention still constituted a major constraint on the ability of the independent African states to raise funds on behalf of the persons that were displaced due to the anti-colonial wars. In response to this in 1964, the Council of Ministers of the Organization of African Unity resolved to appoint a commission to "examine the refugee problem in Africa...."[18] In its Third Ordinary Session, it also invited the Commission to "to draw up a draft convention covering all aspects of the problem of refugees in Africa."[19] In its Eleventh Ordinary Session, the Council of Ministers placed heavy emphasis on the continent's inability to "solve this distressing [refugee] problem alone without the assistance of the international community."[20] The various categories with which the Organization of African Unity was concerned were not included in the 1951 Convention's definition of the term "refugee." Even though the international community would have been able to channel assistance through the "good offices" of the United Nations High Commissioner for Refugees, the independent African states were not satisfied with ad hoc arrangements. They wanted to make the victims of colonial oppression and domination the direct responsibility of the international refugee regime so that, on the one hand, they would be entitled to material assistance and on the other, the strain of their presence on the receiving countries' economic and social infrastructure would be offset.

Thus, in 1969 the OAU Convention Governing the Specific Aspects of the African Refugee Problem was adopted with a broader definition based on the specific African experience, which was characterized by mass displacements resulting from political instability and social unrest. Regional instruments are codified in response to regional needs and the OAU Convention was no exception. It adopted the definition of the 1951 Convention,[21] but added:

> The term "refugee" shall also apply to every person who, owing to external aggression, occupation, foreign domination or events seriously disturbing public order in either part or the whole of his country or origin or nationality, is compelled to leave his place of habitual residence in order to seek refuge in another place outside his country of origin or nationality.[22]

This made sense because one of the weapons used by the colonial forces was to disrupt rural life by targeting crops, watering points and routes of pastoral nomads. The social base of the anti-colonial national liberation movements was also in the rural areas. The peasantry supplied the food for the national liberation movements in most of the anti-colonial struggles in the continent. Hence, one of the strategies adopted by the colonial rulers was to attack villages and sources of livelihood in the rural areas. Their motto was "dry the sea in order to kill the fish." Destruction of food crops was, for example, one of the weapons the Ethiopian government used against the Eritrean peasantry in its futile attempt to subdue the national resistance. By disrupting rural life, the colonial forces hoped to quell the resistance against colonialism. In this heinous colonial strategy, economic destruction was used as a weapon to subdue the anti-colonial struggles by undermining their mass base. There was therefore a rationale for a broader definition that would accommodate all victims who fled colonial oppression and domination. As E.G. Ferris points out, "As governments increasingly use economic oppression as a tool of warfare, the distinction between political and economic motivations for flight breaks down.... Most refugees probably leave their homelands for both political and economic reasons."[23] The OAU Convention's rationale was that under the circumstances during the heyday of the anti-colonial wars, all those who were displaced due to wars, colonial oppression or domination qualified for refugee status.

The definition of the OAU Convention represents a major departure from the 1951 Convention in three areas.

(i) Unlike the 1951 Convention, which envisages a solution to the refugee problem in the context of exile, the OAU Convention envisages a solution to the refugee problem to result from changes that occur in the refugees' countries of origin. Refugeehood is seen as temporary. Postflow interventions are aimed at catering for the temporary needs of refugees by prolonging their refugee status until the conditions that force them to flee, and that prevent those in exile from returning, cease to exist. That is the reason why the OAU Convention is the only instrument that contains substantive provisions relating to voluntary repatriation. It affirms the voluntary character of repatriation and reintegration. It also calls for measures to facilitate repatriation and reintegration, and declares that refugees shall in no way be subjected to any form of punishment in relation to reasons giving rise to their refugee status.[24] In the countries of asylum, refugees are received as temporary guests awaiting a solution to their problems. However, history is rarely made to order. Developments in the last three decades have shown that some of the problems that force refugees to flee their homelands or that prevent those in exile from returning are long-lasting. Nowhere does the Convention mention that a solution to the African refugee problem is attainable in the context of exile.

The OAU Convention's departure from the 1951 Convention in this regard is easy to explain in a historical perspective. The 1951 Convention was passed in response to the refugee situation as it existed in the aftermath of World War II. At that time, the refugees were from Eastern and Central European countries. They were all considered victims of Communism. Since no one envisaged the future decay of the totalitarian states, the main preoccupation of the governments and the organizations that assisted them was with finding permanent homes for the refugees. This was possible with the receiving countries' expanding national economies. Displaced persons and refugees also played a key role in boosting the labour force that was depleted because of the war.

The economic and demographic conditions in the newly-born African states did not only constitute a mirror image of the situation that prevailed in the industrial countries during World War II, but colonial decay was obvious and the repatriation of its victims was considered inevitable.

Hence, a real solution to the African refugee problem resulted from fundamental changes that occurred in the sending countries. Despite the expectation of the states that ratified the OAU Convention, however, many refugee situations have become institutionalized and changes in some of the sending countries were not within sight. This was further complicated since the 1970s when a large proportion of the refugee population was produced by the independent countries. This institutionalization of the refugee problem has an implication on the OAU Convention's definition of the concept of refugee.

(ii) As stated above, the definition of the OAU Convention dispenses with the criterion of "well-founded fear of persecution." By adopting such a broad definition, it leaves the door of the regional refugee regime wide open to various categories of persons who were previously considered migrants or "persons in refugee-like situation," whose needs were either left unmet or were met through ad hoc arrangements. A historical perspective is essential to understand the reason why Africa has adopted a different, unique and generous definition of the term "refugee." The OAU Convention was ratified at the time when most of the former colonies had just achieved their political independence, but when other Africans were still suffering under the colonial yoke. The generosity that permeates the Convention reflects the determination of the newly independent states to help their brethren break the colonial yoke. The memories of colonial domination were fresh. The leaders wanted to extend protection to anyone who fled colonial domination. The lawyers who drafted the Convention and the states that subsequently ratified it viewed colonialism, especially when perpetrated by white minority rulers, as an adequate cause of mass displacement. Refugee status was extended to all persons who fled from colonial oppression. However, this was long before their policies prompted their own citizens to flee in search of international protection elsewhere. When the OAU Convention was ratified, only a few independent states were producing refugees. The major sending countries were the former Portuguese colonies, the minority regimes in Southern Africa, Sudan and Eritrea.

(iii) The OAU Convention contains provision for individual status determination, but host governments seldom apply this procedure except in the case of a few urban refugees who may enter the countries of asylum through airports. Generally, unlike the 1951 Convention, the OAU Convention does not require individual status determination. Refugee status is granted en masse. An individual does not need to show that he or his community has been subjected to ill-treatment in order to be granted refugee status. It is enough that they have fled from a situation that meets the broad criteria enumerated in Article I (2) of the OAU Convention. In the majority of cases, the existence of such conditions is well known in the receiving country, so often no group or individual interviews are conducted to determine causation. Any person who comes from a country where there is war or social unrest is considered a *prima facie* case qualifying almost automatically for refugee status.[25]

The Problems of a Broad Definition

In migration studies, definitions are crucial because obtaining protection by a host country and material assistance by the international refugee regime and states' obligations are determined by whether or not a person is defined as a refugee. If a person is defined as a refugee, this may have a far-reaching implication to the individual, as well as to the sending and receiving countries. Under the present system, the term "refugee" has become a catch-all that encompasses various categories of people who flee their countries of origin for diverse reasons that include: economic hardship, persecution, high population pressure on resources, international or civil war, expulsion, environmental degradation, famine, forcible relocation, etc. These mass movements occur within or between countries. Because the OAU Convention does not require individual status determination, most of these categories have been more or less treated as refugees or as persons in "refugee-like situations," sharing whatever is available in terms of protection and material assistance with "refugees."

In the Northeastern African countries (Sudan, Ethiopia, Eritrea, Somalia and Djibouti) this is complicated by population movements that are caused by economic hardships, which are difficult to distinguish from the other types of movements, for example, those caused by persecution, violence, war, conflicts, poverty, deprivation of freedom of movement, etc. This has necessitated the need to broaden UNHCR's activities in order to serve the new categories whose advent was not envisaged when the Convention was ratified. Through various General Assembly resolutions and decisions of the Executive Committee of the UNHCR,[26] the mandate of the UNHCR has been broadened on an ad hoc basis in order to meet the needs of the new categories that would otherwise lie outside the scope of the office if the definition of the term "refugee" were to be applied strictly.

As the situation stands, hundreds of thousands of African refugees and persons in refugee-like situations have been able to take advantage of the refugee support regime. This is due to the fact that the term "refugee" is a broad concept under the OAU Convention. It embodies diverse categories of persons who leave their areas of habitual residence due to many factors. Various new categories are also included in the international assistance regime by the various General Assembly resolutions since 1958 and decisions of the Executive Committee of the UNHCR, including those displaced by environmental degradation.[27] As a result, a myriad of ill-defined and vague terms such as "distress migrants," "environmental refugees," "economic refugees," "Convention refugees," "persons in refugee-like situations,"[28] "victims of man-made disasters," "de facto refugees," "displaced persons of concern to UNHCR," etc., have crept into the refugee regime, further complicating the already complex situation. As stated earlier, the consequence is that in Africa, especially in Northeastern Africa, the concept of "refugee" has become all embracing and refers to all categories of persons who cross international borders from countries where there is *prima facie* evidence of public disorder. This became more pronounced during the 1980s when hundreds of thousands were displaced due to drought, and when the gap in the existing international organizational structures precluded efficient management and delivery of emergency relief to "persons in refugee-like situation." For example, in 1981 when mass movements involving refugees and displaced persons in refugee-like situations caused by man-made disasters occurred, the Executive Committee of the UNHCR "emphasized …the leading responsibility of [UNHCR] in emergency situations which involve refugees in the sense of its Statute or of General Assembly resolution 1388 (XIV) and its subsequent resolutions."[29] The Executive Committee was referring to the resolution in 1959, which authorized the High Commissioner to extend his "good offices" in contributing to the assistance of refugees "who do not come within the competence of the United Nations."[30] Since then several General Assembly resolutions have been passed authorizing the High Commissioner to include in their assistance program persons who may not meet the criterion of the 1951 Convention. Whenever an emergency arose, humanitarian concern required immediate intervention and the only expedient and realistic course of action was to utilize the existing structures by expanding formally or informally the realm of operation of the UN agencies *in situ*. Often the gap is filled by the United Nations General Assembly, requesting the UNHCR to extend its "good offices" to serve in areas for which it lacks direct mandate.

Because of this, people who would have been considered migrants or people who move due to adversities in their areas of origin to pursue economic activities are often lumped together and referred to as "refugees." In these countries, cross-border migration for trade, employment, search for pasture, water sources, etc., have always been a common feature where there are strong economic and ethnic ties between the border communities. Without cross-border economic transactions, the economic viability of many such communities would probably have been threatened. That is why cross-border economic transactions have always been crucial among border communities all over Africa. Expansion of the refugee concept has meant including such persons in the international refugee regime. It is interesting to note that in these countries, expanding the definition of the refugee concept has had a retroactive effect, even on those economic migrants who would be considered fully integrated by any standards. For example, all Eritreans and Ethiopians in the Sudan, including those who came as migrants in the 1940s, are at present referred to as refugees. The same is also true of Mozambicans in Eastern Zambia.[31] There does not seem to be room for ordinary migrants from countries where there is a *prima facie* case of public disorder to be considered and treated as such. Governments refer to the citizens of such countries as "refugees" and this even includes those who have been living in those countries concerned long before a change of events gave rise to the need for international protection. Such ordinary migrants, depending on the benefits they expect to get, also refer to themselves as refugees. Hence persons who were fully integrated into the national communities may suddenly join the camps or settlements. This can be illustrated by the example of the author's own findings in Somalia and Sudan where there were many persons among the respondents who joined the camps or settlements despite the fact that they had been living in the said countries long before the change of events in their countries of origin as ordinary migrants. In my recent study in the Sudan, I found that 7 percent of the sample household heads had been in the country long before the onset of the events that prompted the flight of the Eritrean pastoralists and agro-pastoralists during the second half of the 1960s. These are not refugees in *sur plus*. They are people who had come as migrants and who had settled permanently without any intention of returning.

The Magnitude of the African Refugee Problem and the International Context

Judging from the plethora of writings that have appeared since the 1980s, the institution of asylum in the advanced industrial countries is under heavy pressure. The thrust of the argument is that the ever increasing numbers of "bogus" asylum seekers, the limited capacity of the institution of asylum, and the need to salvage the institution require far-reaching adaptations by governments. Since the mid-1980s, mounting concern about the increasing number of asylum seekers, mainly from poor Third World countries, has prompted outcries from government bureaucrats, academic analysts and right-wing political streams who urge their governments to make the institution of asylum inaccessible to "less deserving or bogus asylum seekers." As a result, in the future, immigration issues may become significant forces in shaping domestic political processes in Western countries.

By looking simply at the map of exile, it is difficult to understand the gravity of the threat posed by the so-called large numbers of "economic migrants" who allegedly camouflage themselves in the smokescreen of a "fear of persecution." According to the exponents of this view, if European governments do not harmonize their immigration policies in order to develop a common strategy that would curb the "dangerous develop-ments," they see the collapse of the institution of asylum as almost inevita-ble.[32] The question that springs immediately to mind is what will happen to the institution of asylum worldwide if all governments, including those in the Third World countries, do the same? If similar measures are taken by all refugee-hosting governments, the threat to the system will be global rather than regional. In Western countries, the system is threatened by exogenous factors, thus the restrictive policies pursued by the governments in North America and Europe are said to be in response to these threats. It cannot, however, be denied that factors such as degradation of humanitarian values, erosion of sympathy for refugees in the post-Cold War period, increasing xenophobia, lack of political will and ideological motive in the post-Cold War period, economic recession, as well as race considerations, may have direct or indirect influence on the policies and attitudes of the governments in the OECD countries.

Respective governments are trying to make Europe and North America fortresses. The aim is to make the system inaccessible to less deserving asylum seekers, but in reality, even those who need protection against persecution, i.e., bona fide asylum seekers, may find it difficult to gain entry into the system at a time when all asylum seekers from the poor Third World countries are considered *prima facie* as bogus or economic migrants. Some of the restrictions that have been introduced in many European countries are panic responses that are ineffective in screening illegitimate asylum seekers. The goal of "Fortress Europe" is fraught with problems because it has not been possible either to stop people from coming and/or to deport those who have been denied refugee status. The goal of stopping illegiti-mate asylum seekers is not possible to achieve as long as other channels of migration remain closed, and as long as hundreds of thousands are unable to eke out a meagre livelihood in the poor sending and receiving countries. In Western Europe and North America about 75 percent of all asylum applications are denied, but these countries have not deported those who are denied refugee status.[33] If these people are deported to the first countries of asylum, the burden of the latter may be increased considerably. This may also set a trend for emulation by the first countries of asylum. If they see the

rich countries deporting refugees, they may think that they have more
legitimate reason to do so because of their poverty.

**Table 1: Refugees and Resettled and Persons Granted Asylum in
Major Refugee-Receiving Countries, 1990**

	Refugees	*GNP per capita (U.S. $)*
United States	127,997	20,910
Germany	6,518	20,440
Canada	37,820	19,030
Greece	166	5,350
Australia	3,678	14,360
Hungary	2,561	2,590
New Zealand	738	
Netherlands	1,709	15,920
Japan	440	23,810
Norway	3,767	22,290
Austria	3,678	17,300
Spain	527	
Belgium	504	16,220
Sweden	12,839	21,570
Denmark	747	20,450
Switzerland	808	29,880
Finland	638	22,120
United Kingdom	1,100	14,610
France	13,073	17,820

Source: U.S. Department of State, Bureau for Refugee Programs in R.
Rogers and E. Copeland, *Global Refugee Policy: Issues in the 1990s*, draft.

The restrictive policies pursued by the OECD governments do not seem
to be working. Thus the challenge does not lie in making such territories
inaccessible or in a blanket labelling of refugees as "bogus" or, to borrow
Widgren's phrase, "asylum shoppers,"[34] but rather in the ability to develop
a mechanism to exclude less deserving persons from using the institution of
asylum as a channel for migration to prosperity without at the same time
jeopardizing the right of legitimate migrants to seek and get protection.
With increased restriction, access to asylum may become a random occurrence. Those who are able to pay exorbitant amounts to smugglers will still

be able to take advantage of the system of asylum. The weakest or those with a grave need for protection may unintentionally be excluded. The solution advocated by the governments in the West is not only too easy and unrealistic, but in the wrong hands, it may obliterate one of the finest achievements of Western civilization—the institution of asylum.

Table 2: Major Refugee-Hosting Countries in Africa by Refugee and National Populations[86]

	Refugee population (000) (A)	Nationals (B)	GNP per capita ($) (C)
Algeria	198,400	24.4	23,822
Burundi	90,700	5.3	220
Cote-d'Ivoire	70,500	11.7	790
Djibouti	67,400	n.a	n.a
Egypt	37,800		
Ethiopia	783,000	49.5	120
Guinea	325,000	5.6	420
Malawi	909,000	8.2	180
Senegal	55,300	7.2	650
Sierra-Leone	125,000	4.0	220
Somalia	358,500	6.1	170
South Africa	201,000		
Sudan	726,500	24.5	n.a
Swaziland	47,200	n.a	n.a
Tanzania	266,200	23.8	130
Uganda	156,000	16.8	250
Zaire	370,900	34.5	260
Zambia	133,950	7.8	390
Zimbabwe	186,600	9.5	650
Total	5,443,450		

Sources A: U.S. Refugee Committee, *World Refugee Survey* 1991; Sources B and C: World Bank, *World Development Report* (Oxford University Press, 1991)

Compared to the huge number of refugees in some of the poorest regions of the world, the number of refugees and asylum seekers in the OECD countries is insignificant, especially when looked at in relation to the capacity of their national economies. For example, in 1990 the total number of refugees resettled and persons granted asylum in all of the OECD countries was only 225,911 (see Table 1). These figures may not give a true picture of the situation because the number of rejected applications are not included, but even when such figures are included, they are far less than the total number of refugees hosted by the poorest countries in Africa. Between 1986 and 1990 the total number of applications received in Europe, North America and Australia were 1,687,200.[35] This figure is less than twice of the total number of refugees hosted by Malawi, one of the poorest countries in the world. As can be seen in Table 2, the two poorest war- and drought-torn countries in Northeastern Africa (Ethiopia and Sudan) in 1990 were hosting almost the same number of refugees as the number of applications received by all the developed countries in five years. Malawi alone hosts over 900,000 refugees (see Table 2).

If the refugee problem is a global responsibility, as enshrined in the international legal instruments relating to refugees,[36] it would be expected that those with higher capacities of absorption would bear a bigger share of the burden. In reality, however, the amount of the burden borne by a country is determined by geographical proximity to the areas that generate refugees rather than by capacity. This is obviously clear from Tables 1 and 2. The average GNP per capita was U.S. $17,766 for the eighteen refugee-hosting industrialized countries in 1990, while the corresponding figure for the fourteen major refugee-hosting countries in Africa was U.S. $488. The average refugee population per country in the twenty major refugee-hosting countries in Africa was 271,720 in 1990, while the corresponding figure for the eighteen industrial countries was 12,551 (Tables 1 and 2).[37] Hence, if the collapse of the institution of asylum is a sole function of the level of external strain, the real danger of collapse would not have been in the rich countries of the West, but in Africa where the burden is heaviest and the link in the chain is the weakest. African countries, the poorest and most debt-ridden in the world, are hosting hundreds of thousands of refugees (see Tables 2 and 3). For example, the total debt stock in sub-Saharan Africa increased from U.S. $56,285,000 in 1980 to $175,836,000 in 1991. The corresponding figure for the total debt service was $6,298,000 and $10,604,000, respectively. The debt/export ratio increased from 97.1 percent in 1980 to 340.8 percent in 1991 (Table 3). Despite such structural problems and the large numbers of caseloads in the sub-Saharan African countries, neither of the host governments nor academic analysts have joined their colleagues in Europe and North America to sound alarm bells of collapse. However, their silence should not be construed to imply that things are in order. When there are changes of policies in such poor and undemocratic political systems, they tend to take dramatic turns in which the sounding of alarm bells and political actions may take place simultaneously. Sometimes political action may even take place without the knowledge of the outside world. If that happens, the world community may be caught unaware.

Table 3: Sub-Saharan Africa's Debt Profile (U.S. $ millions)

	1980	1986	1987	1988	1989	1990	1991*
Total debt	56,285	116,083	143,531	145,916	154,751	173,737	175,836
Long-term debt	43,555	95,447	121,694	123,826	131,069	146,240	149,151
Short-term debt	9,697	13,607	14,266	15,090	17,302	20,895	20,329
Debt to IMF[†]	3,033	7,030	7,571	7,000	6,380	6,603	6,356
Interest arrears	215	2,523	4,440	6,353	7,965	10,500	9,319
Debt service							
Total debt service	6,298	10,121	8,750	10,090	9,466	10,070	10,604
Long-term debt	4,786	7,652	6,721	7,941	7,340	8,255	9,042
IMF Payments/charg	487	1,689	1,543	1,493	1,596	1,192	1,009
Short-term debt(int)	1,025	780	486	655	531	623	553
Resource flows							
Net resource flows[††]	11,008	10,755	13,144	13,577	17,042	16,842	16,357
Net transfers[††]	5,946	6,578	8,354	8,420	12,603	12,172	11,167
Net transfers (IMF)	730	-954	-863	-461	-734	-527	-430
Debt ratio							
Debt/exports (%)	97.1	325	359.6	361.2	351.9	329.5	340.8
Debt/GNP (%)	28.1	72.4	99.8	98.1	103.5	111.1	106.1
Debt service/ exports (%)[†††]	10.9	28.3	21.9	25.0	21.5	19.1	20.5

*projected; [†]outstanding obligations to IMF; [††]net resource flows are disbursements on long-term flows, minus repayment of principal; net transfers are net resource flows minus interest payments and repatriated profits; [†††]actual debt service.

Source: Africa Recovery, World Bank, World Debt Tables 1991-1992, December 1991African Host Governments' Coping Strategy

How do African host governments manage to cope with the responsibility of hosting large numbers of refugees when their national economies are plunged into deep crises, and when the basic needs of their own citizens remain largely unmet? Hitherto, host governments in Africa have been able to develop an effective coping strategy that has enabled them to negotiate and shift part of the responsibility for catering to refugees and persons in "refugee-like situations" to the international donor community.

The centrepiece of most African governments' refugee policies is based on the principle of minimizing cost to themselves and their citizens. Most of their settlement strategies are formulated to shift the financial responsibility of meeting the needs of refugees within their territories to the international refugee assistance regime and to maximize benefits as much as possible to themselves and their citizens. For example, the settlement policies of African governments are based on spatial segregation where refugees are kept either in camps in care or they are relocated to settlements in isolated sites. The reasons for such settlement strategies stem from the security (real or imagined) and economic needs of the countries of asylum. Placement in spatially segregated sites also facilitates control of refugee communities. The OAU Convention stipulates that refugees should not engage in "subversive activities"[38] and this settlement form helps to prevent such activities from taking place.

Keeping refugees in a designated and spatially segregated site also allows monitoring of refugees' political behaviour. By placing refugees in spatially segregated sites, host governments protect their citizens from competition with refugees for resources such as pasture, arable land, water, housing, transportation, commodities and employment. That is why most of the governments are anathema to self/spontaneous settlement and naturalization of refugees. They prefer putting refugees in camps and settlements where their negative impact on the economic, social and physical infrastructures of the host country and society would be minimal, and where their assistance needs would be indefinitely met whenever necessary by the international refugee support regime. This is clear from the various limitations embodied in their legislation regarding rights of employment, movement, residence, naturalization, business licence, property rights, etc. For example, Sudan and Botswana have entered reservations on Article 26 of the 1951 Convention regarding freedom of movement and residence. Angola, Mozambique, Rwanda, Zambia, Zimbabwe and Tanzania have also entered some form of reservation to Article 26 of the 1951 Convention limiting refugees' right to freedom of movement and choice of residence.

Other reasons why African host governments place refugees in spatially segregated sites include: prevention of integration in host societies,[39] maintenance of ethnic balance, which is crucial for political stability, and control of rural-urban migrations.[40] By placing refugees in spatially segregated sites, governments try to indefinitely perpetuate their status of refugeehood. In the view of African host governments, refugee status ends only with repatriation, while in the OECD countries refugee status may end with naturalization. That is the reason why many of the host governments in

Africa deny refugees the privilege of acquiring citizenship. Camps and settlements are designed to perpetuate refugee status, not to eliminate it. According to the existing international legal instruments relating to refugees, one way to terminate refugee status is through naturalization. This option is nonexistent in almost all African host countries.[41] As stated earlier, African governments receive refugees as guests on a temporary basis. They are only given temporary refuge until the conditions that prompted their flight cease to exist.

The system is not that rigid, though, because there are many refugees who manage to stay outside of camps and settlements where lack of formal citizenship may not affect their economic or social situation. The prerequisite for this, however, is common ethnicity.[42] Generally self-settlement, when it takes place in defiance of government policy, has a tendency to render the self-settled refugees vulnerable to exploitation by the rich members of the local population in return for protection against being rounded up for forcible relocation to camps or settlements.[43] Those who self-settle among their co-ethnics outside camps or settlements tend to be easily integrated into host societies, but they may not necessarily be better off.[44] The fact that there are refugees who manage to reestablish themselves outside the formal settlements does not show that the system is flexible; it only shows that the system is imperfect.

What are the problems associated with this approach? Firstly, camps that have been established en route to permanent solutions have become institutionalized and scarce resources are spent on care and maintenance, resulting in donor compassion fatigue and in loss of refugee independence and initiatives. Secondly, in many countries refugees in settlements have been unable to achieve self-sufficiency. As a result, they have become dependent on international assistance for their survival.[45] Thirdly, confinement of large populations in designated areas has also led to poor land-use practices (overcultivation, overgrazing and deforestation), resulting in soil and vegetation degradation, as well as a drastic decline of productivity.[46] In many cases these confinements have a tendency to render traditional resource management regimes inoperative.[47] Such traditional management regimes are instrumental in any sustainable use of renewable resources.

As stated earlier, the responsibility of hosting refugees is a global concern, but the burden is not shared equally by the signatories of the 1951 and the 1969 OAU Conventions. Nevertheless, despite the inordinate distribution of the burden, there is an effective international division of labour based on cooperation and understanding between the rich and poor countries of the world. The division of labour in the international refugee regime, as in international trade and commerce, is based on the principle of comparative advantage. The countries of first asylum in the Third World

provide land for residence, grazing and cultivation. The rich countries meet
the financial costs of emergency relief (food, water supply and temporary
shelter), investment for establishment of camps' and settlements' infrastructures (roads, primary schools, health care, water supply) and initial
production inputs such as seeds, agricultural implements (oxen, tractors,
hoes, digging sticks, spades, etc.). Administrative supports are also provided in the form of salaries for local staff employed in the refugee sector or
in the national refugee commissions. Even though the UNHCR has been
from time to time faced with budgetary constraints (with the worst budget
deficit of U.S. $40 million in 1989) due to inadequate donor response, funds
have been forthcoming for meeting basic needs of refugees. Without this
coping strategy, the strain caused by the large numbers of different categories of groups, which are often labelled as "refugees" for the purpose of
providing assistance, would have been too much to bear in many of the poor
countries.

Why Do African Host Governments Pursue Open-Door Policies?

Most of the sub-Saharan African countries are in the grip of economic and
social crises, yet they have one of the most generous refugee policies in the
world. African host governments pursue an unprecedented open-door
refugee policy because of the prevailing reality of the continent during the
anti-colonial wars. The OAU Convention Governing the Specific Aspects of
the Problem of Refugees was passed at a time when international response
to the refugee problem was relatively favourable and when demographic
pressures, land shortage, indebtedness, poverty, environmental degradation, etc., were not as pressing as they are today.

It is important to observe, however, that the open-door refugee policy of
many African governments cannot only be explained by their adoption of
the principles enshrined in the OAU Convention because in reality, substantive or procedural provisions are seldom complied with by host countries in their treatment of refugees. This is not to suggest that refugees are
always ill-treated, but the following are some of the important reasons that
may explain the open-door refugee policy of many African governments.
(i) The factors that prompt mass exodus are intricately interlocked. Sometimes it is not easy to distinguish between mass movements caused by war,
economic hardship, violence and natural disasters. All may result in disrup-
tion of public order, forcing people to flee in search of livelihood and
protection outside the area of their habitual residence. If security and
sources of livelihood are accessible within the countries concerned, internal
displacement results. However, if this cannot be achieved within the

country of origin due to a war, drought or lack of life-sustaining opportunities, external displacement may become the only alternative strategy for survival. Since the subjective element of fear of persecution under the OAU Convention is rarely applied, practically all the categories of people displaced by the above factors are lumped together for the purposes of assistance. From a humanitarian perspective, there does not seem to be an acceptable reason for excluding these categories from assistance programs. This is more so in a region where not only the factors prompting flight are complex and difficult to isolate from each other, but where there is neither developed administrative infrastructure nor resources to screen the various categories that are vaguely agglutinated as refugees.

(ii) International cooperation enabled African governments to cope with hosting a mass of asylum seekers and "persons in refugee-like situations." The short-term costs were met by the international donor community without straining the national budgets of the receiving countries.[48] In fact, in some countries (like Somalia during the 1980s) the refugee sector was the only booming industry that provided employment, scarce commodities and foreign exchange.[49] This may be considered a resource by countries where unemployment and shortage of foreign exchange constitute major constraints on economic activities. Thus there are certain sections, often in the upper echelons of national bureaucracies, that benefit from hosting large numbers of refugees and, as result, that may be positively predisposed towards them.

(iii) Another reason that may explain the open-door policies of African governments is their desire to search for a respectable position in the world community. Even those governments with the worst records of human rights performance and who have distinguished themselves with ill-treatment of their own citizens are hospitable to refugees. The explanation must be other than respect for human dignity and humanitarian principles. This may suggest that governments with bad records of human rights performance see hosting a large number of refugees as an opportunity for improving their international image. If this is true, with the increased demands for democracy, we may increasingly witness a move towards restriction. Theoretically, it is expected that there would be a positive correlation between pursuance of open-door refugee policies and democratic governance in a refugee-receiving country because of commitment to humanitarian interests. This is not, however, often the case. One of the reasons why tyrant regimes may open their doors to victims of violence perpetrated by their colleagues across the border is partly to divert international attention from the victims of their own violence and partly as stated earlier, to improve their image in the world by shouldering a share of global responsibility. A poor democratic government accountable to its own citizens may have no such concerns.

One such concern is a host country's citizens' human right to freedom of expression and assembly. In dictatorial regimes, nationals are not allowed to challenge their governments' policies or to protest against such policies. If their governments are positively predisposed to asylum, so would the nationals, at least superficially. They cannot object to their governments' policies no matter how much they disapprove of them. This may be illustrated by the experience of the Sudan during the time of the elected government. The refugees in the country were subjected to unprecedented forms of harassment and round-ups during the period of the democratically-elected government of Syd Sadiq El Mahdi. During the three years of elected government, antirefugee propaganda in the newspapers and on television was more than what was produced or shown in the previous twenty-five years.

This suggests that in poor countries that suffer from lack of adequate resources, citizens' increased accessibility to freedom of expression and assembly is likely to result in them challenging their governments' right to allocate scarce resources to liens when they themselves suffer from such shortages. The only hope is that with democratization, the root and the immediate causes of the refugee problem may be eliminated, allowing refugees to return in peace and dignity. As long as the root and the immediate causes that prompt people to flee remain unsolved, the democratization process in receiving countries may ironically represent one of the factors that may threaten the institution of asylum.

(iv) Governments may also provide asylum to refugees because of sympathy to their cause. During the anti-colonial wars, many of the African host governments were supportive of the national liberation struggles and refugees were either regarded as victims of colonialism who deserve protection or as a potential source of recruitment for the anti-colonial wars. For example, Siad Barre's government in Somalia considered the able-bodied male adults among the refugee population as potential recruits into the Somali armed forces to fight in the Ogaden and later against the opposition inside the country. For example, on February 28, 1989, the UNHCR wrote to the government of Somalia stating:

> The UNHCR assistance programme in northwestern Somalia was seriously disrupted following the outbreak of conflict at end of May 1988. After a number of earlier presentations, on 5 October 1988 the High Commissioner wrote to the Government of Somalia expressing serious concerns about lack of monitoring of the use of humanitarian assistance and *about the arming of refugees, who had thereby become party to the conflict.*[50] [emphasis added]

(v) Common ethnicity is also a decisive factor on how refugees are received, not only by governments, but mainly by local populations. In fact governments are often uncomfortable about receiving refugees who have members of their ethnic groups across the border for fear of disturbing ethnic balance.[51] One of the reasons why the government of Sudan remained committed to the strategy of placing all refugees in camps and settlements despite its failure for two decades to implement such a policy, was for fear of disturbing ethnic balance among the border population, which would in extreme situations threaten national or regional security.[52]

(vi) The open-door refugee policy of African states may also be motivated by humanitarian considerations even though it is difficult to understand why a government that flagrantly violates its own citizens' rights would receive refugees out of respect for humanitarian principles. The answer may lie in the powerlessness of refugees. The OAU Convention prohibits refugees from engaging in any subversive activities aimed against a member state of the OAU (except South Africa).[53] Refugees pose no threat against governments except in cases where they may be recruited by host governments to fight against opposition forces or when they are encouraged by a host government to attack the governments in their sending countries. The Rwandese refugees in Uganda are the case in point. What seems clear is that even though there are some African governments that accept refugees for humanitarian reasons, in the absence of international cooperation, this humanitarian concern is likely to vanish into thin air.

(vii) Many African governments are unable to stop people from crossing their borders, either because their borders are too extensive or they lack resources for patrolling them. This is the case when refugees settle spontaneously among their co-ethnics in border areas. Sometimes nationals may cooperate in hiding refugees even against the decisions of their own governments.[54] It is important to note here that the decisive factor is common ethnicity and adequate resource availability. The relationship between refugees and the nationals, even when they are of common ethnic background, tends to be exploitative.[55] As stated earlier, the rich members of the local population often take advantage of the impoverished refugees.

All the above are important factors for explaining the relatively open-door refugee policy of African governments. It must be noted, however, that the most important reason why the poor countries have been able to host hundreds of thousands of refugees and persons in refugee-like situation is due to the limited but relatively generous assistance provided by the UNHCR in cooperation with UN agencies and with many nongovernmental organizations. Many African national economies would have been overwhelmed by large numbers of refugees if it were not for the intelligently calculated coping strategies formulated by the poor refugee-hosting governments and the favourable international response to their appeal for assistance.

Ending of the Cold War and its Implication on the International Refugee Regime

In the immediate post-World War II period, there were two important motives underlying the development of the institution of asylum. Firstly, governments and civil society in Western countries were horrified by the heinous crimes committed by the National Socialists against innocent civilians. Their lack of preparedness in providing the victims with safe haven and succour was also considered as quite distressing. There was therefore strong opinion in favour of creating an international organization with the special mandate of providing legal protection for victims of persecution. Secondly, after the defeat of the National Socialists, Communism was looked at as a future cause of population displacements. Thus Western governments envisaged a similar scenario of human tragedy unfolding because of Communist oppression or Communist-instigated conflicts.

The institution of asylum as it exists today was, therefore, developed in the context of the Cold War hostilities as a humanitarian instrument of Western foreign policy.[56] The response of Western governments to a refugee crisis was largely determined by their foreign policy interests. Discussing the influence of the Cold War on the evolution of the international refugee regime, Ambassador P.N. Lyman argues:

> The Cold War atmosphere of the period was so important in terms of U.S. policy that when we began formally funding refugee programs under the Displaced Persons Act of 1951, we ruled out giving our money to any organization that had a Communist country or Communist-dominated country as a member. In other words, our original contributions to refugees could not go to the UNHCR because we did not trust, at that point, a United Nations organization in which the Soviet Union would play a major role.[57]

For example, until the enactment of the 1980 Refugee Act, the definition of the term "refugee" in the United States was geared almost exclusively to Communist countries.[58] The Soviet Union and its satellites also looked at the institution of asylum with contempt because in their view it was a creation of Western governments to discredit Communism. As Susan Martin argues, assistance to refugees was equated with assistance given to individuals fleeing from Communism or Communist-instigated conflicts. By definition, individuals coming from Communist countries were automatically granted refugee status with little or no examination about causation.

Financial support for refugee programs was given on the basis of utility in the propaganda war between the great powers.[59]

During the late 1960s and 1970s the arena of the Cold War shifted to the colonial and semicolonial countries of Africa and Asia where the vying great powers saw an opportunity for influencing the course of events in their favour towards strategic interests. The turmoil or the lack of stability that characterized the political situation of many colonial and semicolonial countries during the struggles for national independence and nation building provided fertile ground for great power intervention in the internal affairs of the fledgling states. As a result, the conflicts generating refugees during the 1970s and 1980s were direct or indirect results of superpower conflict for hegemony.[60] It is worthwhile to note, however, that on the one hand, superpower competition for hegemony constituted one of the major factors that generated refugees and on the other, concern for regional stability and the desire to forestall or dispel Soviet influence induced Western states to cooperate in refugee issues. The international refugee regime derives its strength and vitality from this cooperation.

It is important to note, however, that there are also other concerns that motivate states to cooperate on refugee issues. One of the factors that promotes state cooperation is concern for humanitarian principles in which persons who flee their countries of origin because of war, persecution, civil strife, etc., are accorded legal protection and minimal material assistance. The responses of states in the post-Cold War period to refugee needs in the poor countries will show whether or not humanitarian motive is an independent variable. The third factor that promotes cooperation on refugee matters is self-interest of states in domestic affairs.[61]

As stated earlier, with the end of the Cold War hostilities and the decline of Communism, which was the key factor for cooperation of states on matters relating to refugees, most of the underpinnings of the existing institution of asylum are open to question. As noted earlier, historically refugees were seen as victims of Communism or Communist-instigated conflicts. For people in the West, the reasons that prompt people to flee their homes are not easy to understand, let alone sympathize with. As Communism ceased to be a cause of population displacement, people in the West have seriously begun to look at asylum seekers as people on the move in search of economic opportunities.

Many works have already appeared questioning the legitimacy of asylum seekers' motives and the resilience of the institution of asylum in the Western countries to survive the external pressures.[62] As stated earlier, serious efforts are under consideration to develop measures that would avert the threat to the system. All countries in Europe and North America seem to be engaged in salvage operations. What would the impact of these changes be on the African refugee regime and what is to be done to minimize the effect on the institution of asylum?

The Impact of the Ending of the Cold War
on the African Refugee Regime

How would the ending of Cold War hostilities affect the regional refugee regime in Africa? There is no doubt that the denouement of the Cold War hostilities represents one of the most important landmarks of this century.

On the one hand, the ending of the Cold War may usher a new era of cooperation among states, paving the road for peaceful resolution of regional and international conflicts in the world. There are already discernible signs of this. As stated earlier, most of the conflicts that have been producing refugees since the 1970s were directly or indirectly related to superpower conflicts for hegemony. The countries in Southern and Northeastern Africa are, for example, the cases in point. The ending of the Cold War has, therefore, created favourable conditions for ending these conflicts, either because of superpower mediation or because the superpowers have stopped supplying weapons to the warring parties.

However, in the short term, this may have far-reaching effects not only on the refugee assistance regime, but also on development aid to poor Third World countries. Lessening of assistance due to shifting priorities may require the refugee-hosting governments in the poor countries to adjust their existing refugee policies. For example, the way refugees are received and treated in the poor countries of Northeastern Africa is inseparably linked to the international assistance regime, thus lessening assistance for meeting refugee needs and for offsetting the strain that their presence may cause on the economic and social infrastructures of the host countries. These factors may force the governments to reconsider their customary open-door policies.

It is worthwhile to observe, however, that in Africa the effect of the ending of the Cold War is likely to be varied. For example, in Angola, even though the peace process is not completed, mediation has resulted in peaceful settlement of the fratricidal civil war. In Ethiopia, the government was already on the verge of collapse, even when it enjoyed unlimited support from the former Soviet Union and its satellite states. Thus, its collapse seemed inevitable, regardless of the outcome of the Cold War. However, the decline of the Soviet Union and its satellites must have had some important influence not only on the way the war ended without bloodshed in both Eritrea and Ethiopia, but also in influencing the position of the U.S. government towards the opposition. The effect of the Soviet Union's demise on the changes that are taking place in Ethiopia are difficult to state with certainty, but it has been clearly demonstrated that brutal and undemocratic governments are unable to maintain their power without outside financial and military assistance from one of the big powers.

The Eritrean struggle for national independence also cannot be understood outside the context of the Cold War. It was U.S. strategic interests in the Red Sea and in the route to the Indian Ocean, as well as British interests in the sources of the Nile, that prompted the two governments to deny the Eritreans their rightful place in history through the United Nations General Assembly in the heyday of the Cold War hostilities. The Soviet Union and its satellite states were staunchly opposed to the federal arrangement with Ethiopia as contrived by the U.S government, not out of concern for the right of the Eritreans to establish an independent state, but as part of their competition for hegemony in the area against the U.S. In 1977, most of the country was liberated, but the direct intervention of the Soviet Union and some of its satellite states against the Eritrean revolution on the side of the Ethiopian military government delayed victory and caused immeasurable losses of lives and property. The decay of the totalitarian states and the subsequent denouement of the Cold War hostilities also enabled the Eritreans to achieve the goal they fought for the last four decades. The post-Cold War period will also create favourable a international climate for the recognition of the Eritrean state. However, in the post-Cold War period, small states like Eritrea may find it difficult to raise funds for national reconstruction.

In Somalia, the end of the Cold War seems to have had a detrimental effect reflected in total breakdown of the socio-political order due to clan-centred leaderships that are involved in a fratricidal civil war to vie for political power. The country's problem is not directly related to superpower conflict, but it is questionable if the country would have been left to bleed to death in the heyday of the Cold War. With the end of the Cold War Somalia suddenly became strategically marginalized and the world powers have nothing at stake to intervene militarily or otherwise in defence of human lives and property. To a certain extent this may indicate that in the post-Cold War period, strategically marginal countries may be left on their own to put themselves in order. If they are unable to do so, they have only themselves to blame. However, in the colonial and semicolonial societies, many of the problems, including ethnic-based conflicts, are related to colonial legacies and the Western countries cannot exonerate themselves from responsibility. What is happening in Somalia does not in any way show that the various ethnic groups are unable to coexist with each other peacefully. They have done so since time immemorial. However, in the past three decades, Barre's government was playing off one clan against the other with the help of the Soviet Union and later with the help of the U.S. government. It is this legacy, irresponsibility and total lack of respect for human lives by the vying leaderships that account for the loss of lives and property in the country. This may indicate that in the post-Cold War period, countries with no strategic resources will be left alone to sort out their own problems and the problems created by superpower interests during the Cold War. In the future Western governments may be less interested or less motivated to solve conflicts in such marginalized societies. During the Cold War Somalia had some strategic importance to the superpowers because of its geographic position. With the ending of the Cold War hostilities, its strategic location has suddenly become an unattractive feature.

What has happened to the refugees in the country also indicates how fragile the institution of asylum could be in such poor countries in the absence of international support or intervention. In 1990 Somalia was hosting about 358,500 refugees.[63] With the advent of the civil war, many of the refugees either fled for their lives back to their country of origin or perished in the fratricidal civil war. When the civil war broke out, the refugees were under the protection of the international refugee regime, but when their lives were threatened by the war, either directly or indirectly, the international community made no intervention to secure the refugees' physical safety. The question of intervening in the internal affairs of a sovereign state does not arise in Somalia because there was (and still is) no real state worth the name. It was this vacuum that led to the immeasurable loss of lives and property in the country.

The other important post-Cold War consequence is related to access to emergency relief and development assistance to refugees and to the poor governments that host them. The countries in the former Soviet Union, Central and Eastern Europe may no longer be sources of refugee flows.[64] However, given the economic decay and turmoil that pervade these countries, many people may still want to use the asylum channel to migrate to the West. In 1989 about one and a quarter million people had left these countries. The corresponding figure for 1990 was about two million.[65] The implication of this on the international refugee regime is that Western countries may have to provide large financial and technical assistance to these countries, not only in order to avert mass migration to the West, but also because these countries have key strategic importance to the industrial nations in the West.

For example, the G7 group on April 1, 1992 announced a U.S. $24 billion international package to the Commonwealth of Independent States (CIS).[66] The total amount required for reconstruction and development in Eastern Europe and the CIS is estimated at five thousand billion dollars. CIS's strategic significance to industrial Western countries can be easily inferred from what President Bush said when he made a $1.1 billion contribution to the package on behalf of the U.S. government:

> A victory for democracy and freedom in the former USSR creates the
> possibility of a new world of peace for our children and grandchildren. If
> this democratic revolution is defeated, it could plunge us into a world more
> dangerous in some respects than the dark years of the Cold war.[67]

This must be the largest contribution to national reconstruction since the
Marshall Plan. The strategic importance of these newly-born democracies
will no doubt marginalize the strategic importance of many African countries and, if so, their possibility of raising funds for development or for
national reconstruction may prove to be an uphill task. Compared to Africa,
there is no doubt that the countries in the former Soviet Union, Central and
Eastern Europe are of more strategic concern to Western industrialized
countries. The best way Western countries can avert the threat of massive
migration and political turmoil that may result in total breakdown of civil
society in the said countries is by giving massive development aid for job
creation and consolidation of democratic changes. The newly announced
international package indicates the level of Western countries' commitment
to do this.

Most of the 128 infrastructural projects that were presented by fourteen
refugee-hosting governments in Africa at the Second International Conference on Assistance to Refugees in Africa (ICARA II) still remain unfunded.
The total amount of external financial assistance required was only
$362,260,000.[68] As R.F. Gorman states, "In general, donor country attitudes
toward ICARA II were marked initially by a lack of enthusiasm and in some
cases outright circumspection."[69] He further remarks "Pinning down with
precision the donor country response to ICARA II is a bit like trying to
photograph a moving target. At one time donors express interest in particular projects based on a cursory reviews at headquarters, only to shy away
after closer scrutiny."[70] If donor country responses to projects designed to
enable the poor African countries to cope with the burden of dealing with
large numbers of refugees and returnees were characterized by lack of
enthusiasm during the Cold War hostilities, there is even less room for
optimism in the post-Cold War period.

Without directly suggesting a situation of a zero-sum game, these
developments will no doubt have an important implication on the African
refugee regime. Until now, no one seems to have considered the implication
of the end of the Cold War on the institution of asylum in the poor Third
World countries. Whether or not the institution of asylum, which was
developed historically in the context of the Cold War as an instrument of
Western foreign policy against Communism, would still serve in the poor
countries remains to be seen. One of the reasons why African countries have
been able to cope with hosting hundreds of thousands of refugees in spite
of their abject poverty was largely due to the financial cooperation of the

Western countries. Generally, during the Cold War financial assistance to refugee programs was provided on the basis of the purpose it served in the struggle for hegemony. Now there is no need to fight for hegemony against Communism. Will this mean more or less leaving strategically marginal countries on their own? In light of the rapidly eroding sympathies for refugees due to the end of the Cold War and deep economic recession, will humanitarian principles be enough to motivate the donor countries to maintain the present level of commitment or to increase their financial and technical assistance to refugees and refugee-hosting poor countries? The most support for the refugee regime came from the ability to mobilize resources in the West against the Communist threat. With Communism gone, what will happen to this resource? At present the main preoccupation of the West is with the East while the majority of the refugees are in Third World countries.

The end of the Cold War may also bring about a new dimension into the international assistance regime that may affect the general flow of resources and the contributions to refugee programs in refugee-hosting countries. During the Cold War, Communism or Communist-instigated conflicts were blamed for the generation of refugees. In future, the refugee problem will not be blamed on Communism. It will be blamed on violation of human rights. States that lack respect for their citizens' fundamental human rights may therefore be disqualified from receiving development aid if not emergency relief. This may even affect countries that host large numbers of refugees if the same countries are also producers of refugees. In the context of the Cold War hostilities, all refugee-hosting governments, even those with the worst records of human rights performance were given assistance to cope with the responsibility of hosting refugees. In the post-Cold War period, donors may take into account more seriously a host government's records of human rights performance before they earmark their contribution to UNHCR. At present most donor contributions to the UNHCR are earmarked. In future we may see more earmarking and linking of governments' human rights performance to the refugee regime. In Northeastern Africa, for example, the three governments are major refugee producers and receivers. A host country that lacks respect for its citizens' basic human rights, and whose policies generate refugees, may be affected by this emerging trend. If that happens, most of the refugee programs in many African countries may suffer from financial bottleneck, which may force the host governments to reconsider their open-door policies.

The fear of the continent's strategic marginalization has already begun to worry many African governments. In a different context, but on the same issue of development aid, African governments have already begun to "feel that the major donors will be preoccupied with developments in regions which are of more strategic concern to them."[71] Johnsson, for example, argues that "... current and future refugee programs will have significantly less funds and material resources at their disposal than in the past, as a result of which protection problems will be multiplied."[72]

The Need for Legitimate Discrimination in the African Refugee Regime

When is discrimination legitimate and when is it illegitimate? Is there legitimate discrimination? Is not any form of discrimination undesirable?

Discrimination is a relative concept and its legitimacy or illegitimacy is determined by the end it serves. Discrimination is therefore a means and not an end in itself. In this paper discrimination is legitimate when it is applied to make certain privileges inaccessible to less deserving categories of people, either because their accessibility to such privileges would detrimentally affect the exercise of such rights (entitlements) by more deserving categories (the raison d'être of such rights) or simply because the sharing of such entitlements by wider categories would erode the foundation of the right itself, leaving all categories worse off in the long term. By the same, token discrimination is illegitimate when governments make the basic principles of asylum and *nonrefoulement* inaccessible to persons in need of protection, either because of self-interest, inability to develop a mechanism by which to distinguish legitimate from illegitimate asylum seekers, or as a result of degradation of the humanitarian values that constitute the central plank of the institution of asylum expressed in the basic humanitarian principle of *nonrefoulement*. Making asylum and *nonrefoulement* inaccessible would mean returning asylum seekers to countries where they are unable or unwilling to return because of "well-founded fear of persecution by reason of race, religion, nationality or political opinion."[73]

In Africa, especially in Northeastern Africa (Sudan, Eritrea, Ethiopia, Somalia and Djibouti), the central concern is whether or not the institution of asylum can continue to serve in the light of fast-changing world events without applying legitimate discrimination in order to preserve the system for those who need it most. It is a question of denying certain privileges to certain categories in order to maximize accessibility of the right of *nonrefoulement* and material assistance to those in need of protection. Implicit in this argument is that failure to practise legitimate discrimination would in the long term jeopardize or undermine the right of those in serious need of protection. What are the privileges and rights at stake? The right in question is the right to seek asylum against persecution. Do persecuted people have a right to seek asylum? Indeed they do, but the exercise of such a right is dependent on the decision of the country where asylum is sought.

A refugee does not have a right to asylum, but s/he has a right against being involuntarily repatriated to a country where s/he fears for her/his life, security and liberty. The right to seek asylum comes from the principle of *nonrefoulement*. What are the privileges that may be denied to certain categories of persons in Northeastern Africa? These privileges are the option of seeking exit from a life-threatening situation due to natural and man-made disasters (such as earthquakes, storms, floods, insects, pests, forcible relocation, drought, famine, environmental degradation and economic hardship) and to be able to leave one's own country of residence by taking advantage of the international refugee regime, as opposed to leaving for "reasons of race, religion, nationality, membership of a particular group or political opinion," or for the reasons enumerated in the OAU Convention. For purposes of assistance, it is difficult to argue that the two categories should receive different treatment, but that is not the crux of the argument either. The issue is not whether a state should open its territories to less deserving categories. The issue is that states should do this with full awareness of the changing circumstances in the world, including future reduction of international assistance to refugees, otherwise states may throw out all categories in their territories in response to reduced international assistance because one of the basic assumptions underlying host governments' refugee policy is that the international community would share the burden in accordance with the principle of burden-sharing. Deportation of all categories, including those who fled for fear of life, liberty and security, would constitute flagrant violation of the basic human right of *nonrefoulement*. A poor state cannot be expected to keep all the categories of refugees in its territory because in the absence of international assistance, this may constitute a threat to its national security. However, no state is justified in deporting a person when her/his life, liberty and security would be threatened because of the reasons given in the 1951 and the OAU Conventions. The solution to such a dilemma is resorting to legitimate discrimination, whereby only those who were allowed to stay for assistance purposes are denied the privilege of staying. This presupposes, however, that the said state has records of the various categories. At present none of the African host governments has access to such records, thus the whole problem seems to stem from lack of individual status determination. In the past, as long as the costs of emergency relief, investment and recurrent costs were met by the international donor community, the need for screening and discrimination was not felt, but in the post-Cold War period it is only by resorting to legitimate discrimination that poor states can preserve the institution of asylum.

Such discrimination is justifiable because it is exercised in defence of a more important and profound principle—the institution of asylum. The

[handwritten: full-length should begin]

institution of asylum is one of the greatest achievements of the twentieth century and its collapse should be avoided at any cost. In the poor countries of first asylum, the use of legitimate discrimination may be necessary to *[handwritten: OBS!]* assure the continuation of the institution of asylum, which, in poor African countries, is threatened by a system that lumps together different categories of persons as refugees. This suggests that something is wrong with the system and its viability requires a cost-effective procedure of screening *[handwritten: OBS]* various categories that are at present vaguely referred to as refugees. Currently there is no administrative capacity to carry out such an elaborate screening process, but there does not seem to be an easy way out of the dilemma. Crowding the system will inevitably reduce accessibility to those who are in grave need of international protection. Hence the international refugee regime should contribute financial and technical assistance to enable the poor countries of asylum to develop administrative systems to screen categories of refugees.

Double Standards in a Single Regime

As stated earlier, even though the OAU Convention contains a provision on individual status determination, it does not make individual determination of refugee status a requirement. This has left the institution of asylum wide open for various categories of refugees whose reasons for migration may only be tangentially relevant to the factors enumerated in the refugee law instruments. The donor community accepts the principle of mass status determination for the purposes of providing assistance to refugees in the poor Third World countries of asylum, but they themselves stick to the procedure of individual determination. Hence there are double standards of status determination in a regime that derives its vitality and strength from concerted international cooperation and action.

At present the two procedures are fraught with serious problems. In the long term, the threat to the institution of asylum, both in developed and in Third World countries, is embodied in the procedures of status determination of asylum seekers. Individual status determination in the Western countries, as it is applied at present is inefficient, expensive and a source of immeasurable distress, including mental breakdowns, to many asylum seekers. The lives of many asylum seekers are affected by the bureaucratic labyrinth of asylum procedures.

In the developed world, the problem stems from too much and ineffective status determination, while in Africa it stems from too little status determination. In the former, the bureaucratic decision-making process and the inability to remove those persons whose cases have been rejected cost the taxpayers dearly. The cost is estimated at about five to six billion dollars in Western Europe and North America per annum.[74] This is happening in a period when the receiving countries are in the grip of an economic crisis. The xenophobia that is widespreading in many European countries is not only a result of the increased number of asylum seekers, but is also mainly due to the costs incurred in their adjudication, care and maintenance.

By contrast, African countries have been pursuing an open-door policy. The existing national legislations may contain procedures for individual and mass status determination, but the former is seldom applied. In the Sudan the only time individual determination was applied was when a person wanted to be considered for resettlement in a second country of asylum. In fact, in the Sudan, it is sometimes doubtful if there is any status determination at all. People stay in a host country either without applying for asylum or when they apply, no decisions are taken regarding their status. There is a tacit understanding that because they come from a war-torn country or a country dominated by a colonial power, they are referred to as refugees with no examination of causation. A problem appears when the need for protection arises, for example, when refugees are caught outside the residence designated for them. This was a common problem in the Sudan during 1978-88 when refugees in the urban areas were periodically rounded up for deportation to the countryside. The nonethnic Somali urban refugees were also faced with the same problem in Somalia. In both countries, protection was denied to refugees whose status was not determined individually. This problem was faced even by those who were residing in the countries for decades. As long as there was no need for protection or intervention on behalf of the refugees, having no individual refugee status was not a problem. However, whenever the need for protection arose, invocation of status granted as a member of a certain group or groups did not help. The majority of the refugees did not have any evidence to prove their refugee status. This raises a serious problem of protection issues. It seems that the only way to ensure individual protection is through individual refugee status determination.

Mass status determination is cost-effective and imperfect. It has saved many lives, but with increased demand on the international assistance regime. In view of the fact that in the drought-prone countries environmental degradation may constitute one of the major causes of population displacements in the future, a real solution for the problem does not lie in broadening the definition of the term "refugee" or in expanding the mandate of UNHCR or in crowding the institution of asylum, but rather in solving the problem at its source. The only way this could be done is by providing comprehensive development aid that would eliminate the need to cross international borders in search of sources of livelihood. If this happens, only those who fear for their lives, liberty and security would leave their homes in search of international protection.

Is Legitimate Discrimination an Answer?
Discussion and Concluding Remarks

The two basic assumptions central to the African refugee regime are the principle of burden-sharing and the concept of temporariness. No country chooses its neighbours. Therefore, whether or not a country receives refugees is a result of random occurrence. The responsibility of meeting the costs of refugee needs and of offsetting the strain their presence may cause on the receiving country's economic and social infrastructure is, however, expected to be shared by the international community in general, and by the OAU member states in particular. African governments, therefore, receive refugees with the understanding that this will happen.

As far back as in 1968, the African Council of Ministers pointed out this important principle, but it was stated that, in view of the continent's limited economic capacity, more emphasis would be placed on getting assistance from the international donor community.[75] The Conference on the African Refugee Problems in 1967, for example, stated: "The refugee problem is a general African problem, and the burden created by it should therefore be shouldered by all African states and in the spirit of the OAU."[76] This was later enshrined in the OAU Convention where member states are urged "in the spirit of African solidarity and international cooperation" to "take appropriate measures to lighten the burden of the member states granting asylum."[77]

The articulation of the principle of burden-sharing by the African governments in international fora notwithstanding, the principle was never implemented in practice within Africa.[78] For example, in his opening speech to the 1979 Arusha Conference, J. Nyerere stated that there has been no burden-sharing in Africa and he urged the favourably-placed African governments to contribute towards meeting some of the costs incurred by the refugee-hosting member states.[79]

The fundamental assumption for receiving refugees has always been based on the understanding that the burden would be shared by the signatories of the international instruments relating to refugee status. Even though the principle of burden-sharing has never advanced beyond lip service among African governments, it was on the basis of this principle that the international donor community has been allocating resources for meeting the needs of refugees in poor African countries. Without this assistance, most of the refugee-hosting countries would have found the burden too much to cope with. As we saw earlier, the open-door refugee policy of many of the African host governments would have not been possible without such international cooperation and solidarity.

In the context of the Cold War, the costs of emergency relief and self-sufficiency projects were met by the international assistance regime. As we saw earlier, there is good reason to expect that there will be less funds available to the refugee sector in the poor refugee-hosting countries because most of the donor countries may be preoccupied with East-West migration and development issues in the new democracies. Reduced resource flow to support programs for refugees or returnees may have a serious conse-quence on the viability of the institution of asylum as it exists today. If the flow of assistance is drastically reduced, one of the fundamental assump-tions (burden-sharing) on which the African refugee regime rests will be eliminated. This will inevitably make the institution of asylum fragile to the extent of forcing host governments to close their doors to asylum seekers or to return refugees forcibly to unchanged political and social conditions. For example, in 1987 Sudanese Prime Minister Syd Sadiq El Mahdi stated, "refugees constitute 10 percent of the countries' population." He also pointed out "Sudan's limited resources could not cope with any additional number of refugees."[80] Three days after the prime minister's statement, it was reported that the authorities in the Eastern region had "refused to grant asylum to 30 Ethiopians."[81] According to the Commissioner for Refugees, the decision was based on the country's "new policy towards refugees which called upon the international refugee relief organizations to provide refugees with assistance relief in their countries of origin so that their numbers do not increase in the Sudan, particularly when we know that refugees constitute 10 percent of the population."[82] On July 4, 1988 the Minister of Refugees, Syd Hassan Shubu, told the authorities in the Eastern region that "no additional refugees be accepted. Refugee status was to be granted only to war victims."[83] This was designed to exclude victims of natural disasters.

Temporariness is the second fundamental assumption underlying Afri-can governments' refugee policy. Refugees are received as guests. The assumption is that the problems that prompt people to flee their homelands are temporary. As a result refugees are kept in spatially segregated sites where they cannot integrate with the local population. The resources made available to refugees in settlements are also allocated on the basis of this assumption. That is why the OAU Convention envisages a real solution to the African refugee problem to result from fundamental changes that occur in the sending countries. As it is commonly known, however, this assump-tion has been swept away because in many countries the refugee problem has become overinstitutionalized. Refugees who were received with the hope that they would return to their homelands in a matter of few months or even years have been staying in exile for decades. The important question is what happens when the refugees overstay and there is a reduced flow of resources, partly to meet refugee needs and partly to help receiving countries cope with the burden?

Let us assume for analytical purposes that country A is poor and 10 percent of its inhabitants are refugees. They are received with the hope that they would return to their country after a few years. Let us further assume that with assistance from the international assistance regime, the host country was able to implement its settlement policy in which all refugees are placed in spatially segregated camps and settlements. None of the groups is self-supporting. Those in camps are dependent on hand-outs for their survival, while those in settlements produce food crops. All capital investment and recurrent costs for running primary schools, health centres, water supplies, vehicles, tractors, staff salaries, etc., are met by the UNHCR. Let us also assume country A is located, like the many refugee-hosting countries in Africa, in a drought-prone, semiarid zone. Crop failure due to low rainfall is a common occurrence and whenever this happens UNHCR is called upon to provide assistance to enable the refugee communities to tide over seasonal crises. The refugees are placed in spatially segregated sites where migration in search of employment or in pursuit of other income-generating activities is precluded. Also the refugees cannot cultivate new arable land outside the confines of the settlement. This often leads to overcultivation, overgrazing, deforestation and soil fertility decline within the confines of the camp or settlement sites, undermining the possibility that the refugee communities will become self-supporting. As a result, perpetual dependence on international assistance becomes inevitable. The settlements and camps are set up in remote areas to prevent integration. Let us further assume that country A becomes strategically marginalized in the post-Cold War period and a solution to the political problem that prompted the flight of the refugees is not within sight. With the increasing trend of donors earmarking their contributions to UNHCR programs, let us assume the flow of resources to country A is reduced drastically.

What are the options open to country A? In view of its poverty, it cannot cope with the refugee problem on its own. When distribution of hand-outs is stopped in the camps, the refugees will try to leave the camps in search of other sources of livelihood. When crops fail, the refugees in the settlements may also try to drift to urban centres or elsewhere outside the settlements. This may be considered a threat to national security and in extreme situations, country A may consider it legitimate to force the refugees to return to their country of origin, even when the circumstances that prompted their flight have remained unchanged. This situation is hypothetical, but it is grounded on a conceivable sequence of events that may actually unfold in circumstances where a poor country is left on its own to deal with a problem that may constitute a threat (real or imagined) to its national security.

The interesting issue that emerges from this hypothetical scenario is that because most of the returned refugees might have fled their country of origin because of war, drought, famine, economic hardship and environmental degradation, the majority may not face a problem except economic hardship upon return. This will put the lives and liberty of the few who had fled their country of origin due to fear of persecution in great danger. Country A did not have separate records of these persons because their status was determined en mass without any examination of causation and the decision of forcible repatriation was also enforced en mass. One of the most serious weaknesses of mass status determination is that it does not ensure individual protection. The individual refugee is forgotten, which is fundamentally inconsistent with the philosophy of the refugee legal instruments whose main focus is the individual. As long as the financial costs were met by the international refugee regime, African host governments did not mind hosting large numbers of refugees, including those who fell outside the purview of the 1951 and the OAU Conventions.

As stated earlier, in the post-Cold War period, there is no doubt that there will be less funds to finance refugee programs in poor African countries. This has already become the case. For example, even though UNHCR's annual expenditures have increased during the 1980s, the increase is insignificant when compared to refugee population figures. The world refugee population doubled between 1980 and 1990, but UNHCR expenditures were only higher by less than 10 percent in 1990 (U.S. $540 million) than they had been in 1980 (U.S. $497 million).[84]

Reduced international assistance may, therefore, force the poor refugee-receiving countries to close their doors to future influxes or may make life unbearable for refugees in order to induce them to return to unchanged political conditions. The future of the institution of asylum in such poor countries therefore depends ultimately on whether or not they are able to distinguish between the different categories of refugees and consequently make the institution of asylum accessible only to those who are more deserving. In light of lessening international assistance in the post-Cold War period and in the view of economic, environmental and social pressures, there is a risk that host governments may "throw the baby out with the bath water" unless they develop an effective and cheap screening procedure, so that when the need to close the doors arises because of an inability to cope, those who need protection are unaffected.

The tradition of asylum in Africa is among the best in the world, but this should not imply that the resilience of the institution of asylum in these countries is impregnable. In the presence of political will, the resilience of hospitality is affected by economic hardship. Without political will, however, the best economic performance may not mean increased hospitality to refugees. But in the long-run, the best political will is seldom enough if the states in question are plunged into economic and social crises, as many of the African host governments are at the present. That is the reason why something drastic should happen to protect the African tradition of asylum before it is too late. In many countries, the capacity of absorption is exceeded, self-sufficiency programs are not working, refugee situations are overinstitutionalized, and appeals for development assistance have almost fallen on deaf ears. All these may lead to degradation of the long-established principle of asylum.

There is a need to address the problem in a far-reaching and comprehensive way. There are interesting insights that Africa and the international donor community can gain from the Comprehensive Plan of Action (CPA) in Southeast Asia where "fifty nations entered into a set of reciprocal responsibilities" to seek solutions to the refugee problem in the region. The important aspects of the CPA that could be emulated in Africa are, firstly, providing economic incentives to those who do not qualify for refugee status to return to their country of origin. They are helped to become self-supporting. Secondly, UNHCR is mandated to monitor their treatment upon return. As Ambassador P. Lyman states, the CPA is perhaps the highest per capita refugee program in the world because of the enormous amount of counselling, incentives and monitoring involved.[85] In the post-Cold War period and in view of the strategic marginalization of some of the African countries, such programs may not sound attractive to donors, but it seems there is no easy way to preserve the generous tradition of asylum in Africa.

Notes

1. Loescher, "Mass Migration as a Global Security Problem."
2. The broad definition of the term "refugee" by the OAU Convention has already been emulated to a certain extent by some regions outside of Africa. For example, the Cartagena Declaration, which was adopted by central American States meeting in Colombia in 1984, contains a similar formulation as the OAU Convention. It states:

    ... the definition of concept of refugee recommended for use in the region might, in addition to containing the elements from the 1951 Convention and the 1967 Protocol, also consider as refugees those persons that have fled from their countries because their life has been threatened by conflict, massive violation of human rights or other situations that have seriously disturbed public order.

It can also be argued that certain elements of the OAU Convention's definition has influenced West European practice. This is reflected in the acceptance by these states of the so-called de facto refugees even when they don't meet the criterion provided in the 1951 Convention.

3.   Burman, "Environmental Refugees: An Emerging Concept."

4.   Ibid.

5.   Ibid.

6.   Kibreab, "The System of Asylum in Economies Under Pressure."

7.   Ibid.

8.   Kibreab, "Current Events in Ethiopia and Eritrea: Prospects for Repatriation."

9.   Convention relating to the Status of Refugees, July 28, 1951, Article I A (2).

10. Ibid.

11. Ibid.

12. Zolberg, Suhrke and Aguayo, *Escape from Violence: Conflict and the Refugee Crisis in the Developing World*, 25.

13. Convention Relating to the Status of Refugees, Article B 1 (a and b).

14. General Assembly official records, Fourth Session, supp. No. 11 (IA/4104/Rev. 1, 1958).

15. See General Assembly records, Eighteenth Session, supp. No. 11 (A/5511/Rev. 1, 1963).

16. Protocol relating to the Status of Refugees, Article I (2 and 3), January 31, 1967.

17. Goodwin-Gill, *Refugees: The Expanding Mandate of the Office of the United Nations High Commissioner for Refugees*, May 1989:3.

18. Organization of African Unity, Council of Miisters, Res. 11 (II), 24-29.

19. Organization of African Unity, Council of Ministers, Res. 36 (III), 6, Kenya, July 13-17, 1964.

20. Organization of African Unity, Council of Ministers, Res. 149 (XI), September 2-12, 1968.

21. OAU Convention Governing the Specific Aspects of the Problem of Refugees in Africa, Article I (1).

22. OAU Convention Governing the Specific Aspects of the African Refugee Problem, Article I (2), 1969.

23. Trafas Burman, "Environmental Refugees," 23.

24. pects of African Refugee Problems, October 9-18, 1967, Recommendation IV, para. 1-4; OAU Convention Governing Specific Aspects of the Problem of Refugees in Africa, Article V, para. 1-5.

25. This observation is based on the situation of the Northeastern African countries. The praxis may differ slightly in some African countries. However, it was also

pointed out to me by Dr. Shaloka Beyani that the same procedure is applied to determine refugee status in the Southern African countries.

26. Goodwin-Gill, *Refugees*.

27. See El-Hinnawi, *Environmental Refugees*, Nairobi: UNEP, 1985.

28. See Goodwin-Gill, *Refugees*.

29. Ibid.

30. Ibid.

31. Beyani. Personal communication, April 14, 1992.

32. See Widgren, "The Asylum Crisis in Europe and America"; Widgren, "International Refugee Regime: Will It Serve in the 1990s?"; Ministry of Labour, Government Bill on Active Refugee and Immigration Policy, Summary of Government Bill (prop. 1990/91:95), Stockholm, Sweden; A Comprehensive Refugee and Immigration Policy, Stockholm, Sweden.

33. See "Informal Consultations on Asylum, Refugee and Migration Policies in Europe and North America and Australia" in Martin, "East-West Migration: Challenge of the 1990s."

34. There is no doubt that there are people who move from one country to another in search of nonexistent "prosperity." Using such a derogatory phrase is damaging because it derogates without going into the reasons why the problem exists. One of the main reasons that induces asylum seekers to move from one country to another is the level of uncertainty they suffer during the time of waiting for their status to be determined. This does not suggest, however, that there are no individuals who move between countries even when they have already been granted refugee status in one country. I assume these are not many and using such derogatory phrases may have prejudicial consequences on the situation of bona fide asylum seekers.

35. Martin, "East-West Migration," 3.

36. See para. 4 of the Preamble of the Convention relating to the Status of Refugees, 1951.

37. It has to be admitted that the costs of care and maintenance of asylum seekers, as well as the process of status determination in the industrial countries, are much higher than they are in poor African countries. Nevertheless, the figures in the tables show how inordinately the responsibility of hosting refugees is distributed between the signatories of the international legal instruments.

38. OAU Convention Governing the Specific Aspects of Refugees, Article III, paras. 1 and 2.

39. Kibreab, "Local Settlement of Refugees in Africa: A Misconceived Option?"

40. Kibreab, "Integration of African Refugees in First Countries of Asylum: Past Experiences and Prospects for the 1990s."

41. The only exception is Tanzania and in a few cases in Botswana. The latter allowed about 2,500 Angolan refugees to acquire citizenship.

42. Hansen, "Refugee Dynamics: Angolans in Zambia 1966 to 1972"; Lugusha, "A Final Report of a Socio-Economic Survey of Barundi Refugees in Kigoma

Region"; Kulman, *Burden or Boon? A Study of Eritrean Refugees in Sudan*; Wijbrandi, *Organized and Spontaneous Settlement in Eastern Sudan: Two Case Studies on Integration of Rural Refugees*; Freund and Kalumba, *Spontaneously Settled Refugees in Northwestern Province, Zambia*.

43. Chambers, "Rural Refugees in Africa: What the Eye Does Not See"; Kibreab, *Reflections on the African Refugee Problem*.

44. Hansen, "Refugee Dynamics"; Kulman, *Burden*; Wijbrandi, *Organized*; Lugusha, "Final Report."

45. Kibreab, *Refugees and Development in Africa: The Case of Eritrea*; Kibreab, *Wage-Earning Refugee Settlements in Eastern and Central Sudan: From Subsistence to Wage Labour*.

46. Young, "A General Assessment of the Environmental Impact of Refugees in Somalia With Attention to the Refugee Agricultural Programme"; Kibreab, *Refugee Settlements, Resource Management and the Environment in Eastern Sudan*.

47. Kibreab, ibid.

48. See, for example, Organization of African Unity, Resolution on the Problem of Refugees in Africa, Council of Ministers, Res. 149 (XI), para. 2 of the Preamble.

49. Tucker, "The Politics of Refugees in Somalia."

50. UNHCR, "The Situation in Northwestern Somalia"; see also UNHCR's Officer-in-Charge Peter Meijer's letter of June 6, 1989 to J. Marks, Director, SCF (USU) Mogadishu, Somalia, SOM/1438, in which he states, "There are a number of camps where security conditions do not allow UNHCR to verify the civilian nature of beneficiaries and to monitor the use of assistance. It has not proved possible for the Government to relocate refugees outside the affected area."

51. See Sudan's settlement policy, National Commission for Aid to Refugees, Documentation for the June 20-23 conference, Vols. I-III, Khartoum, Sudan, 1980.

52. Ibid.; Kibreab, *Refugee Settlements*.

53. OAU Convention Governing the Specific Aspects of the Problem of Refugees in Africa, Article III, 1969.

54. See Freund and Kalumba, *Spontaneously Settled Refugees*; Hansen, "Refugee Dynamics"; Lugusha, "Final Report."

55. Chambers, "Rural Refugees"; Kibreab, *Reflections*.

56. Martin, "East-West Migration."

57. Lyman, "U.S. Responses to Refugee and Migration Issues: The Challenges of the 1990s."

58. Ibid.

59. Martin, "East-West Migration," 1.

60. Johnsson, "International Protection of Refugees."

61. See Rogers and Copeland, *Global Refugee Policy: Issues in the 1990s*.

62. See, for example, Widgren, "The Asylum Crisis in Europe and North America"; Smyer, "Prospects for Survival of the Refugee System"; Widgren, "The International Refugee and Migration Regime: Will It Serve in the 1990s?"

63. U.S. Committee for Refugees, *World Refugee Survey*, Table 1.

64. Kibreab, *The State of the Art Review of Refugee Studies in Africa*.

65. Martin, "East-West Migration."

66. *The Guardian*, April 2, 1992.

67. Ibid.

68. UN General Assembly, A/Conf. 125/1, January 31, 1984.

69. Gorman, *Coping with Africa's Refugee Burden: Time for Solutions*, 67.

70. Ibid., 72.

71. World Bank, "New Africa Agenda Adopted at the UN."

72. Johnsson, "International Protection," 19.

73. UNHCR Statute, para. 1, 6, Article 1, 1951 Convention relating to the Status of Refugees.

74. Widgren, "The International Refugee and Migration Regime." This includes costs of care and maintenance of asylum seekers.

75. Organization of African Unity, Council of Ministers, Res. 149 (XI), 1968.

76. Conference on Legal, Economic and Social Aspects of the African Refugee Problems, Final Report, May 1968.

77. OAU Convention Governing the Specific Aspects of the Refugee Problems in Africa, Article 11 (4) and para. 8 of the Preamble, 1969.

78. Kibreab, *The State of the Art Review*, 32.

79. Nyerere, opening speech at the 1979 Conference on the Problems of African Refugees, Arusha, May 1979; Nyerere, opening address to the meeting of the OAU Secretariat and Voluntary Agencies on African Refugees, Arusha, March 1983.

80. *Seyyasa* (Arabic newspaper), Issue 538, January 12, 1988.

81. *Axam*, (Arabic newspaper), Issue 6230, January 15, 1988.

82. Ibid.

83. *Ayam* (Arabic newspaper), Issue 6360, July 4, 1988.

84. Rogers and Copeland, *Global*, 14.

85. Lyman, "U.S. Responses."

86. The following numbers of refugees were also hosted by:

Angola	11,900	Benin	800	Botswana	1,000
Cameroon	6,900	Central A.R.	6,300	Congo	3,400
G. Bissau	1,600	Gabon	800	Gambia	800
Ghana	8,000	Kenya	14,400	Lesotho	1,000
Mali	10,000	Mauritania	22,000	Morocco	800
Mozambique	800	Namibia	25,000	Niger	800
Nigeria	5,300	Rwanda	21,500		

Source: *World Refugee Survey*, U.S. Committee for Refugees, 1991.

References

Axam (Arabic newspaper), Issue 6230, January 15, 1988.

Ayam (Arabic newspaper), Issue 6360, July 4, 1988.

Beyani, S. Personal communication, Oxford, April 14, 1992.

Chambers, R. "Rural Refugees in Africa: What the Eye Does Not See." Paper presented at the African Studies Association Symposium on Refugees, London, September 13-14, 1979.

Conference on the Legal, Economic and Social Aspects of African Refugee Problems, Final Report, Addis Ababa, October 9-18, 1968.

El-Hinnawa, E. *Environmental Refugees*. Nairobi: UNEP, 1985.

Freund, P.J., and K. Kalumba. *Spontaneously Settled Refugees in Northwestern Province*. Zambia: University of Zambia, Institute for African Studies, 1985.

Goodwin-Gill, G.S. *Refugees: The Expanding Mandate of the Office of the United Nations High Commissioner for Refugees*. Geneva: UNHCR, 1989.

Gorman, R.F. *Coping with Africa's Refugee Burden: Time for Solutions*. Boston: United Nations Institute for Training and Research, Martinus Jijhoff Publishers, 1987.

Guardian, The, April 2, 1992.

Hansen, A. "Refugee Dynamics: Angolans in Zambia 1966 to 1972." In *Disasters 3*, no. 4 (1974).

Johnsson, A.B. "International Protection of Refugees." Paper commissioned by the Program on International and U.S. Refugee Policy, Fletcher School of Law and Diplomacy, Tufts University, 1991.

Lyman, P.N. "U.S. Responses to Refugee and Migration Issues: The Challenges of the 1990s." Seminar presentation in the series "Critical Issues in International and U.S. Refugee Law and Policy," Fletcher School of Law and Diplomacy, Tufts University, 1991.

Kibreab, G. *Refugees and Development in Africa: The Case of Eritrea*. Trenton, New Jersey: The Red Sea Press, 1987.

_____. "Local Settlement of Refugees in Africa: A Misconceived Option?" In *Journal of Refugee Studies* 2, no. 4 (1989).

_____. *Wage-Earning Refugee Settlements in Eastern and Central Sudan: From Subsistence to Wage Labour*. Trenton, New Jersey: The Red Sea Press, 1990.

_____. "Integration of African Refugees in First Countries of Asylum: Past Experiences and Prospects for the 1990s." Paper commissioned by the Program on International and U.S. Refugee Policy, Fletcher School of Law and Diplomacy, Tufts University, 1991.

_____. *The State of the Art Review of Refugee Studies in Africa*. Uppsala Papers in Economic History, Research Report No. 26. Uppsala: Uppsala University, Department of Economic History, 1991.

_____. "The System of Asylum in Economics Under Pressure." In *Hundred Flowers Bloom: Essays in Honour of Bo Gustafsson*, edited by K. Ullenhag. Stockholm: Almqvist & Wiksell International, 1991.

_____. "Current Events in Ethiopia and Eritrea: Prospects for Repatriation." Seminar presentation in the series "Critical Issues in International and U.S. Refugee Policy," The Fletcher School of Law and Diplomacy, Tufts University, 1992.

_____. *Refugee Settlements, Resource Management and the Environment in Eastern Sudan*. Forthcoming.

Kulman, T. *Burden Or Boon? A Study of Eritrean Refugees in Sudan*. Amsterdam: VU University Press, 1990.

Loescher, R. "Mass Migration As a Global Security Problem." In *Refugee World Survey* (1991).

Lugusha, E.A. "A Final Report of a Socio-Economic Survey of Barundi Refugees in Kigoma Region." Dar es Salaam: Economic Research Bureau, 1981. Unpublished manuscript.

Martin, S. "East-West Migration: Challenge of the 1990s." Paper commissioned by the Program on International and U.S. Refugee Policy, The Fletcher School of Law and Diplomacy, Tufts University, 1991.

Children Fund (USA). Mogadishu, Somalia, SOM/1438, June 6, 1989.

Ministry of Labour. "A Comprehensive Refugee and Immigration Policy." Stockholm, Sweden: Ministry of Labour, 1990.

Ministry of Labour. "Government Bill on Active Refugee and Immigration Policy, Summary of Government Bill" (prop. 1990/91:95). Stockholm, Sweden: Ministry of Labour, 1990.

National Commission for Aid to Refugees. *Documentation for the June 20-23 Conference*, Vols I-III. Khartoum, Sudan: National Commission for Aid to Refugees, 1980.

Nyerere, J.K. Opening speech at the Conference on the Problems of African Refugees. Arusha, Tanzania, 1979.

_____. Opening address to the Meeting of the OAU Secretariat and Voluntary Agencies on African Refugees. Arusha, Tanzania, 1983.

Organization of African Unity. Council of Ministers resolution 11 (II), February 24-29, 1964.

_____. Council of Ministers resolution 149 (XI), September 2-12, 1968.

_____. Council of Ministers resolution 36 (III), 6, July 13-17.

_____. Resolution on the Problem of Refugees in Africa, Council of Ministers resolution 149 (XI).

_____. Convention Governing the Specific Aspects of the Problem of Refugees in Africa, 1969.

Rogers, R., and E. Copeland. "Global Refugee Policy: Issues in the 1990s." Fletcher School of Law and Diplomacy, Tufts University, 1991. Unpublished manuscript.

Seyyasa (Arabic newspaper), Issue 538, January 12, 1988.

Smyer, W.R. "Prospects for Survival of the Refugee System." Paper commissioned by the Program on International and U.S. Refugee Policy, Fletcher School of Law and Diplomacy, Tufts University, 1992.

Trafas Burman, E. "Environmental Refugees: An Emerging Concept." In partial fulfilment of the MALD Paper, Tufts University, 1991.

Tucker, J.B. "The Politics of Refugees in Somalia." In *Horn of Africa* 5, no. 2 (1982).

United Nations General Assembly official records. Fourth Session, supp. No. 11 (IA/4101/Rev. 1).

_____. Eighteenth Session, supp. 11 (A/5511/Rev. 1), 1963.

_____. A/Conf. 125/1, January 31, 1984.

United Nations High Commissioner for Refugees. Convention relating to the Status of Refugees, July 28, 1951.

_____. Protocol relating to the Status of Refugees, January 31, 1967.

_____. "The Situation in Northwestern Somalia." Geneva: UNHCR, 1989.

Widgren, J. "The Asylum Crisis in Europe and America." Paper commissioned by the Program on International and U.S. Refugee Policy, Fletcher School of Law and Diplomacy, Tufts University, 1990.

_____. "International Refugee Regime: Will It Serve in the 1990s?" Seminar presentation in the series "Critical Issues in International and U.S. Refugee Law and Policy," Fletcher School of Law and Diplomacy, Tufts University, 1991.

Wijbrandi, B. *Organized and Spontaneous Settlement in Eastern Sudan: Two Case Studies on Integration of Rural Refugees.* Amsterdam: Free University of Amsterdam, Faculty of Economics, 1986.

World Bank. "New Africa Agenda Adopted At the UN." In *Africa Recovery* 5, no. 4 (1991).

Young, L. "A General Assessment of the Environmental Impact of Refugees in Somalia With Attention to the Refugee Agricultural Programme." In *Disasters* 9, no. 2 (1985).

Zolberg, A., A. Suhrke and S. Aguayo. *Escape from Violence: Conflict and the Refugee Crisis in the Developing World.* New York: Oxford University Press, 1989.

4

The Refugee Problem in West Africa: Some Responses to Legitimate and Illegitimate Migration

A. Essuman-Johnson

The issue of forced migration has been a major problem around the world, particularly in Africa. Of an estimated world refugee population of approximately fifteen million, five million are in Africa. The African refugee population has been unevenly distributed, particularly in areas where there has been the most conflict. In the Horn of Africa, refugees have moved from Ethiopia to the Sudan, from the Sudan to Ethiopia, from Somalia to Ethiopia and vice versa. Central Africa also generates many refugees from Zaire, Uganda, Rwanda and Burundi. Refugees also come from South Africa, Namibia, Angola, Mozambique and Zimbabwe due to apartheid and postindependence internal conflicts. In North Africa the conflict between Morocco and the Polisario over Western Sahara between Morocco and the Polisario has created a refugee flow from Western Sahara into Algeria.[1]

It appears that Africa's refugees are mainly in regions of the continent other than West Africa. For a long time West Africa has not known the kinds of conflict that has generated refugees elsewhere on the continent. Until recently, West Africa was not a major refugee-producing region. It was more of a resettlement region for refugees from Southern Africa, the Horn and Central Africa. Until the recent conflict in Senegal/Mauritania and Liberia, which brought West Africa to the attention of the international press, West Africa played host to refugees from the Sahel region who were displaced by the harsh environment of the Sahara.

West Africa has had a history of generating its own refugees, though not on the scale seen in the Horn and Southern Africa. West African refugees are expelled as a result of political struggles for control of the state, which is the case in Ghana, Nigeria, Benin, Togo and Cameroon.[2] Politicians whose governments are overthrown by military coups have moved across borders to escape arrest by the new leaders. Similarly, conspirators who fail in their attempts to overthrow incumbent governments have also sought refuge in neighbouring countries in West Africa, Europe and the United States. Refugee movements are usually taken for granted and not noticed, except for mass expulsions.

Legitimate and Illegitimate Migration

Migration within the West African subregion has existed for a long time. Burkinabes have migrated to work in the cocoa farms in Cote d'Ivoire and in the gold mines and on cocoa farms in Ghana. Nigerian traders settled in Ghana and other West African Countries like Togo and Liberia, while Liberians also settled in Ghana to work in the ports. Ghanaian fishermen have moved as far as Senegal, Liberia and Cote d'Ivoire to settle and fish.

This paper explores the various types of migration in West Africa that were considered legitimate in the colonial era, but which are regarded as illegitimate in the postindependence era.

Protest Migration

In West Africa protest migrations formed an important dimension of the revolt against colonial rule,[3] particularly in French West Africa where the primary objective was to escape from socio-political difficulties. This was especially true of communities along or close to Anglo-French boundaries.

The protest migrations included the exodus of various ethnic groups from Senegal into Gambia. From French Guinea during the period 1900 to 1945, large numbers of Mende-speaking people crossed into Sierra Leone to protest against conscription into the armed forces and other objectionable policies of the French colonial masters. In the Cote d'Ivoire, which from 1936 to 1947 included the area of the present-day Burkina Faso, the exodus involved southern groups like the Sanwis and Affemas, as well as groups from Bondougou, Ouagadougou, Bobo-Dioulasso and Betie. The exodus also affected the Lobi, the Mossi, Kusasi and Dagari. There was a large-scale exodus into British Nigeria of Yoruba, Gun and Bariba refugees from French Benin and Hausa and related groups from French Niger.

All these movements, which occurred mainly between 1914-45, demonstrated that for comparatively weak groups, exodus was as much a means of expressing discontent as armed uprising was for relatively more power-ful people when faced with a resented alien political power.

It is important to note that these and other similar protest migrations left the French colonial authorities with a loss of tax revenue and labour. Needless to say, the French loss was a gain for the British, for it was in their territories that the migrants invariably sought refuge. In the British territo-ries the refugee communities often constituted labour reservoirs, contribut-ing to the growth of agriculture and, in the Gold Coast, to the cocoa and mining industries. For example, the ground-nut industry in the Gambia benefited from the Senegalese and Guinean labourers who originally migrated for primarily political reasons. Of similar benefit to the cotton industry in the Imeko district of Abeokuta province were the Dahomean immigrants, many of whom became excellent cotton growers. Ultimately, therefore, the larger the emigrations, the more extensive the loss to the French and the greater the gain to the British of more producers and taxable adults.[4]

The French considered these protest migrations illegitimate and asked the British governors to repatriate the migrants, but since it was advanta-geous for the British to receive these labourers, they turned a deaf ear to such demands and considered such migration legitimate. That set the pattern for migration along the West African region. Push and pull factors combined to make people move from one country to the other. Furthermore, colonial borders were not that rigidly patrolled and movement across borders did not require too much documentation.

Postindependence Migration

With independence came the struggle for national identity and a newfound sovereignty that needed to be jealously guarded. As the new states em-barked on their national development effort, they set up legal norms for determining who are citizens and who are aliens. Acts have been passed on aliens in the host country. Ghana's Aliens Act was enacted in 1963.[5] The Act sets out the basis for legitimate and illegitimate migration into Ghana. Under the provisions of the Act, every person entering Ghana has to appear before an immigration officer at the border post or within two days of his arrival. If the immigration officer is satisfied that the person is not a prohibited immigrant, has a valid passport and a requisite visa or an entry permit, the person may be allowed to enter Ghana and granted a permit to remain in the country for a specified period.[6]

Where a residence permit has been granted, the Minister of Interior, with the approval of Cabinet, can revoke the residence permit or impose new conditions to the permit. The residence permit only allows aliens to remain in the country; the Act specifies that they need a licence to work. The Act states:

> No person shall employ any alien in Ghana except in accordance with a license in writing granted by the Minister. A license granted by the Minister shall specify the number of persons of a specified description authorised to be employed thereby, and may specify different numbers for different classes of employees.[7]

Such aliens are considered legitimate migrants because they have a residence permit and can legitimately engage in commercial business ventures. Aliens are considered illegitimate migrants and subject to deportation if a court recommends it; if a court decides they are destitute, have no visible means of support, are of unsound mind; if they are prostitutes, prohibited immigrants, do not have valid permits, or have violated any of the conditions on which permits were granted; or if their presence in Ghana is, in the opinion of the Minister, not conducive to the public good.[8] Ghana's Aliens Act is similar to other legal norms in all countries of the subregion.

The Political Context

The Aliens Act's application in the West African region has been influenced to a great extent by the political and economic circumstances of the country. Under the government of Dr. Kwame Nkrumah, Ghana's policy toward aliens from other African countries was greatly influenced by political considerations. Following Ghana's independence in 1957, it was largely influenced by Nkrumah's famous declaration on the eve of independence that "the independence of Ghana is meaningless unless it is linked up with the total liberation of the African continent."

Following the 1958 conference of Independent African States in Accra, it was resolved to give every assistance to African freedom fighters struggling to achieve independence for their countries. From then on Ghana adopted a rather open-door policy toward all Africans seeking refuge. Ghana was all too willing to grant them legitimate immigrant status—that of freedom fighters and refugees. Accra became the mecca for African freedom fighters who came to look for financial assistance and inspiration. They were from Southern Africa, Rhodesia and territories still under colonial rule. There were also politicians from independent African states who were either guilty of crimes or feared unjust treatment at home.

These political refugees from independent African countries were to cause a rumpus over the 1965 Organization of African Unity (OAU) Summit in Accra.[9] Some African governments condemned Ghana for harbouring subversive agents and organizing training camps for them. The countries whose exiles were in Ghana (including Cote d'Ivoire, Niger, Burkina Faso and Benin) indicated they would not attend the Accra summit unless Ghana changed its African policy.[10] To save the conference, Ghana had to give assurances and guarantees to expel undesirable aliens to countries of their choice that were prepared to receive them, or to send them away from Accra during the period of the conference.

Ghana's open-door policy was in line with Nkrumah's policy of pan-Africanism and sought to champion African liberation and unity. Ghana became a magnet for many Africans in the West African region and Southern Africa. When the struggle against apartheid intensified in the early 1960s and the flow of Southern African refugees increased, Ghana issued a Commonwealth passport, which was an ingenious device to suggest that they are Commonwealth citizens, but which was regarded internationally as a special version of a Ghana passport. They were issued in the name of the Ghana Ministry of Foreign Affairs and were very useful travel documents because they were internationally regarded as a commitment by the Ghana government to receive their holders back to Ghana at any time.[11]

Aliens Compliance Order

Ghana's first republic's open-door policy toward aliens has been rather unique in light of its distinction between legitimate and illegitimate migrants, which is marked by the possession of residence permits. This authorizes noncitizens to reside in the country of their sojourn. This distinction has created many problems among the West African states. Those states that want to implement the distinction have resorted to Aliens Compliance Orders, which require noncitizens without residence permits to leave the country by a certain date. Most of the West African governments have at one time or the other asked noncitizens to leave. These states include Ghana, Nigeria, Togo, Cote d'Ivoire, Liberia and Sierra Leone. The most notable expulsions have been those of Nigerians from Ghana in 1969, Ghanaians from Nigeria in 1983 and 1985, Burkinabes from Ghana, Ghanaians from Togo, Cote d'Ivoire and Sierra Leone, and Beninois from Burkina Faso.[12]

In November 1969, an estimated 300,000 immigrants were given fourteen days by the government of Dr. Busia to legitimize their residence in Ghana or leave the country. The majority were Nigerians, Burkinabes, Togolese and Liberians. Many of them were long-term residents—farm labourers who helped create the cocoa boom of the 1950s, and other labourers and petty traders who were attracted to Ghana by that boom. Others had responded to the Nkrumah government's open-door policy toward other Africans. The wretched drama of the trecking thousands during the weeks following the order signalled the crisis that was beginning to develop in Ghana's postcolonial economy.[13]

Similarly in January 1983, an estimated two million West Africans, mainly Ghanaians, Malians, Burkinabes and Liberians, also hurried to beat a two-week deadline given to illegal immigrants to leave Nigeria.[14] These immigrants were drawn to Nigeria by a demand for their labour during the oil boom of the mid-1970s. They were expelled amidst accusations of being criminals, prostitutes and unemployed vagrants.

The expulsions set up a strain in relations among member states of the Economic Community of West African States (ECOWAS). Countries whose nationals were affected raised issue with violations of the ECOWAS Protocol on Free Movement of Persons. The Executive Secretary of ECOWAS, Dr. Aboubakar Diaby-Quattara, declared that the expulsion order was not a violation of the ECOWAS Protocol. President Mathiew Kerekou of Benin, Chairman of ECOWAS, visited Lagos and met with his Colleagues in the Nigerian government. They issued a joint statement assuring West Africans that the expulsions would have no adverse effect on the development of ECOWAS. Apart from the strong condemnation by the governments whose nationals were most affected—Ghana, Togo and Liberia—the reaction of other West African governments was one of muted disapproval.

There were significant dissident voices within Nigeria, even though the press supported the Shagari government's expulsion order and attacked hostile foreign press coverage of the exodus. Notable among these dissidents were chief Obafemi Awolowo and Dr. Nnamdi Azikiwe, leaders of the opposition Unity Party of Nigeria (UPN) and the Nigerian People's Party (NPP). They warned of the damage the expulsion would do to Nigeria's continental image and role. Similarly, when the military government of General Buhari again expelled an estimated 700,000 illegal immigrants in April 1985, a small number of people, most academics, recognized the futility and emphasized their total failure in achieving any of the objectives for which they were intended.[15]

The Expulsion Context

These expulsions occurred in difficult economic times. Studies in contemporary African immigration have pointed out historical precedents that go far back into precolonial times. Contemporary immigration in the subregion is cross-border and rooted in the region's integration into the global economy and in the colonial era's policies of economic expansion. Immigration continues to be propelled by the structures created by these policies, which are still maintained by postindependence governments. Most migrants are job seekers. Zachariah and Conde[16] have shown that a substantial migrant population of job seekers have been in West Africa since the early part of this century. The migrants to Nigeria and Ghana in the 1950s and 1970s were seeking jobs in booming economies. In 1975, 2.5 million West Africans lived in eight countries (excluding Nigeria) not their own, and 1.3 million of those were workers. If Nigeria had been taken into account Zachariah and Conde's figures would have been even larger.

The expulsions were of job seeking migrants rather than refugees. Migrants are attracted to a destination because of jobs and a healthy economy—pull factors—but refugees are forced to leave their countries of origin by famine, political strife and war—push factors. Until the flare-up between Senegal and Mauritania, the Sahel drought and the Liberian civil war, West Africa had very few refugees.

Policy Toward Asylum and Residence

Given West Africa's history of expelling migrant workers, there is a significant difference in the way refugees have been treated, as in the case of the Sahel drought victims and Liberians who have sought refuge.

The drought and famine in the Sahel in the 1970s forced people to leave their homeland to seek refuge elsewhere in the subregion. Such people have been called environmental refugees. Jodi Jacobson[17] speculates that there are already ten million unrecognized environmental refugees worldwide. Because the UNHCR does not recognize them as refugees, their plight has been difficult. These environmental refugees, most of whom are from Mali, Burkina Faso, Niger and Chad, took refuge in the neighbouring countries to the south—Ghana, Nigeria and Cote d'Ivoire.

These environmental refugees started arriving in Ghana in 1984. Their presence became more conspicuous in 1985, just about the time Ghanaian migrant workers in Nigeria were asked to leave. The official attitude towards them was one of benign neglect. They were left to fend for themselves and adopt various survival strategies while the refugee committee of the Christian Council of Ghana arranged assistance for them. Approximately two thousand refugees from the Sahel took refuge in Ghana. They were mostly nomads from Mali, Burkina Faso and Niger, who belonged to two broad ethnic groups, the Fulani and Tuareg. They are all Muslim nomadic herdsmen and warriors from the Sahara and the Sahel. The Tuareg see themselves as raiders, while the Fulani, who maintain cattle, are nomads who graze their herds in the bush from late June till early October and then take their cattle to cultivated land from October to the end of the harvest in February.

Arrival and Reception

On arrival in Ghana, the Fulani normally roam the northern and upper east and west savannah bush with their cattle. Most of the Tuareg had no cattle left, so they headed for the urban centres of Kumasi and Accra to find means of survival. The departments of immigration and social welfare left these refugees from the Sahel to fend for themselves. Voluntary organizations organized food and clothing for them.

The Tuaregs' main source of sustenance was begging for alms in the Muslim tradition. They indicated that problems of language and lack of capital to do petty trading were the main reasons for not being able to find work.

Assistance to the Refugees

In writing on rural refugees in Africa, Betts[18] points out that over the past two decades the UNHCR has tried to collaborate with the governments of asylum to develop an increasingly efficient system of organized settlements. The aim has been to provide assistance, security and a standard of living at least comparable to that of the local indigenous population until the refugees are able to decide whether they wish to return to their country of origin or become permanent members of their host country. According to Betts, the majority of African rural refugees have never come within this system and many have deliberately avoided it. He points out, however, that this form of spontaneous settlement within a familiar ethnic environment provides social rewards that far outweigh the advantages of formal settlement and requires only properly organized local services, particularly health and education. Betts cites the 1979 OAU Conference on Refugees at Arusha to buttress the point. The conference report noted:

> However complications arise in such situations [spontaneous settlement] since it is estimated that well over 60 percent of rural refugees are in this category and that the assistance provided for them is nil or negligible. Spontaneous settlement is often interpreted as spontaneous integration and thus all is assumed to be well. Traditional hospitality, especially between next of kin, solves the problem. This belief is convenient. It absolves government and aid agencies from doing something about this. If they are not causing any political problems, the temptation is to leave well alone....Spontaneous integration may mean extreme poverty and insecurity, eking out precarious and marginal existence through casual labor and migration. They are disorganized. They may not present themselves to officials or visiting missions. They may indeed constitute a rural subproletariat, powerless, inarticulate and unseen.[19]

The situation of the Sahel refugees in Ghana fits very well with the above. Interviews with those refugees who had settled in the bush and in unfinished buildings in urban areas indicated that their main concerns were food and clothing. Those with cattle were concerned about health care for themselves and their animals. One group said that in Burkina Faso, the government checked water-holes for contamination and wondered if Ghana would do same for them. They complained that their water was contaminated or that they had to walk long distances for water in the dry season.

Official Attitude and Assistance

When the refugees from the Sahel started to arrive, the government took a rather lukewarm attitude toward them. The state agencies did not know what to do. The Department of Social Welfare began registering the refugees, but made no effort to assist beyond that stage. Officials claim that there was no cooperation from the refugees. The government also gave the national mobilization program the responsibility of establishing relief camps. The camps were to have been sited at Sege in the Greater Accra region and Hiawa in the western region. Sege has an ongoing pilot agricultural program, but due to problems in logistics, the camps were never set up. The main reason given was the lack of funds and cooperation from the refugees, but the refugees' attitude could be explained by the fact that as nomads, they were not interested in being settled in a camp to adopt agricultural practices.

There was, therefore, no organized official assistance for these refugees. As far as Ghana's laws are concerned, there is no domestic law or administrative regulation on asylum and refugees. However, the Ministry of Interior, in cooperation with the UNHCR, has developed administrative practices to deal with refugee problems. Ghana has acceded to the 1951 UN Convention on the Status of Refugees and the 1967 Protocol, and is also a party to the 1969 OAU Convention Governing the Specific Aspects of the Refugee Problem in Africa. These international conventions are not considered part of Ghana's domestic laws. There is no domestic legal definition for the refugee/asylum seeker. The Ministry of Interior uses the extended definition contained in the OAU Convention as a basis for its categorization on a case-by-case basis. In principle, a person who has been given refugee status in another country in cooperation with the UNHCR, would be accorded the same status in Ghana.

Like the UNHCR, the Ghana government does not consider the refugees from the Sahel as refugees. They are considered indigent aliens and informal immigrants who should be attended to by the Department of Social Welfare, charitable organizations and individuals.

Unofficial Assistance

As a result of their nonrecognition as refugees by the UNHCR and the
Ghana government, assistance for these victims of the Sahel drought and
famine has fallen on the shoulders of voluntary organizations and church
groups. The Christian Council of Ghana is the main organization that is
providing assistance to these refugees. The council's refugee committee
provides food such as millet, cassava, beans, maize, rice and sugar twice a
week. The refugee committee also has a medical team that provides free
medical care on a weekly basis. The Christian Council has been encouraging
the refugees to work in small-scale ventures like leather work by providing
them with the raw materials. They are encouraged to use their skills to
become self-sufficient rather than relying on hand-outs.

Problems with Authorities

Government authorities are inclined to leave refugees alone if they are not
causing any political problems. This is the case with those refugees who
have settled among compatriots in the zongos and in unfinished houses in
urban areas. These are mainly Malians, Burkinabes and Nigerians. There
have been problems with the Fulani who brought their cattle and grazed
them in the northern savannah. The main problem was complaints from
Ghanaian farmers that the cattle were destroying their farms. The authorities feared that the cattle were potential carriers of rinderpest and anthrax.
The Ministry of Agriculture launched Operation Cow Leg to drive alien
herdsmen to the borders—the governments of Burkina Faso, Niger, Mali
and Nigeria were informed.[20] A national task force was set up to supervise
the program, which was expected to last three months. The Ministry was
concerned about the uncontrollable movement of the nomads and their
cattle, so they were held in quarantine and made to compensate farmers
before they were escorted out of the country.

Ghanaians' Attitudes as Hosts

When the refugees from the Sahel started arriving in Ghana, they were
warmly received and Ghanaians were at their charitable best. In many cases
the chiefs in the zongos arranged accommodation for them and people were
generous with their support. The zongos are the urban areas in which most
aliens settle. In an Accra suburb called Medina, the zongo chief said, "Their
sleeping mats, blankets, cooking pots and other household accessories were
freely given by charitable Ghanaians. They normally line up in front of my
house and signal that they are hungry and I give them the little I can."[21]

But after awhile, the Ghanaians' warm hospitality began to cool. Some Ghanaians viewed the refugees as people whose main aim was to beg for alms as the only legitimate means of earning a living instead of finding lucrative jobs to do. Others pointed out that the refugees who came in the early 1960s were hard-working, energetic and prosperous people who worked as "water boys" and porters in the market. Some Ghanaians felt that the refugees from the Sahel were lazy in comparison. Others argued that they should be forced to work on the farms and rehabilitated by the government, and if they refused, they should be deported back to their country of origin.

These sentiments are to some extent reactions to the manner in which the begging was done, which generally irritated Ghanaians.[22] In Ghana the only people who are seen as legitimate beggars are cripples or old people with no family to support them. In Muslim communities where the Sahel refugees lived, however, begging by children is accepted and giving alms is considered a duty, but the aggressiveness of the begging created irritation and not sympathy.

Other Ghanaians feel that the Sahel refugees are racist and do not like working for black people. There is the case in Accra of a Tuareg boy who refused a Ghanaian's job offer by saying that he would not work for a black man. In another instance a Chadian refugee, who worked for a white woman and a Ghanaian man, left when the woman left for Europe and returned only when she returned. This apparent sense of superiority of some Tuaregs may be due partly to their consciousness of racial differences and partly to a nomad's contempt for the lifestyle of settled people. Despite all these difficulties, some Ghanaians remain warm towards the refugees. They argue that the refugees should be allowed to stay in Ghana because of the OAU charter, which seeks to unite Africans, as well as for humanitarian reasons.

The Liberian Refugees

The Aliens Act is the only mechanism in the West Africa region that distinguishes between legitimate and illegitimate migrants. Because the region has seldom seen the kind of refugee movement that occurs elsewhere on the continent, there are no domestic laws on refugees. However, West African governments have reached an understanding over the years with the UNHCR on refugee issues. They have treated those they consider as refugees differently from aliens and, as illustrated in the case of the refugees from the Sahel, even though governments did not accord them refugee status, they allowed them to stay on as long as they posed no political problems.

The governments and host populations have been very forthcoming with assistance. The case of the Liberian refugees is a good example. Following the 1990 Liberian civil war, Liberians started seeking refuge all over the region. In December 1989 the neighbouring countries of Sierra Leone, Guinea and Cote d'Ivoire took large numbers of refugees. Guinea initially reported an inflow of 13,000 Liberians, but by March 1990 it had an estimated 66,000 to 80,000 refugees. Cote d'Ivoire reported some 55,000 Liberian refugees by December 1989. By the end of 1990 an estimated 700,000 Liberians left their country as a result of the conflict, and another one million were displaced within Liberia.

When the conflict became protracted and no faction could establish a government, the Economic Community of West African States (ECOWAS) became concerned and embarked on diplomatic efforts to bring peace to Liberia. They set up an ECOWAS monitoring group to intervene militarily to stop the carnage in Liberia. The group was made up of 2,000 troops from Nigeria, Ghana, Sierra Leone and Gambia, who landed in Monrovia Port in August 1990. As a show of concern for Ghanaians trapped by the conflict, the Ghana government dispatched a ship to evacuate them from Monrovia. This organized evacuation of Ghanaians led Ghana to host a large number of Liberian refugees. The ships that were sent to evacuate Ghanaians from Monrovia and Freetown ended up bringing back Ghanaians and Liberians who were stranded at the two ports. An earlier group of Liberian refugees left Monrovia to avoid the impending attack from the Charles Taylor rebel forces and arrived in Ghana in May 1990.

Liberian refugees at the camp at Gomoa Buduburam near Accra gave vivid accounts of how they got to Ghana. Most of them immediately left their homes when bombs fell and destroyed part of their homes, or when they saw neighbours being interrogated, taken away and shot dead. They left Monrovia without anything except their clothes, and walked along the highway towards Sierra Leone.

After crossing into Sierra Leone they joined the Ghanaians they had accompanied along the highway because they heard that a Ghanaian ship was in Freetown to evacuate Ghanaians. They introduced themselves as Ghanaians born in Liberia and were evacuated to Ghana. At Accra airport they were screened and those who admitted that they were actually Liberians were sent to the newly-created refugee camp at Gomoa Buduburam. The largest group of Liberians came with the Ghanaians evacuated from Freetown and Monrovia by the Ghana vessel *M.V. Tano River* on September 3, 1990. By the end of September there approximately 7,000 Liberians at the camp, with an estimated 2,000 self-settled in Accra.

Providing assistance to the Liberian refugees has gone through a good deal of politicking due to the novel nature of the refugee situation in Ghana and the lack of policy guidelines for assisting refugees. Ghana had no previous experience with hosting refugees in a camp. There was no state agency with the expertise to handle such a situation. It was also not clear to various nongovernmental organizations whether the Liberians could be called refugees, given the fact that most of them had been evacuated to Ghana by the Ghana government. The Ghana government regarded them as refugees, but has not given them refugee status en mass because there is no refugee law in Ghana, only a law for aliens. The government was therefore very slow in seeking international assistance for the Liberian refugees.

The host population took the initiative by providing lots of food and other items for their upkeep. The UNHCR could not assist initially due to its financial crisis. At that time the UNHCR's local office was due to be closed down in December 1990 and its continued operation was uncertain. The Adventist Development and Rehabilitation Agency (ADRA) assisted by distributing food parcels to the refugees.

The Ghana government asked for international assistance for the upkeep of the camp. The camp has a management committee that administers the assistance received. The EEC provided some funding for food and other necessities until December 1990. Providing food for the camp is now largely the responsibility of the International Committee of the Red Cross (ICRC), which has provided funds that the UNHCR was unable to raise. The ICRC's assistance operates through the Ghana Red Cross.

There was a disappointing response from the international community regarding assistance to Liberian refugees ever since an appeal for financial assistance was launched by the UNHCR in February and June 1990. In September 1990, only U.S. $5.7 million was raised against the initial target of U.S. $11.3 million. What little assistance was received was given to the neighbouring countries of Sierra Leone, Guinea and Cote d'Ivoire. The Liberian refugee problem came at a particularly bad time on the international scene. The UNHCR was going through a very serious financial crisis and was cutting back on its field staff as much as possible. The organization's High Commissioner had resigned and a row had developed over his successor. The crisis also coincided with the Iraqi invasion of Kuwait, and the West's attention was focused on providing assistance to deal with that situation.

Under the circumstances, the Ghana government and other host governments in the subregion have done what they could to provide sustenance for the Liberian refugees. After the initial show of concern and donations by the host population, things have subsided and now assistance is only coming from nongovernmental organizations and the Red Cross. We have taken a broad look at the basis for distinguishing between legitimate and illegitimate migration in the West African region. Laws regarding aliens have been used as a basis for the various expulsions that have taken place in Ghana, Nigeria, Togo, Cote d'Ivoire, Senegal and Mauritania. Subsequent migrations are of job seekers, and the region has a long history of similar migrations. The expulsions have been seen as an economic measure aimed at freeing certain jobs for citizens.

Such expulsions have, however, not included refugees. Even though the region has not seen the kind refugee flows that are common in the Horn, East, Central and Southern Africa, governments have generally been forthcoming with assistance to refugees or people in refugee-like situations. The care of the Sahel and Liberian refugees shows how the government, the host population and international agencies have organized assistance for refugees. There is a clear distinction between illegal aliens who are expelled when the economic bubble bursts and refugees who are either given assistance despite the country's economic hardships, or left to find their own means of survival. The exception are environmental refugees, who are sometimes viewed as refugees and, at other times, as illegal aliens in Ghana for economic reasons.

Notes

1. W.I. Zartman, *Ripe for Resolution: Conflict and Intervention in Africa* (New York: Oxford University Press, 1985).

2. Ghana has had a stream of politicians taking refuge in Togo, Cote d'Ivoire and Burkina Faso as a result of coups in 1966, 1972, 1979 and 1981. Opponents of Togolese President Eyadema have also taken refuge in Ghana.

3. A.I. Asiwaju, "Migration As An Expression of Revolt: The Example of French West Africa Up to 1945," *Tarikh* 5, no. 3 (1977):31-43.

4. Ibid.

5. Republic of Ghana's Aliens Act, 1963, Act 160.

6. Ibid., Section 5.

7. Ibid., Section 10.

8. Ibid., Section 12.

9. *West Africa*, July 10, 1965.

10. *West Africa*, May 1, 1965.

11. Sven Hamrell, ed., *Refugee Problems in Africa* (Uppsala: Scandinavian Institute of African Studies, 1967), 58-59.

12. S.K.B. Asante, "ECOWAS and Free Movement of Persons," *West Africa*, July 1978.

13. Yaa Frempomaa Yeboah, "The Crisis of International Migration in an Integrating West Africa: A Case Study of Nigeria and Ghana." Paper presented at a seminar at the Institute of Development Studies, University of Sussex, Brighton, England, October 1985.

14. The order that was announced by Ali Baba, the Minister of Internal Affairs, on January 18, 1983, was modified on January 25 as follows: "That all aliens who are unemployed, as well as those employed in unskilled labour, such as cooks and stewards, drivers, watchmen, gardeners, nannies, etc., must leave within the period of 14 days as allowed in my earlier announcements. Those who are self-employed in petty trading, tailoring, hairdressing and similar traders, must also leave within the same period." Quoted in Yaa Frempomaa Yeboah, "The Crisis of International Migration in An Integrating West Africa: A Case Study of Nigeria and Ghana."

15. See Aribisala, "The Aliens Explusion Order Revisited: "A Minority Viewpoint," *Spectrum* (November/December 1983); "Tai Solarin," *Satellite* (February 11, 1983); Opoola, "Thoughts on the Aliens' Exodus," *New Nigerian* (February 21, 1983).

16. K.C. Zachariah and J. Conde, *Migrations in West Africa* (London: Oxford University Press, 1981), 53.

17. Jodi Jacobson, *Environmental Refugees: A Yardstick of Habitability* (Washington: Worldwatch Institute, 1988).

18. J.F. Betts, "Rural Refugees in Africa," *International Migration Review* 5, no. 1-2 (1981):213-14.

19. Ibid.

20. *West Africa*, May 2, 1988, p. 813.

21. Interview with the Chief of Medina.

22. The method involved young boys and girls who held onto the clothes of the world-be benefactor until the person gave them some money. The women held their emaciated babies to passing motorists, pointing to their mouths to indicate that they were hungry.

5

Definitions of Legitimacy: Afghan Refugees in Pakistan

Grant M. Farr

Much of the discussion of refugee migration, including notions of refugee laws and norms that legitimize these migrations, are framed in the context of refugees in the developed world. In this context, refugee status is determined by laws of nations with strong state structures, in which there are relatively clear legal definitions that determine the nature of citizenship, immigration, political asylum and rights against forced repatriation that characterize the status of a refugee. As a consequence, determining whether refugee migrations are illegitimate or legitimate is *relatively* straightforward in countries with strong and developed state governments. Difficulty in judging which refugees are legitimate, as in the recent case of the Haitian refugees, occurs frequently when refugee status is ambiguous because the legal or bureaucratic norms do not clearly apply.

Yet in most of the world, the migration of refugees is into areas where nations have not developed clear definitions of statehood. In many of these Third World countries, the concept of a nation-state has not emerged because of the lack of strong centralized institutions of government and/or because of strong regional, tribal or local political structures that resist the development of national identity. In much of the world, especially Africa, Asia and parts of the Middle East, state governments rule largely in the capital, and perhaps the major cities, but have little salience in rural areas where tribal or other socio-political structures operate, and where people's allegiances are to what anthropologists have called "primordial" sentiments, rather than to national state governments.[1]

119

In these situations, concepts of illegitimate and legitimate migration become less clear, since national and international laws have little, if any, relevance to the refugees or to their hosts. Rather, definitions of legitimate and illegitimate migrations are rooted in local folk histories, cultural traditions and religious sentiments that provide definitions of neighbouring tribes or ethnic groups, strangers, travellers or migrants as good or evil, welcome or unwelcome, and that spell out traditional norms of hospitality, rights of refuge and ethnic or tribal relations. In this context, the legitimacy of refugee migrations into neighbouring countries must be understood in terms of these local or regional cultural values, customs and norms, although national or international law and regulations may continue to have relevance as the refugees confront international refugee relief organizations.

This chapter will examine the case of the Afghan refugee migration into Pakistan. The chapter will show that the status of the Afghan refugees in Pakistan, and thus their legitimacy, is defined by a number of overlapping contextual layers that include the ethnohistory of the peoples in the region; the traditional relationships between the nomadic tribes of Afghanistan and the agriculturalists of the Indus plain, the area that is now Pakistan; the religious definitions that derive from Islam, and, lastly, from the modern definitions of refugee status that derives from international refugee law. How an Afghan refugee views himself, how an Afghan refugee seeks aid, develops political coalitions, whether or not he will repatriate, and how he is viewed by Pakistan are consequences of these definitional frameworks.

Background

Since the Marxist coups in Afghanistan in 1978 and the subsequent Soviet invasion of Afghanistan in late 1979, over five million Afghans have fled to neighbouring countries, approximately one-third of the fifteen million pre-1978 population. Although exact counts of refugee populations are hard to come by, despite many attempts at accurate numeration,[2] it is now estimated that over 3.2 million Afghan refugees are in Pakistan, primarily in the border areas of the Northwest Frontier Province (NWFP) and in the province of Baluchistan. While some refugees have voluntarily returned in the three years since the Soviet army withdrawal in February 1989 to regions of Afghanistan that are now safe, refugee flow to Pakistan has also continued from other parts, especially those areas where sectarian fighting has intensified. As a result, the refugee population has remained relatively stable since 1985.

The burden of supporting these refugees has largely been on the host country, although Pakistan has also received large amounts of material aid to care for the refugees. The Afghan refugees have created considerable civil, economic, social, ethnic and ecological problems for Pakistan.[3] The presence of the Afghans has now become a major issue in Pakistani politics. Repatriation of the Afghans will clearly be problematic, since the Afghans have slowly integrated into Pakistani society over thirteen years. The United Nations High Commissioner for Refugees (UNHCR) has recently encouraged Pakistan to consider offering citizenship to the large group of Afghans who will not return, a step Pakistan is obviously reluctant to take.

The vast majority of the Afghan refugees in Pakistan, as much as two-thirds of the total refugee population, are situated in the Northwest Frontier Province. Two other provinces, Baluchistan and a small area of the Punjab, have been designated by the Government of Pakistan as refugee-receiving areas. Over 320 official camps have been established to receive refugees.[4] Each camp was originally designed to hold 10,000 refugees, but the size of the migration has swollen the camp size to over 150,000 in some cases.

In addition to the care and feeding of the refugees, the Government of Pakistan has been concerned with issues of security and accountability. Determining who are legitimate refugees, their rights in Pakistan, where they should live and travel and what kinds of occupations they can engage in became issues in the early 1980s when the huge waves of refugees started to arrive and the immediate humanitarian concerns had been largely met.

When refugees arrive in Pakistan most are registered through an office established by the Government of Pakistan in 1980 to deal with these problems. This office, the Chief Commissionerate of the Afghan Refugees, issues identity documents that are necessary to obtain refugee assistance, such as clothing, food, cooking utensils, tents and, at one time, a cash stipend. In the early 1980s, the cash supplement amounted to fifty rupees (approximately U.S. $3.70) per refugee per month, with a limit of 500 rupees per family. The cash stipend was phased out by 1985, in part because it was politically unpopular among the local Pakistanis, many of whom were economically less well off than the refugees.

Beyond initial items provided to establish a household, those who register are entitled to regular issue consisting of a packet of dry food (mostly wheat) and kerosene for cooking and heating. These rations are donated by the international community, including the World Food Program. The cost of refugee relief in Pakistan is nearly $500 million per year, or about $1 million each day. This amount is financed by contributions from foreign governments and a wide array of private voluntary organizations. Much of the foreign government aid is channelled through the United Nations High Commissioner for Refugees (UNHCR), which plays an important role in partnership with the Chief Commissionerate of the Afghan Refugees.

The population characteristics of the Afghan refugees show that three-quarters of the refugees are women, children and the elderly. Since a guerrilla resistance war has been occurring simultaneously with the refugee migration, men bring their families out to the camps of Pakistan and then return to fight. As a consequence, males of fighting age, which begins in the early teens, are largely absent from the camps. In addition, war fatalities have decreased the population of young men, so that there are large refugee camps made up solely of widows and orphans. According to the Chief Commissionerate of the Afghan Refugees' figures published in January 1987, 75.6 percent of the registered refugees in Pakistan were women or children.[5] The refugee population is characterized by a high birth rate. Fifty-seven percent of the refugees are children under fifteen, and of those, 40 percent are under the age of five. A large and growing segment of the Afghan refugees in the camps have been born in Pakistan and are being raised outside of Afghanistan.

Many of the refugees have left the camps and are now living in the major Pakistani cities. Since they are relatively poor, they live together in the poorer sections of the cities and have created Afghan ghettos. The Government of Pakistan has not restricted the Afghans to the camps, but has unsuccessfully attempted to keep them from the cities. For instance, it has made Afghan business or ownership of property illegal in most parts of Pakistani cities, but Afghans have found ways to circumvent these rules. In addition, the Government of Pakistan requires that the refugees receive the monthly rations at their designated camps in an attempt to keep the refugees in the camps. Of course, the Afghans simply return to camp one day a month to receive their rations and then return to their homes in other parts of Pakistan.

The Afghan refugees pose a dilemma to the people of Pakistan. At some levels, Pakistani tradition points towards acceptance of the Afghans and tolerance of their presence in Pakistan. Other levels suggest that the Afghans should be feared, mistrusted and expelled from Pakistan at the earliest moment. Likewise on the part of the Afghans, Pakistanis can be viewed as gracious and generous hosts, brothers in culture and religion, or as mortal enemies to be conquered and not to be trusted. Clearly, the mix of Afghans and Pakistanis on the very hot, humid and crowded Indus River plain is an explosive combination that needs analysis.

The acceptance of the Afghans as refugees, and possibly as potential citizens, is tied to how the Afghans' migration is viewed by Pakistan, the Afghans and the world community. Specifically, whether the Afghans' migration to Pakistan is illegitimate or legitimate is the very point of the issue and will be a key element in its resolution whether they settle or repatriate.

Historical Background

The modern state of Afghanistan began in 1747 when Ahmad Shah came to power as the first Afghan ruler.[6] Afghanistan means "the land of the Afghans," the name used to refer to the Pushtun tribes of the southern and eastern areas of the country. There are many ethnolinguistic groups in Afghanistan. Louis Dupree, the father of modern Afghan studies, mentions twenty-one.[7] The country is generally split into three major ethnic divisions: the Central Asians of the north, who are largely Turkic speakers; the Persian speakers of the central and western parts; and the Pushtun of the south and the east. The Pushtun make up approximately 40 percent of the population of Afghanistan and, except for a brief period in 1929, they have ruled the country.

The development of a nation-state, especially through the institution of national government, has largely eluded Afghanistan. The country was ruled until 1978 by a series of monarchs,[8] except for the brief period in 1929. The kings were all Pushtun and all from the Mohammedzai tribes of southern Afghanistan. However, a true nation-state was never fully developed and the people outside the capital continued to lead lives regulated by local norms and customs that derived from local ethnic, tribal or religious traditions. Among the Pushtuns, for instance, strong tribal laws and customs (*Pushtunwali*) dominated, advocating strong norms of male equality, independence, pride, revenge, hospitality and manhood.

Most explanations for the failure of state building in Afghanistan focus on the country's diverse ethnolinguistic mix, its difficult topography, and the presence of strong tribal, village or other regional social structures that demand strong loyalty.[9] Clearly, trying to build a cohesive nation in a land with hot arid deserts and mountain peaks over 18,000 feet, and where inhabited central valleys are only open a few months a year, made the task impossible. But recent work has argued that the failure of state building is more a function of the central government's inability to get its act together, as Shahrani explains:

> The real difficulty with the development of state structure in Afghanistan has been the government's inability or unwillingness to try to establish an organic relationship with its citizens based on just and equitable treatment ... a mechanical relationship based on the expanding corrupt bureaucracy was nothing more than a castle built on sand.

In addition to the problems created by weak and corrupt government institutions and strong tribal cultures, Islam has also played a role in the failure to develop a strong nation-state in Afghanistan. Islam, it has been argued,[10] has played a dual and contradictory role in Afghanistan, at times used by the government for sanctifying its actions, and at other times as a whipping boy standing against modernization. Islam can also provide a unifying force, especially when used to confront external non-Islamic enemies like the British in the nineteenth century or the Soviet Union in the 1980s. In times when there was no external enemy, however, Islam often became a force for those to organize against the state, since Islam is an appeal to the community of all true believers and thus antistate at its core.

In Afghanistan the tribal groups that have exercised the most independ-ence and the greatest roadblock to state formation, even though they have participated actively in the various governments of Afghanistan, are the Pushtun who live in the border areas on both sides of the Afghan-Pakistan border.[11] The Pushtun tribes are divided roughly between the southern tribes centred around Kandahar in Afghanistan called the Mohammedzai, and the tribes in the northeast centred around Peshawar, known as the Gilzai. These tribes have ruled Afghanistan since the founding of the country. In Pakistan Pushtun tribes live mostly in the border areas of the Northwest Frontier Province and in Baluchistan. In Baluchistan the Pushtun now number more than the Baluch, a fact that is causing increasing ethnic tension in that province. The Pushtun made up about 40 percent of the population in pre-1978 Afghanistan and over 80 percent of the Afghan refugee population now in Pakistan.

Historically, the Pushtun tribe (or subtribe) that ruled Kabul was almost always a branch of the Mohammadzai. They dominated the other tribes, as well as the other ethnic groups in Afghanistan. As a result, tribal leaders and their followers have often had to flee the mountains of Afghanistan fearing persecution from tyrannical rulers of Kabul. Throughout much of the nineteenth and the early part of the twentieth century, Afghans fled to the plains of the Indus River valley, the area that is now Pakistan. In exile they were either kept as prisoners by the British or offered political asylum, depending on who they were and how the British felt at the time. Peshawar, the present capital of the Northwest Frontier Province of Pakistan and the centre of the present Afghan refugee population, was often home to Afghan tribal leaders who had fled during this turbulent period of Afghan history.

As a result, the Afghans, especially the Pushtun, have come to view the area of the Indus plain, now Pakistan, as a traditional and legitimate area of refuge. The Afghan tribes have historically been contemptuous of the agriculturalists of the Indus valley and have conquered this area several times. The Afghans view this area of Pakistan as part of greater Afghanistan. The present Afghan migration into Pakistan is unprecedented, both be-cause of its size and cause. It is nonetheless seen by the Afghans as part of a historical tradition and therefore, to some degree, as a right. By this logic, the migration of the Afghans into Pakistan is considered legitimate by the Afghans, although it may be seen as illegitimate by the Pakistanis.

Cultural Similarities

The cultural similarities of the peoples on both sides of the Afghan-Pakistan border also play a part in the definition of the present migration. Since the people on both sides are Pushtun, they share a common language and cultural tradition. To the Pushtun and other Afghans as well, the Afghanistan-Pakistan border, often called the Durand Line, does not constitute a legitimate national boundary. To resolve the exact nature of the boundary between British India and Afghanistan, the British sent a mission led by Sir Mortimer Durand to Kabul to meet with Amir Abdur Rahman. The British were concerned especially about the Pushtun tribes in that area and felt that they needed to establish a clear line demarcating who controlled what. Abdur Rahman, for his part, was concerned about the British road and railway construction in the border area. He felt that the British might be headed for Kandahar and Kabul. He concluded, therefore, that it was time to establish the boundary to keep the British from taking parts of Afghanistan.

The exact nature of this boundary was not terribly important for half a century, since neither the British nor the Afghan government were able to control the Gilzai, Pushtun and other tribal groups who lived in this border area. The dispute over the Durand Line, however, became critical at the time of the partition of British India in 1947 when the country of Pakistan came into existence, and the Durand Line became the official boundary between Pakistan and Afghanistan. The Afghans have never accepted this as an international boundary and once went to war with Pakistan over this issue. To the Afghans, it divides into two parts the Pushtun people, who insist that they are one united people, despite continuous and bloody wars among themselves.

The issue of a Pushtun homeland, the Pushtunistan issue, is in fact an important point of contention between Pakistan and Afghanistan. The war over the boundary in 1957 resulted in Pakistan closing the border to Afghan travel, isolating Afghanistan from any seaport. This issue, a united Pushtun homeland, is important in the definition of legitimate migration of the Afghans into Pakistan. Since the Afghans, at least the Pushtun, believe that they are simply crossing from one area of their tribal homeland into another area, they are by their own definition not refugees and certainly not making an illegitimate migration. However, the Government of Pakistan, which recognizes its border with Afghanistan as the legitimate border, views the Afghans' migration quite differently.

Islam and Refugees

Almost all of the population of Pakistan and Afghanistan are Muslim.
About 80 percent of both countries are followers of the Orthodox or Sunni
sect. Small Christian, Sikh, Hindu and other communities are found in the
two countries, but Islam dominates. Islam, in its present ideological formation, not only provides a religious and theological direction for the two
countries, but also has taken on a definite political meaning. At this time in
Pakistan and Afghanistan, as in much of the rest of the Muslim world,
religious symbols and ideology dominate the political discourse to the point
that the two institutional spheres almost completely overlap.

In the Afghan refugee community, leadership is dominated by either
traditional religious clerics or newly-minted fundamentalist[12] radicals with
ties to radical Islamic movements in other parts of the world. As a result,
Islamic ideology dominates the actions and discourse of the leadership of
the resistance movement and the refugee community. Secular leaders,
including members of the former ruling class and westernized intellectuals,
have been ostracized and even killed in some situations. Relief workers
attempting to deal with the Afghan refugee community on topics that are
considered un-Islamic, such as women's issues, find great resistance and
often armed resistance.

Arabic religious terms are used by the Afghans for important positions
in the society. The resistance fighters are referred to as *mujahedin*, holy
warriors, and the war against the government in Kabul is referred to a *jehad*,
holy war.

Likewise, the refugees are also viewed in an Islamic context. Seeking
temporary refuge from religious persecution has a sacred place in Islam.
The prophet Muhammad fled from Mecca to Medina to seek refuge in 622
A.D. to escape from enemies. This event has become sacred in Islam and is
referred to in Arabic as the *hijra*, and marks the beginning of the Islamic
calendar. Refugees in Islam are called *Muhajarin*,[13] especially those who
have fled because of religious persecution.

It has been said that refugees may be more prominent among the
believers of Islam than in other religions.[14] Certainly several of the largest
refugee migrations in recent time have been from and/or to Islamic countries, including Afghanistan, Palestine and Kurdistan. However, refugees
have a main place in the theology of the other religions as well, although the
Islamic understanding of being a refugee is somewhat different. Since
Muhammad was a refugee, *hijra* is viewed as a profound event in a
Muslim's life, with important religious significance. In fact, if the situation
warrants it, *hijra* is looked upon as a supreme religious imperative and
without fleeing one cannot be properly called a Muslim.[15]

This analogy to the prophet Muhammad's flight sanctifies the refugee migration from Afghanistan into Pakistan and thus defines the Afghan migration as legitimate, both for the Afghans and for their host, Pakistan. Obviously, the religious legitimation of the Afghan migration into Pakistan is clearly more salient to the segments of Afghan and Pakistan society for which religion is most important. This explains, in part, why the Afghans are embraced by the religious groups in Pakistan and their followers, particularly the Jama'at Islami, an Islamic political group that has great influence on the present government, and why the Afghans are treated with open derision by the Pakistan secular middle class to whom religion does not have strong appeal.[16]

The analogy to the flight of the prophet Muhammad also increases the Afghans' expectations of repatriation. Muhammad returned triumphantly to Mecca in 630 A.D. after eight years of exile. By the same analogy, the Afghans *Muhajarin* should return triumphantly to Afghanistan. This expectation remains to be fulfilled.

Legitimacy and Modern International Law

Another aspect of what defines legitimate and illegitimate migration has to do with the definition of a refugee that derives from modern international law. These laws are relatively new and are important in the Afghan case because of the presence of the UNHCR and other international refugee relief agencies who must, by mandate, only serve those who can legitimately claim refugee status according to this international definition.[17]

This modern definition of a refugee derives from the period immediately following World War II, as millions of displaced persons wandered around Europe and in the following decades during which most of Eastern Europe came under Communist control. Much of the canon of modern refugee law was written during this period.

The Western concept of a refugee has also been affected by the recent refugee migration from Third World countries to Europe and America in the last two decades as a direct result of collapsing colonial empires. Inhabitants of former colonies flee to the colonial centre to avoid political persecution or economic ruin. Thus America has in the last two decades accepted many refugees from Southeast Asia and Latin America, while Britain has received people from the Indian subcontinent and from former colonies in Africa and elsewhere.

These refugees have several things in common. They have left their homelands in the Third World to move to a more modern and affluent country. While many have fled terror and oppression, many have also come for reasons of expected financial gain or financial survival. And many have fled because in their home country they were associated with the former colonial power, an association that both made their flight possible and necessary. Finally, these refugees move with the expectation that they will never return to their homeland.

The 1951 United Nations Convention relating to the Status of Refugees and its 1967 Protocol are the primary sources of international refugee treaty law. Under the 1951 Convention, a refugee is defined as any person who:

> ... owing to well-founded fear of being persecuted for reasons of race, religion, nationality, membership of a particular social group or political opinion, is outside the country of his nationality and is unable, or owing to such fear, is unwilling to avail himself of the protection of that country; or who, not having a nationality and being outside the country of his former habitual residence as a result of such events, is unable or, owing to such fear, is unwilling to return to it.

> (*United Nations Convention Relating to the Status of Refugees, 1951*, Art. 1[a] [2], 189 unts, 137)

In the case of the Afghans, this definition becomes important when Afghans come into contact with international agencies, particularly the United Nations High Commissioner for Refugees (UNHCR). Pakistan never signed the 1957 Convention on Refugees, but has agreed to "continue to be guided by the provisions of the...Convention as regards the protection and treatment of the refugees."[18]

To make this definition work, Afghan refugees entering Pakistan must register with the Chief Commissionerate of the Afghan Refugees, a branch of the Government of Pakistan. Being a registered refugee entitles one to a place in one of the refugee camps and to rations. However, many refugees do not fit the legal definition and are forced to live in the growing settlement of illegal refugees. These illegal settlements are usually in areas surrounding legal camps or in the older parts of the major cities, where the presence of large numbers of Afghans is viewed as undesirable by the local Pakistani.

Implications for Pakistan and the Regional Repatriation

All of the definitions of illegitimacy or legitimacy of the Afghan refugee migration to Pakistan include, implicitly or explicitly, expectations of repatriation. Historical, cultural, religious and legal definitions of the refugee all assume that the situation is temporary and that the refugees will return to Afghanistan at some not-too-distant point in the future. Thus for the Afghans and Pakistanis, the issue of the refugees' repatriation has become paramount. The resolution of the Afghan situation has come to mean one thing for Pakistan—the successful and complete repatriation of the Afghans out of their country.

Most Pakistani officials involved with the refugees believe that as many as 30 percent of the Afghans will stay in Pakistan. Recent studies have indicated that the number staying will be at least double this.[19] Clearly, the repatriation of the Afghan refugees will depend on the nature of the political settlement in Afghanistan, the level of damage to the economic infrastructure in the country, the level of security that can be guaranteed, the nature and amount of external material aid to help the return migration, and the situation in Pakistan.

The nature of the economic aid to the refugees has important implications on the probability of successful repatriation. Much of the attention of the various refuge aid groups, including Pakistan's Chief Commissionerate of the Afghan Refugees, has been on developing self-help programs for the refugees that will shift their economic burden from Pakistan to the Afghans. This is thought not only to be economically smart, but to have psychological and sociological benefits by creating self-sufficiency in the refugee communities.

Afghan refugees, however, have been consistently penetrating the local Pakistani economies on their own initiatives. Although this has occurred primarily in the areas of high refugee concentration in Pakistan, Afghan labourers, shopkeepers, truck drivers, craftsmen and traders are now found in most parts of Pakistan.[20] As early as 1982 several internal UNHCR reports described the economic activities of the Afghans in Pakistan. In a survey done in refugee camps in the Kohat district of the NWFP, 72 percent of the adult males had some type of employment in the local Pakistani economy, and 87 percent of all refugee families surveyed had at least one wage-earning member.[21] Some of these occupations included kitchen-gardening workers, day labourers, craftsmen, traders, tailors, merchants, and trucking and shipping workers.

Trucking and shipping has been an important source of income to the Afghans. During the 1970s in Afghanistan, there was an expansion of road construction, and many traditional shippers purchased heavy trucks with the help of West German credit. Many of the refugees fleeing into Pakistan brought their trucks with them. The Pakistani authorities have registered these vehicles under temporary registration to allow the Afghans to continue to operate. This policy was made in part because Pakistan has had a shortage of commercial vehicles.

In the NWFP alone there are over 893 heavy trucks, 55 buses, 173 mini-buses, 152 tractors, 411 cars, cabs, jeeps and pick-ups registered to Afghans. There are probably at least that number unregistered. The UNHCR also estimates that the Afghans have brought with them into Pakistan 45,000 camels and 25,000 donkeys for commercial purposes.[22]

The Afghans have also opened retail shops in several urban centres and along major highways. Usually small, these shops are nonetheless gaining a growing foothold in the bazaars of Peshawar, Quetta and Islamabad. Many Afghan craftsmen now work in Pakistan and the best tailors of traditional clothes in Pakistan are now Afghans.

The Afghans' penetration into the economy has created a serious problem for Pakistan. Until recently this problem has been mitigated by the fact that many Pakistani men have been working abroad. It is estimated that there were up to 3.5 million Pakistanis working outside of Pakistan, mainly in the Middle East countries of the Persian Gulf. These workers remit billions of dollars to Pakistan. Some of this money is then privately invested in small infrastructural businesses and construction projects that in turn create jobs for Pakistan. Afghan refugee labour has moved into these jobs.

Time is running out, however, as the Pakistani labourers are returning in large numbers as the Gulf work dried up. Competition for jobs in Pakistan is increasing, surplus labor is driving down wages and lowering the standard of living for most workers, Pakistani and Afghan. Afghans have the resources of refugee aid to fall back on that the Pakistanis do not, and a considerable amount of resentment is growing.

To counter the penetration of the Afghans into the Pakistani economy, the UNHCR, with the assistance of other world relief agencies, has attempted to start refugee self-help projects in the camps. It is thought that this would not only solve the problem of the Afghans workers competing in the Pakistani economy, but would also keep the Afghans in the camps. A growing concern has been the increasing number of refugees who do not and will not live in the camps.

Refugee self-sufficiency projects, on the other hand, are a double-edged sword for Pakistan. While these projects may produce income, enabling the refugees to become more self-sufficient, the self-help projects also further the integration of the refugees into Pakistan and thus decrease the chance of successful repatriation.

Afghan Refugees and Ethnic Politics

Internal ethnic divisions in Pakistan have been an important obstacle to stability since its founding. At this time, ethnic nationalist issues and separatist movements loom as major stumbling blocks to long-term stability. Pakistan has historically been dominated by the Punjab, and Punjabis dominate in government, the military and business. The other ethnic groups have long resented this domination, and separatist movements have taken place in all of the provinces of Pakistan outside of the Punjab. The Afghan refugees complicate the ethnic picture and exacerbate these divisions.

The ethnic and regional tensions arise partly as a consequence of uneven development within Pakistan. The Punjab and some areas of the Sind are the most developed regions; Baluchistan, the least developed. Pakistan has attempted to resolve this imbalance through such means as a national quota for public jobs and by putting money into development projects in the depressed areas, especially Baluchistan. It is feared that the addition of the Afghan refugees, who themselves are highly sensitized to the politics of ethnic dominance, will shift the precarious balance that has been painstakingly achieved.

However, among the two provinces with the most refugees, only Baluchistan has seen an increase in ethnic tension. Since most of the Afghan refugees are Pushtuns, the migration has tipped the balance of the population so that there are more Pushtuns in Baluchistan than Baluch. This has caused resentment and fostered several Baluch separatist movements.

In the NWFP, the Pushtun nationalism has periodically been a political force and is always near the surface in local and national politics. While it might be expected that the addition of over two million fellow Pushtuns in the province would increase Pushtun nationalism, this has not been the case. Rather, recent rioting in the Peshawar has pitted Pakistani Pushtuns against Afghan Pushtuns. This demonstrates that, despite cultural similarities, Afghan Pushtuns are different from Pakistani Pushtuns.

Conclusion

As a result of the coups of 1978 and the political chaos that followed, over five million refugees have fled to the neighbouring countries, over 3.2 million of these to Pakistan. How these refugees are treated, their effect on Pakistan and their chance of repatriation is determined by how they are viewed by themselves, Pakistan and the world community. The legitimacy of these refugees is defined differently by each party involved. The definitions of refugee status in this situation derive from the historical relationship between Afghanistan and Pakistan (or British India before 1947), traditional rivalries between the Pushtun tribes and other ethnic groups, Islam and modern refugee law. Whether the Afghans successfully and voluntarily repatriate—now the paramount issue to all sides, will depend on which definition is salient.

Finally, the Afghan case points to the larger issue of defining legitimate or illegitimate migrations in the Third World. With the lack of strong national governmental institutions, migrations of peoples from one area to another must be viewed in the context of local folk histories, regional cultures and traditions of the people of that area. What they define as legitimate in their terms (not Western terms) will determine how the

refugee situation evolves. This lesson is clear to international organizations
that deal with refugees.

Notes

1. Geertz, ed. *Old Societies and New States.*
2. The size of the refugee populations in Pakistan and Iran is a point of some
    debate and several attempts to enumerate and reenumerate the refugee popu-
    lation have been made (N. Dupree 1988).

    Current estimates have the Afghan refugee population in Pakistan at 3,257,600
    in 1990 and 2,850,000 in Iran (*Refugees*, 22-23).
3. Azhar, "Afghan Refugees in Pakistan: The Pakistani View."
4. N. Dupree, "Demographic Reporting on Afghan Refugees in Pakistan," 845-
    865.
5. Afghan Refugee Commissionerate, *Humanitarian Assistance Programme for Af-
    ghan Refugees in North West Frontier Province, Pakistan*, 68.
6. Fletcher, *Afghanistan: Highway of Conquest*, 40-45.
7. L. Dupree, *Afghanistan*, 59-64.
8. Monarchy in Afghanistan, as in most of Asia, is considerably different than the
    European model, a remnant of feudalism and thus based on ownership of land.
    In Afghanistan, the concept of a monarch is an extension of tribalism and kin-
    based relationships. Therefore, a monarch's legitimacy rests on his position as
    the head of the ruling tribe or kin group.
9. Shahrani, "Afghanistan: State and Society in Retrospect," 42.
10. Shahrani, "Afghanistan."
11. Pushtun is also pronounced Pukhtun, the Peshawar area. They were called the
    Pathans by the British, a name now also used by the Pakistanis.
12. The term "Islamist" is now preferred to the term "Fundamentalist." For a good
    work on the religion and the Afghan war, see Roy (1985).
13. Pakistan also has other groups of Islamic refugees, particularly the refugees
    from what is now India, who arrived at the time of partition in 1947. These
    refugees are called *Muhajars*. They have done well in Pakistani society, espe-
    cially in Karachi.
14. Ansari, "Hijra in the Islamic Tradition," 3-20.
15. Ali, *The Holy Qur'an: Text, Translation and Commentary*, 8:72.
16. For a good discussion of refugee status definition in the Afghan case, see
    Centlivres and Centlivres-Dumont (1988), Farr (1990) and Edwards (1986).
17. For a good discussion of Afghan refugees in the context of international law, see
    the work of Pye and Brian (1990).
18. Pye and Brian, Jr., "Refugees and International Law," 21-40.

19. Farr, "Afghan Refugees in Pakistan: Definitions, Repatriation and Ethnicity," 134-143.

20. Ackerman, *Economic Activities of the Afghan Refugees.*

21. Sardi and Taskinud-din, *Nutritional Status, Socio-Economic Factors.*

22. Ackerman, *Economic Activities.*

References

Ackerman, M. *Economic Activities of the Afghan Refugees.* Peshawar, Pakistan: UNHCR, 1983.

Afghan Refugee Commissionerate. *Humanitarian Assistance Programme for Afghan Refugees in North West Frontier Province, Pakistan.* Peshawar: Afghan Refugee Commissionerate, January 1987.

Ali, Abdullah Ysusf, ed. *The Holy Qur'an: Text, Translation and Commentary.* Brentwood, Maryland: Amana Corporation, 1989.

Ansari, Z. I. "Hijra in the Islamic Tradition." In *The Cultural Basis of Afghan Nationalism,* edited by E. W. Anderson and N. Hatch Dupree, 3-20. London: Pinter Publishing, 1990.

Azhar, S. "Afghan Refugees in Pakistan: The Pakistani View." In *The Cultural Basis of Afghan Nationalism,* edited by E.W. Anderson and N. Hatch Dupree, 105-114. London: Pinter Publishing, 1990.

Centlivres, P., and M. Centlivres-Dumont. "The Afghan Refugee in Pakistan: Ambiguous Identity." In *Journal of Refugee Studies* 1, no. 2 (1988):141-152.

Dupree, L. *Afghanistan.* New Jersey: Princeton University Press, 1980.

Dupree, N. "Demographic Reporting on Afghan Refugees in Pakistan." In *Modern Asian Studies* 22, no. 4 (1988):845-865.

Edwards, D. "Marginality and Migration: Cultural Dimensions of the Afghan Refugee Problem." In *International Migration Review* 20, no. 2 (1986):313-325.

Farr, G. "Afghan Refugees in Pakistan: Definitions, Repatriation and Ethnicity." In *The Cultural Basis of Afghan Nationalism,* edited by E. W. Anderson and N. Hatch Dupree, 134-143. London: Pinter Publishing, 1990.

Fletcher, A. *Afghanistan: Highway of Conquest.* Ithaca, NY: Cornell University Press, 1965.

Geertz, C., ed. *Old Societies and New States.* New York: Free Press, 1963.

Pye, A.K., and W.J. Brien, Jr. "Refugees and International Law." In *The Cultural Basis of Afghan Nationalism,* edited by E.W. Anderson and N. Hatch Dupree, 21-40. London: Pinter Publishing, 1990.

Roy, O. *Islam and Resistance in Afghanistan.* Cambridge: Cambridge University Press, 1985.

Sardi, M., and Hamid Taskinud-din. *Nutritional Status, Socio-Economic Factors.* Peshawar, Pakistan: UNHCR, 1982.

Shahrani, N. "Afghanistan: State and Society in Retrospect." In *The Cultural Basis of Afghan Nationalism*, edited by E.W. Anderson and N. Hatch Dupree, 41-49. London: Pinter Publishing, 1990.

UNHCR. "World Refugee Map." In *Refugee* 71 (1990):22-23.

6

Hong Kong Chinese:
Facing the Political Changes in 1997

Lawrence Lam

Hong Kong, with a total land area of some 1 068 square kilometres and a population of over six million, is located on the southeastern coast of China, adjoining the Chinese province of Guangdong. Hong Kong has the highest population density of any community in the world, 4,210 persons per square kilometre, as compared to Bangladesh's 1,600 and the United States' 23.[1] To tourists, this island is as modern a city as one can find anywhere in the world—skyscrapers and high-rise apartments perch stolidly at the base and on the slopes of the hills, while Hollywood-style mansions checker the landscape. However, it is unlikely that tourists realize that almost every other person in Hong Kong is either a refugee or the offspring of refugees who left the mainland after the Communist victory in 1949.[2] In 1949-50 three-quarters of a million Chinese, mainly from Guangdong province and Shanghai, arrived in Hong Kong, outnumbering the local population of 600,000. These "refugees" and their offspring have contributed tremendously to making Hong Kong's economy one of the fastest growing in the region,[3] and giving Hong Kong people the distinction of having the highest GNP per capita in the region.[4]

Starting with the postwar entrepôt trade, Hong Kong gradually became the leading Asian manufacturing centre in the 1960s. Although manufacturing was still important to its economy in the 1970s, Hong Kong was further transformed into a major financial centre of the region.[5] It has enjoyed tremendous economic growth since World War II. In 1981 it ranked third after Japan and Singapore in GDP per capita in Asia. Rapid economic development has led to improved living standards and educational levels.[6]

However, this economic prosperity has not deterred Hong Kongers from emigrating. How does the return of Hong Kong to China in 1997 enable students of migration and/or policymakers interested in regulating migration flows to prepare for and explain the possible outflow of legitimate or illegitimate migrants from Hong Kong seeking "refuge"?

Although the 1984 Sino-British Joint Declaration on the future of Hong Kong has solemnly declared that on July 1, 1997, Hong Kong will become a Special Administration Region of China under the spirit of "one country, two systems," with a high degree of autonomy, complete with an independent judiciary, a freely circulating foreign press, no foreign-exchange controls, no tariffs and an economic and institutional system that will not be changed for at least fifty years, thousands of Hong Kongers have emigrated to Canada, the United States and Australia, creating a brain drain of skilled labour and other much needed professional and managerial personnel to sustain the economic growth.[7] This migration resembles what Kunz has aptly conceptualized as "anticipatory refugee movement."[8]

The cogent question remains: what events will lead to a possible mass exodus of Hong Kongers? This paper attempts to address these questions with a focus on Hong Kongers' confidence in the political transition that is in contradistinction to their traditions of "utilitarianistic familism and low civic/political involvement."[9] The difficulties or, more aptly, the impossibilities in differentiating between legitimate and illegitimate migration under the process of political change—decolonization[10]—will be discussed within the context of looking at the early warning signals to better prepare for and/or anticipate refugee movement.[11]

Hong Kong: A Migrant Community

Population movement is not new for Hong Kong. The depoliticization of Hong Kong Chinese has, at several times in the territory's history, led to their decision to flee rather than to participate in the process of political change.[12] Since 1842 refugees have migrated to Hong Kong, seeking asylum in times of conflict and work in times of famine. The colony has provided a haven for waves of immigrants from China at various intervals in its history, whether for economic or political reasons, whether the movement was temporary or permanent, and whether they were recognized as refugees or economic migrants.

Hong Kong's population growth is often affected by influxes of migrants from China. China has been a predominant source of legal and illegal immigration to Hong Kong.[13] Although immigration to Hong Kong from China has been generally under control since the People's Republic of China was established in 1949,[14] there have been occasional tides of migrants from China, who fled from its ever-changing political climate. While the series of Communist-inspired riots in the 1960s during the Cultural Revolution and the bloody crack-down in Beijing's Tiananmen Square in June 1989 have resulted in Hong Kongers seeking "refuge" in Canada, Australia and the United States as "immigrants," Hong Kong itself became the haven for Chinese from China, who sought asylum from imprisonment and exile to rural areas.[15] The most recent immigrants were tempted by job prospects on the new airport construction project, or were lured by "snakeheads" (illegal immigrant smugglers) to job opportunities. Thousands of Chinese from Guangdong entered Hong Kong illegally.[16] The number of illegal immigrants entering Hong Kong shows no signs of decreasing, in spite of tight border controls; intensive police checks of identity cards; the abolishment of the "philanthropic touch base" policy that allowed illegal immigrants from China to stay in Hong Kong if they were able to reach the urban areas;[17] heavy fines and sentences (HK $250,000 and three years in jail) for employers who hired illegal immigrants; immediate repatriation on arrest or, if found working illegally, after serving a mandatory prison sentence of fifteen months. (Illegal workers constitute about 30 percent of the prisoners in Hong Kong's jail.) On the contrary 11,512 Chinese illegal immigrants were arrested between January and May 1992, representing a whopping 42.2 percent increase over 1991.[18] The number of illegal immigrants caught will probably exceed more than 30,000 by the end of 1992, compared with 25,422 in 1991.

On the other hand, substantial emigration of professional and managerial personnel from Hong Kong since talks began in 1982 on the Sino-British Joint Declaration has become a cause for concern. It is estimated that between 50,000 to 60,000 Hong Kongers have left, 25 percent of whom would be in the professional, technical, administrative and managerial category.[19] *HKStaff*, a human resources journal published in Hong Kong, reported a 22 percent increase in emigration over the past year, as indicated by the number of applications for certificates of no criminal conviction required by all receiving countries.[20] In spite of the government's projections that between 10 percent and 30 percent of these economic emigrants would be returning to Hong Kong after they have acquired citizenship or passports from their receiving countries, the potential for a mass exodus far exceeds the likelihood of mass returns.[21] This brain drain is sustained by the perceived political security in preferred destinations—Canada, the United States, Australia or Singapore. In other words, the emigration of Hong Kongers seeking security insurance of a second passport ("If things go wrong here after 1997, there is a safe place to go") has been precipitated and sustained by widespread anticipation of insecurity when Hong Kong's sovereignty is returned to China.[22] Hong Kongers invariably perceive and believe this insecurity to be imminent.

Staying: The Economic Rational Perspective

In Hong Kong, questions of going or staying are always on people's minds. Surveys consistently indicate that, in spite of abundant job opportunities, many Hong Kongers, particularly professionals, plan to leave[23] because they have no confidence in Hong Kong's future when China takes over.[24] Those who fled the Communist Chinese once before have very real fears. They are, therefore, preparing themselves this time for a timely escape. It has been observed that "wealthy Hong Kongers have been placing savings abroad and seeking the expected protection of foreign passports, while others are working much harder than ever before to make themselves desirable emigrants. There is a sense of urgency."[25] Fear of loss of freedom, a lack of confidence in the stability of post-1997 Hong Kong, and fear that the door of emigration may close at any time are common factors in the decision making.[26] The most recent survey[27] indicated that only about 43.3 percent of Hong Kongers said they were not worried about Hong Kong's politics after the transfer of sovereignty, while one in five Hong Kongers were either waiting to decide or had made up their minds to leave. Most of them were from the vital middle and managerial class.

On the surface, it seems to be extremely unlikely that China would ever mess with the goose that lays the golden eggs, especially since there already is a high degree of economic integration between the mainland, Guangdong province and the colony. There are numerous statistics that show how Hong Kong's pivotal economic role is remaking southeastern China into one of the world's fastest growing areas.[28] Much of the new wealth and economic development in China have been concentrated in the coastal provinces, especially around Hong Kong. Hence, in the words of Lu Ping, China's senior official for Hong Kong matters, Hong Kong will remain a "golden bowl."

The importance of this "golden bowl" or "goose" to China is clear for several reasons. About two-thirds of China's exports to the United States come through Hong Kong. The three-way trade (China, Taiwan, Hong Kong) hit U.S. $68 billion in the first ten months of 1991, while three-way investment reached $36.4 billion, according to the Hong Kong Trade Development Council. Hong Kong accounts for about two-thirds of the direct foreign investment in China and China is reported to have as much as $15 billion invested in Hong Kong. Approximately three million Chinese workers labour in Hong Kong-run enterprises in China and receive their pay cheques from Hong Kong firms. Hence, Hong Kong's economic utility to China would make it hard to imagine that China would intentionally sacrifice the growing economic interests with Hong Kong to reap the bitter fruit of confrontation. In other words, China is already, in economic terms, the biggest stockholder in Hong Kong, and it behoves Beijing not to drive down the value of those shares. It would defy common sense for policies and developments in China to undermine these interests. The corollary of this is that Hong Kong's future security and prosperity lies with the Hong Kongers' collective effort to increase the territory's economic utility to China, making the costs of Chinese repression so high that Beijing will have to guarantee Hong Kong autonomy and freedom to run the economic engine for China.

Despite the current global recession, economic activities in Hong Kong do not seem to be affected. In 1991 and early 1992, the price of residential property rose rapidly, the stock market reached a historic high, the real rate in GDP was 5 percent in 1992, there was an agreement between Hong Kong and China for the construction of a new Hong Kong airport, and China's economy was increasingly integrated with Hong Kong's. All these factors should have boosted the confidence of Hong Kongers, particularly in the aftermath of the bloody, tragic event of June 4, 1989 in Beijing's Tiananmen Square.

Hong Kongers may not be able to enter the labour market of a host society at professional, administrative and/or managerial levels comparable to the ones they left in Hong Kong. Kirkbride and his associates[29] found that downward mobility and underemployment were in fact common, and that close to 80 percent of these Hong Kongers had difficulty even acquiring jobs in the same profession, while others received a reduced salary level and were employed at a lower rank. One might think that these economic prospects would have persuaded and convinced them to stay in Hong Kong. What, then, are the real reasons for Hong Kongers' determination to acquire security insurance by emigrating?

Going: Importance of a Safety Net

Many Hong Kongers' determination to leave Hong Kong prior to the transfer of sovereignty in 1997, or to acquire foreign passports for security insurance to guarantee a safe passage, cannot be rationally explained in economic terms. A senior art director and his family received approval for immigration to Canada, based on his wife's job prospects, although he may find it difficult to continue in his profession. He explained his family's decision to leave: "We are moving for insurance. It is a question of a safety net versus making more money and a career. I prefer safety."[30] Similarly, regardless of the promises made in the Sino-British Joint Declaration to maintain the free-wheeling capitalistic enterprises and social systems in Hong Kong, together with a high degree of autonomy, and in spite of Hong Kong's economic utility and importance to China, many Hong Kongers believe that "China will gradually milk the Hong Kong cash cow dry through heavy taxes and whatever other means she can certainly come up with."[31]

The crisis of confidence over Hong Kong's future did not begin with the bloody crack-down in Tiananmen Square. The determination to leave is related to a complex set of factors. The Joint Declaration between China and Britain provides no clear evidence of easing the uncertainty. Many Hong Kongers consider China an anachronistic, inefficient and tyrannical state, especially those who have felt the back of China's hand and who have been repressed and persecuted after the 1949 revolution and the establishment of the Peoples' Republic of China.[32] Furthermore, there is a widespread belief and deeply-felt realization that from the British government's viewpoint, conflicts with China are to be avoided at all cost, especially since the price won't be paid by Britain but by the Hong Kong people.

The overwhelming concern for Britain is to engineer a graceful and trouble-free exit in 1997. Hong Kongers' scepticism of Britain assuming its responsibilities is further fuelled by Great Britain's reluctance to grant more than a limited number of full British citizenships and the right of abode to key workers in Hong Kong (who are legally British subjects in Britain) and by the fewer than expected number of applications to emigrate to Britain.[33] The British government's silence on its role and responsibility towards Hong Kong once the Union Jack is lowered for the last time in 1997, as well as its failure to object to those parts of the Basic Laws that deviate seriously from the spirit of the Joint Declaration, undermine Hong Kongers' confidence in Britain even further. The perceived threats from China jeopardize Hong Kong's planned construction of a HK $15 billion airport[34] have given credence to Hong Kongers' belief that Britain is washing its hands of the colony and is prepared to do nothing, even if China blatantly reneges on the "promises." Hence, Hong Kongers prepare for the possibility of being hung out to dry in the event that things go wrong. They believe they have to depend on their wits and efforts to negotiate and secure a way out by acquiring "escape route passports;" legitimately or otherwise.

The Commission for Canada in Hong Kong has been swamped by potential applicants.[35] Each year, more than 60,000 hopeful emigrants wait for their files to be processed, and the flow at the Commission's offices is constant, five days a week. It was reported that in the months after the Tiananmen Square crack-down, the Commission used freight elevators to move thousands of applicants who inundated their offices.[36]

Prospective emigrants anxiously seek information about the latest loopholes, as well as immigration regulations and tips that will help them get through the byzantine course faster. Their anxiety and sense of urgency are reflected in the booming immigration consultation business in Hong Kong. In one case, a businessman was charged Can. $25,000 to have his application form filled out, another $25,000 to have it submitted, and yet another $25,000 when the visa was issued. This was by no means an isolated incident as evidenced by a Toronto lawyer, Martin Pilzmaker, who faced more than fifty immigration-related charges when he committed suicide in April 1991.

Bogus migrant plans and stories of immigration stings are indeed legendary in Hong Kong.[37] There are reported cases of pregnant Hong Kong women who flew to Canada to give birth, so that the infants would have automatic Canadian citizenship. Families will use this to their advantage in a subsequent immigration hearing because it is believed that a family with a child carrying a Canadian passport is likely to be given special consideration. International commuters (known as "astronauts" or "spacemen" in local parlance), who shuttle frequently between their families in their adopted lands and their businesses in Hong Kong, and "courier parents," who get visas simply so that their children can emigrate, are among the many who want to gain security and an escape route because they lack confidence in Hong Kong's future.

Of course, everyone hopes that the transition and the transfer of sovereignty will be trouble-free and that things will go well after 1997, that Hong Kong will be stable and prosperous, that its people will continue to possess all their rights and freedoms, and that China will scrupulously observe the commitments made in the Joint Declaration. However, as surveys have indicated, 20 percent to 25 percent of Hong Kongers are waiting to decide or have already decided to leave due to fear of the future alone.[38] Nevertheless, there are hopeful signs that the promises and the provisions in the Joint Declaration will be taken seriously and observed. These include the following.

China's Reaction to the Political Development in Hong Kong

It is desirable for and advantageous to China to maintain Hong Kong's economic utility by assuring its commitment to Hong Kong's autonomy and freedom. This will further China's own economic development and modernization program and, more importantly, set an example to prove the "wisdom" of "one country, two systems" for Macau and Taiwan. Nevertheless, no one seems to know when democratic evolution in Hong Kong may trigger a vigorous response from Beijing. As well, there is no straightforward way of balancing Hong Kong's economic utility to China without politically antagonizing Beijing.

In September 1991 when Hong Kong held its first direct elections to the colony's Legislative Council, the liberal democrats who have been critical of China's human rights records swept the polls, winning seventeen of the eighteen seats. Since then, they have been demanding a greater say in government, insisting on a faster pace of democratization in Hong Kong, obtaining seats on the Executive Council (an appointed body equivalent to a cabinet), and increasing the number of Legislative Council seats directly elected by the public to half of the sixty seats in 1995.

China's response to this political democratization was swift, blunt and unequivocal. China stated that only one-third of the Council's sixty seats can be directly elected before Hong Kong reverts to Chinese rule in 1997. The liberal democrats of the United Democrats Hong Kong (UDHK) have been categorically branded as "subversives." China has hinted that they won't be allowed to participate in government after 1997, and has warned Britain not to give them any more political power by including them on the Executive Council. The warning to Britain not to undermine, intentionally or not, China's ultimate control and authority over Hong Kong also served as a reminder to Hong Kongers that it is in their own interest not to make further demands for political democratization.

These warnings were clearly given in the editorial of a Beijing-backed newspaper, *Wen Wei Po*, on the day the newly appointed governor of Hong Kong, Mr. Patten, was sworn in. It cautioned that "if the governor doesn't consult with China, things will be very difficult. The road will be filled with thistles and thorns and he will bring vexation upon himself."[39] Meanwhile, pro-China political and labour organizations severely criticized the UDHK's lobbying efforts in the U.S. Congress to introduce a separate Hong Kong policy and to consider making the approval of China as a most favoured trading nation conditional upon improvement in human rights. These were actively encouraged and explicitly endorsed by the Democratic Alliance for Betterment of Hong Kong.[40]

The political activities of the New China News Agency (acting as the de facto embassy in Hong Kong) and the recollection of repressive actions taken by China's People's Liberation Army beyond the border, weigh heavily in the minds of Hong Kongers. They believe their days of living in a free-wheeling capitalistic system are indeed numbered. Hong Kongers have reasons to be sceptical of the provisions and promises made in the Joint Declaration between China and Britain.

The New Airport Agreement

Chinese officials have repeatedly said in public that Hong Kong is Britain's problem before 1997, and if major projects and institutional changes go beyond 1997 or have any impact on the Special Administrative Region after that year, consultation with China will be required. As of July 1, 1997, Hong Kong will become China's responsibility and no other country will be able to intervene. British officials have not challenged that stance, and it appears that they are happy if China assumes sole responsibility for Hong Kong, letting them off the hook. However, the twists and turns relating to the agreement for the construction of a new airport in Hong Kong have reinforced Hong Kongers' feeling that Britain has already abandoned them.

Consultation between China and Britain for the construction of the new airport in Hong Kong is required to ensure that the post-1997 government will not face "bare cupboards." After numerous meetings and memoranda of understanding reached in the Joint Liaison Group, China stubbornly withheld final approval of the project's financial arrangements. On the surface, it was argued that China and Britain had different interpretations of the term "consultation." British officials interpret consultation as seeking informed advice and input from China, while Chinese officials insist that it means negotiations before reaching a final agreement. As of now, it is clear that British officials are doing what China says for fear that a diplomatic commotion may upset confidence in Hong Kong. However, Hong Kongers see this "misunderstanding" as an indication of China's determination to assert its authority over Hong Kong's affairs before 1997. Furthermore, Hong Kongers believe that the underlying reason China is withholding its approval—after an agreed-upon amount of money is set aside for the post-1997 administration—is to pressure the Hong Kong government to take action against any further political democratic development of UDHK and, above all, not to give these liberals any more political power by bringing them onto the Executive Council.

Regional Relationship with Beijing

Undoubtedly, economic development has brought increasingly close ties that bind Hong Kong with Guangdong. Beijing is nevertheless wary of Guangdong becoming too independent of central control and forging its links with capitalist Hong Kong.[41] Hong Kong and Guangdong will be linked by a six-lane superhighway in 1994. Driving from Guangdong to China's border with Hong Kong has given the impression that people living in that region are experiencing a boom similar to Hong Kong's in the 1970s. The scarcity of land and labour in Hong Kong makes Guangdong a perfect partner, with Hong Kong providing capital, technology, management and marketing skills to Guangdong. The economic integration between Hong Kong and Guangdong has revived what was historically a close relationship between the two and has prompted business circles in Hong Kong to talk about the inevitability of a vanishing border.

While Guangdong is pressing for greater autonomy and closer links with Hong Kong, Beijing has recently rejected a proposal by the Guangdong government for setting up a Guangdong-Hong Kong coordination group to handle joint social, economic and transport matters. Beijing wants the State Council's Hong Kong and Macau Affairs Office, which is under the exclusive control of central government in Beijing, to be the sole body for handling such issues. The rejection of the proposal has been defended on the basis that, according to the Joint Declaration, Hong Kong will be under the central government's jurisdiction rather than a provincial authority.

The lingering argument of the division of power between Beijing and Guangdong province has further eroded Hong Kongers' confidence because there are already a multitude of agreements between Hong Kong and Guangdong on such matters as border liaison, illegal immigrants and water supply. These are important agreements to Hong Kong, yet the lines between agreements with Guangdong and agreements with the central government are unclear. However, it is apparent to Hong Kongers that whatever suits Beijing will certainly prevail. This was the case during the Yang Yang affair after the Tiananmen Square crack-down when Hong Kong angered Beijing by allowing the swimmer to go to the United States rather than returning him to China. Beijing demanded that Hong Kong immediately repatriate him as an illegal immigrant. In reprisal, China ordered Guangdong authorities to refuse to accept illegal immigrants from Hong Kong, but the original understandings and agreement concerning repatriation of illegal immigrants, though not published and signed as formal treaties, were resumed between Hong Kong and Guangdong. It was speculated that resumption of the repatriation agreement was made with the understanding that Hong Kong will not shelter those identified by China as "bad elements."

This intrusion of Beijing was a sobering experience for Hong Kongers, highlighting the colony's vulnerability. In addition, while many parts of China remain desperately poor, economic prosperity and new wealth in the Guangdong province will become a magnet for millions of Chinese from other areas of China, who are attracted to the booming cities. Any bitter disputes between Hong Kong and China can be resolved in China's favour by the mere threat of opening the border and refusing to accept repatriated immigrants. The May-June Chinese exodus of 1962 and the Beijing-inspired disturbances of 1967 are reminders to many Hong Kongers that there is no place to hide from Communist Beijing's fury. Any sense of complacency is destined to lead to despair.

It is true that whatever happens in China will inevitably have repercussions in Hong Kong. China's political uncertainty, as a result of the continuing struggle between conservative hardliners and so-called reform-minded pragmatists in Beijing, as well as the power struggle between the central government and Guangdong, will influence Hong Kong's economic security and prosperity, but, hopefully, it will not play havoc. Guangdong's failure to develop any effective measures to combat widespread corruption in spite of its vested economic interest, has decreased Hong Kongers' confidence in post-1997 Hong Kong.

Many Hong Kongers have first-hand knowledge of and encounters with corruption. They are required—at times ordered—by mid-level officials in Guangdong to pay a certain percentage of their investment for the privilege of doing business in China.[42] Thefts of luxury cars in Hong Kong—Mercedes Benzs, BMWs, Toyota Crowns—whisk an average of six cars per day across the South China Sea into mainland China, and result in insurance payments of more than HK $14 million in claims every three months. These thefts are believed to be linked with Chinese officials in Guangdong. For example, it was reported that Hong Kong police efforts to stop car thieves who were sailing away within Hong Kong's territorial waters with a brand new Mercedes Benz in November 1991, were countered by uniformed members of China's People's Armed Police, who pointed their assault rifles at the Hong Kong police and ordered them to leave.[43]

As a matter of fact, many Hong Kongers said that their worry and anxiety were directly related to these mid-level Guangdong officials' attitudes towards capitalists. In other words, Hong Kongers are afraid that economic activities in Hong Kong would be thwarted and that Hong Kong business people would be labelled and treated as exploiters of the proletariat. Many of them have not forgotten stories of being incarcerated in the notorious labour reform camps that were operated in the spirit of *Lao Dong Gai Zao* (reform and reeducate through manual labour).

The Question of Citizenship

The question of citizenship is related to how China has defined it and its implications for Hong Kongers who obtained citizenships from other countries and then returned to work in Hong Kong. Immigration statistics from Hong Kong indicate that the total number of expatriates had risen to 276,000 in April from 149,000 in 1982.[44] Filipinos make up the largest expatriate group (81,000) followed by Americans (23,000). Canada and Australia, where many Hong Kongers have emigrated in recent years, are among the top ten countries with the largest numbers of citizens in Hong

Kong. The estimated number of Hong Kongers who hold Canadian passports and are currently living and working in Hong Kong is as high as 40,000, many of them born in the colony.[45]

However, with the exception of Filipinos, this estimate of expatriates is certainly low. Many Hong Kongers, while holding another country's passport, also hold Hong Kong identity cards, which allow them to live and work in Hong Kong as legal Hong Kong citizens and residents. They are not being counted as expatriates. Meanwhile, holders of the Hong Kong identity card will be recognized by the Chinese government as citizens of the Special Administrative Region in post-1997 Hong Kong. There is considerable anecdotal evidence that as many as 20,000 to 30,000 Hong Kong residents hold Canadian, Australian or U.S. passports. The Chinese government has defined them as Chinese citizens, according to its interpretation of the Joint Declaration and the Basic Laws.

Countries such as Canada and Australia, which allow dual citizenship, are no doubt attractive to Hong Kongers, since dual citizenship gives them the option to return and work in Hong Kong. Most important of all, such passports are believed to give them safe passage if circumstances change for the worse in post-1997 Hong Kong. However, what appears to be largely overlooked is the provision that Hong Kongers cannot be guaranteed consular protection when they are in the country of their other citizenship.[46] Even more critical is the fact that China has indicated it will treat them all as Chinese citizens, regardless of what passports they hold, and that they may not be entitled to consular protection in the post-1997 Hong Kong.[47]

What will happen to these expatriates if the transfer of sovereignty is not as trouble-free as expected, and if the administration of post-1997 Hong Kong, for political and/or ideological reasons, introduces measures that go against the "golden bowl" and "economic utility" of Hong Kong? It is likely that Filipino domestic servants in Hong Kong will be required to leave— that is, they will be *liberated*, in class terms. Non-Chinese residents in Hong Kong will follow, whereas the Hong Kongers, defined as Chinese citizens, regardless of the passports they hold, will not be allowed to go. As Chinese citizens, they will be subject to the same restrictive rules and regulations of exit and entry control as mainland Chinese. While diplomacy launched by Canada, the U.S., Australia and the U.K. may eventually persuade Beijing to allow their respective citizens to leave Hong Kong, these expatriates will resort to well established and well organized smuggling rings to escape.[48] Other Hong Kongers are likely to join the mass exodus of expatriates. They will leave Hong Kong using any means available, including false documents or passports, which will lead to a repetition of the illegal immigration to Canada in the 1950s[49] or the exodus of boat people in the 1970s. This will be the likely scenario, especially if family members sponsored by expatriates abroad are not included in the category of family class immigrants, as currently defined in Canada, the U.S. and Australia.

The Lesson of the Boat People

Hong Kongers' attitude towards the boat people began as a surge of humanitarian sympathy that changed to strong ambivalence before becoming outright hostility.[50] The change reflects the perception that they are caught between China and the Vietnamese. The continuing arrival of Vietnamese asylum seekers are perceived to be forever taxing and imposing a burden on Hong Kongers.

Furthermore, the plight of the boat people in the camps and the international community's seemingly ineffective and inefficient efforts to bring an end to the crisis make Hong Kongers reflect on their own fate in post-1997 Hong Kong. Many expect their fate may be even worse than that of the boat people because they believe the international community will be unlikely to antagonize China by intervening on their behalf in what China has repeatedly claimed will be an internal matter. *Legal Daily*, China's official mouthpiece newspaper, recently condemned the International Commission of Jurists' human rights report on Hong Kong as "blatant interference in Hong Kong affairs," which is indicative of China's determination to reject any interference in its sovereignty over Hong Kong. The article reiterated that "there is only one Chinese nation, and Hong Kong compatriots are part of the Chinese nation.... the fate of Hong Kong cannot be renewed.... this will not be stopped by any power."[51] The high number of emigrants from Hong Kong in recent years represents what Kunz[52] has conceptualized as an anticipatory refugee movement. Hong Kongers view any attempts to change the declared provisions of freedom and autonomy stipulated in the Joint Declaration as conclusive signs leading to further changes immediately before or after the transfer of sovereignty in 1997, which will certainly trigger a mass exodus.[53]

Conclusion

Hong Kong's ability to live and prosper in the long and at times menacing shadow of Communist China, despite a large and diverse population that includes thousands of illegal immigrants and refugees from China, has been a remarkable feat.[54] As 1997 nears, everyone hopes that things will go well and not get out of control. Unlike the Falkland Islands, which Britain believed were worth fighting for, no one expects Britain to go to war with

China over Hong Kong. Meanwhile, many Hong Kongers do not believe that Britain will even make any strong affirmation to fulfil its responsibilities to Hong Kong before or after 1997. Hong Kongers realize that Britain won't be able to do anything for them after 1997. The prolonged debate on the issue of right of abode, which resulted in Britain reluctantly granting only 50,000 Hong Kongers (primarily in the professional, administrative and managerial categories) the right of residence in Britain, made Hong Kongers nervous. It was reported that on his recent visit to Hong Kong, former governor Lord MacLehose was unable to satisfactorily explain what would happen if things go wrong after 1997.[55] Of course, this only increased Hong Kongers' anxiety.

Some informed observers[56] believe that it is unlikely Beijing will harm the valuable Hong Kong economy because of the effects on China itself, and because it may immediately lead to chaos and instability in the Portuguese colony of Macau, which is scheduled to be reverted back to China in 1999. Negative measures will also definitely jeopardize the possibility of Taiwan's political reunification with China. Hong Kongers' fear and lack of confidence are clear indications of a possible mass exodus. The warning signals are surfacing and they cannot be summarily ignored or dismissed for political expediency. Many Hong Kongers are finding legitimate and illegitimate means to assure themselves of a safe passage.

Possible crack-down on the political activities of the UDHK, which is already labelled as subversive, disputes between the central government and the regional administration, corrupt mid-level officials and cadres who may assume key administrative positions in post-1997 Hong Kong, and the unpredictable politics in Beijing—singly or in combination—will trigger an exodus. Such an exodus, a trickle or en masse, chaotic or orderly, of refugees or illegal migrants, depends upon appropriate actions taken by the international community.

Assuring Hong Kongers a safe passage (notwithstanding China's claim that such action will be a violation of its sovereignty and interference in its internal affairs), instituting an orderly departure program, and soliciting the cooperation of neighbouring countries to offer Hong Kongers temporary refuge, together with adjustments made in receiving countries' immigration regulations and refugee status determination processes, will certainly serve as a cautionary note, so that China will be less likely to act against Hong Kongers. More importantly and appropriately, a concerted effort will bolster Hong Kongers' confidence and assure them that they will not be forgotten or become political or economic pawns. At the very least, the exodus—if it does happen—will not be as desperate and chaotic as that of the boat people.

Notes

1. Yeh, "Foreign Labour in Hong Kong: Trends, Impacts and Implications."

2. Levenstein, *Escape from Freedom.*

3. Morantz, "Pawns of the Past."

4. Stern, "Review of the Comprehensive Plan of Action for Indochinese Refugees."

5. Chen, "The Economic Setting."

6. Yeh, "Foreign Labour in Hong Kong."

7. Cheng and Ng, "Hong Kong's Brain Drain and the Ethos of the Chinese Migrant"; Nash, "The Emigration of Business People and Professionals from Hong Kong."

8. Kunz, "The Refugee in Flight: Kinetic Models and Forms of Displacement."

9. Emmons, *Hong Kong Prepares for 1997—Politics and Emigration in 1997.*

10. Zolberg et al., *Escape from Violence.*

11. Gordenker, "Early Warning of Refugee Incidents."

12. Lau, *Society and Politics in Hong Kong.*

13. Skeldon, "Hong Kong and Singapore as Nodes in an International Migration System."

14. Cheng and Ng, "Hong Kong's Brain Drain."

15. Levenstein, *Escape.*

16. Yeh, "Foreign Labour"; J. Wong, "How China's Snakeheads Ship their Human Cargo," *The Globe and Mail* (April 11, 1992).

17. Lui, "Undocumented Migration in Hong Kong."

18. J. Leung, "Arrest of Mainlanders Expected to Hit 30,000," *South China Morning Post* (May 30, 1992).

19. Cheng and Ng, "Hong Kong's Brain Drain."

20. Scott, *Political Change and the Crisis of Legitimacy in Hong Kong.*

21. Scott, *Political Change*; Daphne Cheng, "Office Fails to Lure Home Professionals," *South China Morning Post*, international edition (July 10-16, 1992).

22. Cheng and Ng, "Hong Kong's Brain Drain."

23. Ibid.

24. Emmons, *Hong Kong Prepares for 1997.*

25. *The Banker* (September, 1989).

26. Kirkbride et al., *Emigration from Hong Kong: Evidence from Professionals.*

27. A. Ho, "Wasting Words as the Brain Drain Continues," *South China Morning Post* (June 5-11, 1992).

28. Morantz, "Pawns of the Past"; Lampton, "Hong Kong and the Rise of 'Greater China': Policy Issues."

29. Kirkbride et al. "Emigration from Hong Kong."

30. Morantz, "Pawns of the Past."

31. Ibid.; F. Ching, "Britain Must Begin to Prepare a Policy for Post-1997," *South China Morning Post* (May 22-27, 1992).

32. Lam, "Searching for a Safe Haven—The Migration and Settlement of Hong Kong Chinese in Toronto"; Levenstein, *Escape.*

33. Nash, "The Emigration of Business People and Professionals."

34. P. Goodspeed, "Hong Kong's Last Governor Has Tough Task," *Toronto Star* (July 15, 1992).

35. B. Cook, "U.S. Expat Population Doubles," *South China Morning Post* (June 26-July 2, 1992).

36. Morantz, "Pawns of the Past."

37. Malarek, *Haven's Gate: Canada's Immigration Fiasco.*

38. Ho, "Wasting Words."

39. Goodspeed, "Hong Kong's Last Governor."

40. Lampton, "Hong Kong and the Rise of 'Greater China'."

41. Falkenheim, "Changing Patterns of Regional Administration in China: Implications for Hong Kong."

42. Lam, "Searching for a Safe Haven."

43. Goodspeed, "Satellites May Find Stolen Luxury Cars—Car Theft Rings Plague HK," *Toronto Star* (July 15, 1992).

44. Cook, "U.S. Expat Population Doubles."

45. Lary et al., "Hong Kong Migration to Australia and Canada: A Comparison."

46. Ibid.

47. Morantz, "Pawns of the Past."

48. *Montreal Gazette* (April 12, August 8, October 16, 1990); *Calgary Herald* (August 8, 1990); *South China Morning Post* (March 7, 1992); *The Globe and Mail* (April 11, 1992).

49. Hawkins, *Canada and Immigration.*

50. Chan, "Hong Kong's Response to the Vietnamese Refugees: A Study in Humanitarianism, Ambivalence and Hostility."

51. *South China Morning Post*, "China Rejects Rights Report: Interference" (June 22-29, 1992).

52. Kunz, "The Refugee in Flight."

53. Ibid.

54. Levenstein, *Escape*; Morantz, "Pawns of the Past."

55. Ching, "Britain."

56. Burns, "The New China News Agency"; Lampton, "Hong Kong."

References

Burns, J. "The New China News Agency." A paper presented at the workshop, China in Transition: Implications for Hong Kong, York University, Toronto, June 11-12, 1992.

Cannon, M. *China Tide*. Toronto: HarperCollins, 1989.

Chan, Kwok B. "Hong Kong's Response to the Vietnamese Refugees: A Study in Humanitarianism, Ambivalence and Hostility," *Southeast Asian Journal of Social Science* 18, no. 1 (1990):94-101.

Chen, Edward K.Y. "The Economic Setting." In *The Business Environment in Hong Kong*, 2d ed., edited by G. David. Hong Kong: Oxford University Press, 1984.

Cheng, S.M., and S.H. Ng. "Hong Kong's Brain Drain and the Ethos of the Chinese Migrant." A paper presented at the International Conference on Migration, Centre for Advanced Studies, National University of Singapore, February 7-9, 1991.

Emmons, Charles F. *Hong Kong Prepares for 1997: Politics and Emigration in 1987*. Hong Kong: Centre for Asian Studies, University of Hong Kong, 1988.

Falkenheim, V. "Changing Patterns of Regional Administration in China: Implications for Hong Kong." A paper presented at the workshop, China in Transition: Implications for Hong Kong, York University, Toronto, June 11-12, 1992.

Gordenker, L. "Early Warning of Refugee Incidents." In *Refugees and International Relations*, edited by Gil Loescher and Laila Monahan. New York: Oxford University Press, 1989.

Hamrin, Carol L. "Current Political developments in China: Implications for Hong Kong." A paper presented at the workshop, China in Transition: Implications for Hong Kong, York University, Toronto, June 11-12, 1992.

Hawkins, Freda. *Canada and Immigration*. Montreal: McGill-Queen's Press, 1988.

Kirkbride, Paul S., et al. "Emigration from Hong Kong: Evidence from Professionals." Hong Kong: Hong Kong Institute of Personnel Management, 1989.

Kunz, E.F. "The Refugee in Flight: Kinetic Models and Forms of Displacement." *International Migration Review* 7 (1973): 124-46.

Lam, L. "The Attitude of the Local Population Towards Vietnamese Boat People in Hong Kong." In *Refuge* 9, no. 3 (February 1990).

_____. "Repatriation: A Solution to Vietnamese Boat People Problems in Hong Kong?" In *Refuge* 11, no. 1 (October 1991).

_____. "Searching for A Safe Haven: The Migration and Settlement of Hong Kong Chinese in Toronto." In *Reluctant Exiles: Migration and Overseas Hong Kong Chinese Communities*, edited by R. Skeldon. New York: M.E. Sharpe and University of Hong Kong Press. Forthcoming.

Lampton, David M. "Hong Kong and the Rise of 'Greater China': Policy Issues." A paper presented at the workshop, China in Transition: Implications for Hong Kong, York University, Toronto, June 11-12, 1992.

Lary, D., et al. "Hong Kong Migration to Australia and Canada: A Comparison." A paper presented at the conference, Immigration and Refugee Policy, York University, Toronto, May 2-5, 1992.

Lau, Siu-Kai. *Society and Politics in Hong Kong.* Hong Kong: The Chinese University Press, 1992.

Levenstein, A. *Escape from Freedom.* Westport, Connecticut: Greenwood Press, 1983.

Liu, Terry Ting. "Undocumented Migration in Hong Kong." In *International Migration* 21, no. 2 (1983): 260-70.

Malarek, V. *Haven's Gate: Canada's Immigration Fiasco.* Toronto: Macmillan, 1987.

Morantz, A. "Pawns of the Past: Frightened by the Future, Hong Kongers Bid An Ambivalent Farewell to Their Larger-Than-Life Home As They Head for Canada." In *Equinox* (November/December, 1991).

Nash, A. "The Emigration of Business People and Professionals from Hong Kong." In *Canada and Hong Kong Update* 6 (Winter 1992): 1-4.

Scott, I. *Political Change and the Crisis of Legitimacy in Hong Kong.* Hong Kong: Hong Kong University Press, 1989.

Skeldon, R. "Hong Kong and Singapore As Nodes in An International Migration System." A paper presented at the International Conference on Migration, Centre for Advanced Studies, National University of Singapore, February 7-9, 1991.

Stern, Joseph B. "Review of the Comprehensive Plan of Action for Indochinese Refugees." A report to the Canadian International Development Agency, International Humanitarian Assistance Division. Ottawa: CIDA, November 1991.

Wong, J. "How China's Snakeheads Ship Their Human Cargo," *The Globe and Mail,* April 11, 1992.

Yeh, Anthony Gar-on. "Foreign Labour in Hong Kong: Trends, Impacts and Implications." A paper presented at the Expert Group Meeting on Cross-National Labour Migration in the Asian Region: Implications for Local and Regional Development, United Nations Centre for Regional Development, Nagoya, Japan, November 5-8, 1990.

Zolberg, A.R., et al. *Escape from Violence.* New York: Oxford University Press, 1989.

7

New Directions in Migration: The Case of Peru

Oscar Schiappa-Pietra

Introduction

This paper refers to the political and legal means for distinguishing the migratory flows originated in Peru. From the very beginning, it becomes necessary to note that the specific norms and procedures, as well as the reasons for its limited development, can only be understood if placed in close relation with the many different variables which give Peru the character of a very complex politico-social environment. In fact, this country constitutes an extraordinary field laboratory for research on the part of different disciplines of Social Sciences.

The weaknesses and complexities of the Peruvian reality impose strict conditions to the viewpoint on this paper, causing its contents to contrast with the more refined development the matter has reached in other countries.

After making a synthetic reference to some relevant geographical and historic factors, this paper describes basic outlines of the four different types of emigration processes which presently take place in Peru, making reference—as far as reality permits—to the existing political and legal norms and procedures relevant for the purpose.

Some References of the Peruvian Historic Process

Peru is a nation located in the West Coast of South America, that limits with Ecuador. Its territory emerges from the shores of the South Pacific, goes through the steep mountains of the Andes and ends in the Amazon jungle. This country has been the historic core of magnificent cultures of ancient times, having had as its most qualified political expression in the so-called Incas' Empire. The Spanish conquest on the XVI Century meant a new rupture in the original but complex ethnocultural processes and the imposition of cultural patterns which remain nowadays adding tension to the itself diverse native traditions.

The geographical diversity of the Peruvian territory entails a plurality of ethnocultural universes. To this, and to the fragmentation of the territory due to varied geographical accidents, are added other variables which sum up to the complexity of the Peruvian historical process: the inequitable distribution of wealth, which interlocks with ethnical differences; the permanent exploitation of the country to favour cities, the disproportionate growth of population[1] in contrast with the lack of resources to take care of its basic needs; the excessive dependence of the country on World Powers, mainly the United States; the lack of political stability and the crisis of the whole social institutions; the nonexistence of a State capable of imposing its authority by means of basic consensus in the midst of a social diversity, etc.

As a result of so complex a context, social relations have been guided then by illegitimate discrimination, by imposition and vertical subordination. In contrast with modern societies, social and interpersonal relations in Peru are usually characterized by lack of coordination and horizontal "complementation." Concrete expressions of such reality have been the constant occurrence of forced population displacements, as well as the individual asylum in churches or Embassies.

While in the Incas' Empire, there existed specific mechanisms to move entire populations and individuals from one territory to another, for production, military or colonization reasons. The Spaniard Conquest brought to America the Western legacy, but caused harm to the original institutions. The *mitimaes* institution was kept, by which natives were forced to work in mines or lands of Spanish authorities. The intensive use of this modality implied eradicating entire populations from its habitats.

The wretched living conditions—particularly salubrity-wise—created an extraordinarily propitious environment for the dissemination of the new germs carried by the conquerors, the same which in previously unexposed populations caused devastating epidemics. "According to Cook, around 1520 the Peruvian population was close to 9 million; a century later, our diminished population hardly reached 600,000" (Comision Especial Del

Senado 1989, 229). In Mexico, because of similar historical and biological processes, population decreased from roughly 30 million in 1519 to 3 million in 1568.

Upon breaking up the colonial link with Spain, in 1821, no substantial variation occurred as to the actual relations of power and production. African negros were brought as slaves while Semi-forced forms of labour were maintained in large estates and mines, but slavery was formally abolished in 1854. The latter caused a decrease in the offer of available labour force to work in the Coast large estates, for which reason Chinese coolies and Japanese servants were brought.

Twenty-five years ago in the Peruvian agriculture subsisted a typical semi-feudal social and economic structure, from which it has been inherited up to today remnants of social relations of servile type that get to the point of implying populations displacements of eventual character.

The progressive physical integration of the national territory by means of communications media and cultural widespread, together with the global crisis of socio-productive structures and sudden increase of the population growth rates, generate since forty years ago—and more intensely since the 70's—a radical expansion of migratory flows. In 1940 the traditional structure of population concentration determined that only less than a fifth of total population liven in urban areas, while at the present time, only close to half the population still live in rural areas. Worst of all, due to the deepening of the national crisis —continuation of the economic bankruptcy and arousal of chronic political violence—the intensification of internal and international emigration flows can be foreseen.

From the above stated it can be gathered that the sequence of violent situations in the history of Peru has been constant, and hat through them has been built the unstable political structure it has today. Since always, military domination and subordination of the civil elements have been historically constant situations.[2] On an institutional and legal framework formally liberal and democratic, a political system has been built infested with authoritarianism and absolute inequality between citizens. In the field of Social Sciences it has been written much about the colossal divorce existing between the *formal Peru* (described by law and speeches, without much practical operation) and the *actual Peru* (the day-to-day , the really existing).[3]

During the last 25 years, the global situation in Peru has been characterized by general deterioration of life conditions of its population and the breaking out of extreme forms of political violence. Within an integral perspective of human rights, which does not only confine its attention to violations by State agents and does not end in the sphere of civil and political rights, it becomes evident that this country faces an extremely complicated situation, which comes to the point of even jeopardizing its historical viability.

In such context, where only poverty and violence prosper—we insist—migratory flows have been accentuated and diversified. As in many other Latin American countries and poor nations, thousands of citizens migrate to opulent nations to find better economic horizons and personal progress. In such flow leave the most qualified technicians and contractors, reinforcing in this way the conditions which thwart national development and accentuate the growing asymmetry existing today in every field of international relations.

Furthermore, within Peru's same national borders, a very intense process of economical migration has been developing, due to which during the last 50 years the profile of population distribution has radically changed. This internal economical migration has been reinforcing the centralised development that concentrates itself in a few large cities, while the population of rural areas is decreasing.

Peru was traditionally a receptive nation for some flows of immigrants. During colonial domination many Spaniards came to live in Peru; after the Independence slaves were brought from Africa, coolies from China and rural workers from Japan. During World Wars I and II the Peruvian Government lined up with the Alien Enemies Policy designed by the United States: the immigration of European people was not promoted. As a result of mob riots, during World War II, stores belonging to the Japanese immigrants were assaulted. In recent decades, for reasons of tourism, foreign investment, or international cooperation actions, external non-permanent migratory flows, continued to arrive. However, it is evident that Peru, at least during the current century, has not received any quantitatively important immigrant flows. Nowadays, in the midst of a generalized crisis, even diplomatic missions have reduced to the utmost the presence of officials of their nationality.

Within the very weak institutional structure of the Peruvian Government, the political and juridical regulation of migratory processes—and the resulting delimitation between legitimate and illegitimate discrimination—constitutes truly *an exotic matter* to which no significant attention has been paid. And that is so despite the fact Peru has been—an again is, for internal reasons—involved in migratory processes of some singularity. There is no exaggeration in asserting that the Peruvian Government lacks an integral migration policy and a specialized agency to plan and execute it. The *Dirección General de Migraciones* (General Migrations Office) is the fundamental instance on the matter, but its field of action is reduced basically to primary administrative functions, directed under paradigms of control and openly police-oriented. In the academic field, the situation is not less regrettable: the Refugee Law is not taken into account in Law Schools, and in part because of it, there are absolutely no professionals capable of designing, analysing or executing modern global policies on the matter.

1980: Between Constitution and War

In 1980 many things changed in Peru. That year the military gave back the Government to civilians, by means of an orderly process with general elections. But, simultaneously, the subversive group Communist Party "Shining Path" (PCP-SL), started its armed struggle against the nascent Democracy, hanging dead dogs in street lighting poles with slogans against the then rulers of the Peoples' Republic of China. A few years later, with methods somewhat less ferocious, another subversive group, the Movimiento Revolucionario "Tupac Amaru" (MRTA) started its armed actions.

That year, the new and modern Constitution came into effect but, paradoxically, at the same time started to loose applicability, due precisely to the onset of an internal war which had not been foreseen months before, when it was drafted.

Soon war extended to the Central Andes, in the poorest area of the country. At first some quechua-speaking peasant communities lent attention and certain support to the groups of youths from *Shining Path* that visited them, haranguing to get followers in favour of their cause.

The violent reaction of military officers which were originally moved to those areas to confront the *Shining Path* took no delay, and thus an atmosphere of frontal tension was generated between the troops and the population. As a result, according to many documented reports, there are many cases of extrajudicial executions , forced disappearances and tortures, attributable to State agents. On the other hand, there are thousands of extremely cruel assassinations perpetrated by the armed subversive groups (largely by *Shining Path*).

The drug traffickers nourish the process of violence, as they seek to disrupt all means of Government or social control in order to act without charges, while Peru remains the main coca-growing country in the world. With the passage of time, and due to lessons learned after many frustrations, as well as due to increasing international pressure against the Peruvian Government, the militarists are beginning to show a better behaviour and more concern about human rights, and people are recovering its confidence in them.

From an heterodox perspective of human rights, today the main violating agent of same is *Shining Path*, in Peru. Thanks to the rapprochement of the military with the population and the creation of an army of peasants (called *ronderos*), the warlike and human rights situation is going through important changes. In this context, *Shining Path* has become almost the only agent to cause refugees and displaced populations, while the former inhabitants of some villages are choosing to return to their place of origin, provided adequate protection is given by some nearby military base.

Some Features of Recent Migratory Processes in Peru

The situation of political violence has reached in Peru a level of extreme severity, which deserves the label of *non-international armed conflict* and the intensive application of the International Humanitarian Law. The ICRC is actively involved in providing humanitarian assistance to the combatants and the population, but no formal recognition of the specific legal statute applicable in such context has been given by the Government, despite that in recently passed decrees and official press releases it is admitted that Peru is affording a warlike situation.

Within present Peruvian reality, different types of migratory processes can be distinguished, taking into account causing factors and internal or international character of each situation. The main types, named according to the population magnitude involved, are:

- internal economic migration;
- international economic migration;
- displacement; and,
- refuge.

Internal Economic Migration

As mentioned above, this one constitutes the most traditional and massive modality among migrations in Peru. The usual pattern includes transfer of population, in an individual fashion, in small family circles, or progressively in larger groups, from the country to some of the few large cities. In a more recurrent way, transfer occurs from country sites of the Andean highlands to the populated areas of the Coast.

During the last decades these processes have had such an immense character, in quantity and quality, that the have surpassed the scarce possibilities of planing and assignment of resources on the side of the Government. Such reality has abruptly reduced the country population, has significantly deteriorated conditions of habitability within the cities, and is in the strictest sense promoting greater impoverishment of the society as a whole.

The continuation of these migratory flows generates greater tension on the factors of the structural crisis, thus nourishing the process of political violence and deterioration in the quality of human relations.

It is evident that the main and most effective political measure which can be imposed to stop and revert such migratory flows is promoting development in the poorest localities. The prescription seems simple, but its realization results extremely complex, due to the variety of internal and international (inequity in international economic relations, mainly) factors that conspire generating some kind of vicious circle. The lack of such perspectives of development prevents the Government or any other public entity from carrying out re-emigration programs.

On the legal aspect, little can be done immediately to change such situation. In the framework of a political system of relative democracy, as the one that has existed in Peru since more than a decade ago, the constitutional and legal order guarantee freedom of passageway and, in a general way, the whole set of fundamental rights which are essential for the individual self-determination. There are no specific laws to limit the unwinding of such migratory flows, neither are there known judicial precedents of such nature. In fact, the adoption of restrictive legal norms on free passageway within the national territory could easily attempt against the whole human rights standing.

International Economic Migration

This is a phenomenon which massive character appears recently, as it was initiated approximately one decade ago. Although there are no precise estimates on its magnitude, it becomes evident that the country is facing a process of great decapitalization of technicians, professionals and qualified labour force, due to this massive emigration. Even though there are evident causes of internal order—generically, the global deterioration of living conditions—it is as well a process that with different tints is taking place in all poor nations, and particularly in Latin America as a whole. It is undoubtedly a consequence of the increasing global asymmetry which characterize the current International Relations.

The traditional destinations are, in order of magnitude: the United States and some West European countries. However, on recent months emigration to Japan and other countries of Southeast Asia is becoming massive, by forging certificates (to prove a really nonexistent presence of Japanese ancestors) and plastic surgery (to make eyelids look like typically oriental). Although ads appear in local newspapers offering jobs in Japan, and being it foreseeable they appeal to these illegal methods, Peruvian authorities adopt no restrictive actions to prevent them. No public information has been provided about deportation of Peruvian illegal immigrants in Japan.

As to flows heading for the United States, two trends may be distinguished:

- relatively legal migrations, made with visa (at least tourist visa, for temporary stay and not allowed to work) and through a direct itinerary by plane;
- absolutely illegal migrations, made without a visa and through an indirect itinerary (by land, making stops in different countries) to go stealthily by the Mexican border.

The criteria of selectivity for granting United States visas has been gradually intensified, which obviously increases pressure to migrate in an absolutely illegal fashion. Nevertheless, it is important to note that in the U.S. Consular offices there is great arbitrariness in the qualification of applications and very frequently a kind of treatment that batters the applicants' human rights. To this, many other violations to the same fundamental rights are added, which occur when illegal migrants reach their destinations.

Within the first modality, a significant percentage of migrants extend their stay after the visa is due, and take up a job, generally in conditions of overexploitation. We need not further explain these situations as much has been written and said about same.

The second modality results particularly serious as to the countless risks that must be faced by people who choose this as a last option to realize their dream of progress in the United States. In the so-called transit countries[4], assaulting or robbery to these migrants is a general rule, sometimes by police authorities themselves, of the respective countries. There are also many cases of migrant women being raped and records on some homicides as well. To this are added, obviously, the enormous difficulties they must face when and after crossing the border between Mexico and the United States.

The majority of this transit countries require visa to stay within their territory, and usually these migrants lack same, ratifying its condition of absolute and repeated illegality. They become ideal prey to all kinds of extortion and ill-treatment, as there are no international norms or procedures of specific character to protect them, and because the total illegality of their condition favours impunity for their abusers.

For Peruvian authorities it has not been up to now significant political priority coordination with other Latin American countries to improve and standardize policies and norms, for the treatment and protection of illegal migrants in transit. As a general pattern, coordinations are carried out at consular level, only on a bilateral basis, mainly regarding individual cases, without great political backup or availability of resources.[5] South American Governments act still under the traditional patterns of reciprocity and rhetoric, designing mechanisms of economic integration which up to now have worked almost exclusively as wishful thinking, whilst discussion on migratory policies is neglected.

As to migration toward Europe, the past liberality of the majority of these countries (not requiring visa to go in, for example) made illegal stay and working easy, but such situation is changing dramatically. The high cost of transportation, language difficulties, cultural differences and lack of family ties in destination points determine these flows to be less in volume (compared to those heading for the United States), although recently a significant increase is being registered.

In recent months the expulsion of Peruvian citizens has been intensified in several European countries, including cases like Spain, that required no visa. In order not to affect other fields of bilateral relations, Peruvian authorities decided to adopt a conciliatory or even obliging position with those countries. At the request of the Peruvian Government, starting this year, Spain has imposed the requirement of visa for all incoming Peruvians and vice versa, being debatable the efficiency of this element. It may be worthy to mention that this is the only case in which the reciprocity condition has been imposed, in the context of the bilateral relations with the European countries that require visa to Peruvian immigrants.

Besides all restrictions to transcontinental migratory flows, agreed upon by the European Community countries, there is prejudice regarding the fact that Peruvian passengers introduce coca illegally.[6]

Notwithstanding the fact that a significant percentage of Peruvians live out of their country, national authorities don't understand yet that such reality deserves to be reflected in the policy and lawmaking processes, in order to make it easier for those people to maintain links of different types with their country of origin. Consequently, there are no laws specifically referred to this new reality, neither judicial precedents relevant to the subject. On the other hand, there are no specific laws or procedures to allow distinction between legitimate and illegitimate discrimination within the limits of international economic migration.

In fact, Peru is a country that has maintained during the last decades a rather conflicting relationship with the rest of the international community. Nationalist policies have motivated periodical expropriation of foreign properties without offering immediate solutions regarding indemnification, and in the social conscientiousness there is a tendency to see the foreign investor as a thief. This question has reached an interesting anthropological dimension through the myth of the *pishtaco*: some American or European employees of agroindustrial enterprises were radically rejected by Peruvian workers, who accused them of kidnapping their children to throw them into their machines to keep them greased.

Traditionally, Peruvian laws and public policies expressed a very deep-rooted isolationist vision that radically separates internal from international and minimizes importance of the latter.

Near the Peruvian border with Chile, hundredths of Bolivian citizens have settled seeking better living conditions. Many of them are illegal migrants, but through informal means have obtained Peruvian identification documents without resigning to their nationality. Neither the Peruvian Government nor the Bolivian one have taken specific actions in this respect.

The Displacement

Under this category are considered all people (mainly groups of populations) who have had to flee from the political violence, but remain inside their national territory. This is a very new process in Peru, as it was started twelve years ago when the armed conflict lead by *Shining Path* aroused. The zones in conflict are basically rural locations of Andean highlands, and the displaced people are mainly poor quechua-speaking peasants. Besides carrying in their souls wounds opened by violence and having to migrate with no resources or clear destinations, they must face the shock of the crash between their culture and urban-Western and crossbreed.

Until around 1989, the flows of displaced originated from the crossfire situation between two groups in which Andean populations were located, having on one side the military; and on the other, *Shining Path*. Furthermore, in many cases, the flight of populations was due to the brutal interventions of the military. More recently, according to testimonies gathered in-situ, situation is changing thanks to new orientation of the military in anti-subversive war, and recent flows are basically caused by the barbarism of *Shining Path*. Moreover, some populations are being registered to return to locations in which there is some military presence (to protect population from the attacks of *Shining Path*).

The settlement of the displaced in the poor marginal areas of the cities— mainly Lima, the capital—is characterized for its absolute precariousness, with total lack of basic services and essential conditions of dignity to subsist. To the usual racial discrimination is added the originated by the fact they come from combat zones, which makes them be seen as suspicious of being *terrucos* (popular expression which means combatant of *Shining Path*). It is very frequent for the displaced to lack identification documents, which makes their integration to society virtually impossible in conditions of legality; in the case of children, this frequently implies denial to be admitted in public schools, therefore in no position to exercise their human right to education.

The subject of the displaced as a specific social category for assistance and protection purposes, was usually not taken into account by Government authorities or other institutions—such as the NGOs—until 1991. This has caused a situation of total abandonment and lack of protection to the displaced population to endure.

For the same reason, there are no approximate statics available concerning the number of displaced people in Peru, but a reasonable estimate could be around 300 thousand.

There is presently a National Commission for Displaced Population, created by the Government, with participation of the Peruvian NGO Association, the Catholic Church, the Ministry of Defence and other institutions, which is elaborating a diagnose and proposal of strategy to take integral care of the basic needs of the displaced. Furthermore, in July 1991, the Peruvian Government requested the Secretary General of the United Nations to authorize participation of different agencies of the universal system to support the national efforts in favour of the displaced. The UNDP, UNIFEM, UNICEF and WHO are already lending some support to said National Commission and a substantial increase in such support is expected in coming months. Meanwhile, in February 1992 the UNHCR sent a Working Group to Lima to evaluate the possibility of undertaking participation of their international organization, but no concrete results are yet known.

Having in mind the situation of displaced population in Peru and Colombia, the Interamerican Institute of Human Rights announced in its presentation before the recent Second International Meeting of the Follow-Up Committee of CIREFCA, held in April 1992, the summons of an International Conference about Displaced Populations in the Andean Region, to take place during 1993.

Inasmuch as displacement does not constitute yet—for municipal or International Law—a specific category, there are no juridical parameters to distinguish between legitimate and illegitimate discrimination of those migrants. As we have already stated, within the formal framework of the Constitution and prevailing laws in Peru, there is freedom of passageway and relative prevalence of every other civil and political rights, for which reason there are no open restrictions against the displaced as such.

In the technical area, the National Commission for Displaced Population is discussing the convenience of making a difference between the displaced and the rest of the population, in order to give specific assistance and protection. The subject encloses special complexity, as even though legitimate discrimination may contribute to improve the living conditions of the displaced and to offer them security and identification documents, that could bring about risks of rejection among their neighbours—who would feel set aside despite their similar needs—or increase their vulnerability in face of the harassing of *Shining Path*. Furthermore, in some exceptional cases, legitimate discrimination would result superfluous inasmuch as local institutions are getting to take adequate care of the basic needs of the displaced. In conclusion, it would only be valid to appeal to legitimate discrimination for assistance and protection purposes, based on the analysis of the specific situation of each group of displaced population, and no general rules should be applied in this respect.

Refugees

Due to the situation of violence, some hundreds of Peruvians have left the country and taken in the refugee status. There are no approximate figures on the magnitude of these flows, but only in the neighbour country of Bolivia there are around 350 people in that condition, according to unofficial reports given by UNHCR officers. Probably the total number of Peruvian refugees is in total not higher than one thousand.

According to the same UNHCR sources, there is a relationship of great cooperation in this matter on the part of the Bolivian Government, and as much as an indifferent attitude on the side of the Peruvian Government. The UNHCR emphasizes the differentiation between the *political persecuted*, and the members of *Shining Path* involved in criminal acts, as only the first ones are eligible to obtain the refugee status, in the light of the Convention, the Protocol and other international standards. In Peru, Government agents do not usually realize political persecution, but there is a possibility that in some cases for lack of information or for ideological prejudice a person is accused by mistake of belonging to *Shining Path*, which situation gives rise to an application for asylum in another country.

A rather unique fact of Peruvian reality is that many of the people who apply for asylum are running away from threats by *Shining Path* and not from persecution by Government agents. It so happens that in general the Government lacks the basic capacity to offer protection to persons threatened and the subject has not even deserved significant attention from the high Government authorities. Recently, some important grassroot leaders, have been threatened and even murdered, originating well-known cases of application for asylum in other countries.

Due to the lack of interest (or of possibilities) on the side of the Government, there is not enough information in Peru about the treatment given its citizens that apply for asylum in other countries, neither on situations of eventual illegitimate discrimination against them. It is vaguely known there are people who choose to run away from violence under the condition of economic migrants, while there are others who with no base claim being subject to political persecution to obtain the refugee status, but there is a total lack of more precise data.

On the other hand, it is evident that due to its situation of global crisis, Peru results of very little attraction as country of asylum, and no applications for such purpose have been presented during the last months.

During the last decade Peru faced the problem of approximately 10 thousand Cubans who abruptly went into the Embassy of Peru in Havana. Although in the majority of cases they wanted to go to the United States, many of them were sent to Peru, situation that generated discontent and thanklessness among them, and created a relation of little appreciation on the side of Peruvian people. Technically, these people were not refugees, so the Peruvian Government only recognized them under the unique qualification of *Non-Immigrant Refugees*.

To take care of such situation a Subdelegation of the UNHCR was established in Peru, which ceased operations when the problem of those Cuban people was basically solved, in 1989. On that date, the problem of the Peruvian displaced had already acquired great proportions, but such circumstance was of no use to change the decision of the UNHCR.

Epilogue

The complex situation of human rights violations and the migratory flows, in Peru, are in many aspects determined by the underdevelopment situation of the country. Besides the internal political process and its consequent responsibilities, Peru is victim of an unjust International Order which is causing its asphyxiation.

In face of situations like the one Peru is affording, more international attention should be given to the relatively unprotected migrant groups, such as international economic migrants and displaced people.

Within the regional priorities of the UNHCR, South America is not important at all. What is more, in the context of Central America, during the recent Second International Meeting of the Follow-Up Committee of CIREFCA, some delegates expressed their concern on the possibility that UNHCR would give up participating in the Joint Support Unit UNHCR-UNDP of CIREFCA, as it would mean a significant withdrawal from the taking over of responsibilities in the regional pacification process. As far as the Peruvian case is concerned, the UNHCR, with orthodox fidelity to its mandate presently takes care of refugees only, and gives no signs of willingness to get involved in the problem of the displaced. This happens despite the fact Peru constitutes from far the main current concern of the UNHCR in the context of South America.

It is evident that the mandate of the UNHCR has to be expanded to adequate itself to the new migratory situations that arise in the international scenery. For Peru it results positive, although at the same time regrettable, that other agencies of the United Nations pay attention to problems of forced migration other than refuge, while the UNHCR continues to hide behind the formal gown of the limits in its institutional mandate.

Furthermore, the UNHCR performs a very poor job of the Refugee Law diffusion, which hardly contributes to encourage specialization or professional interest on the matter, within the context of South America. This situation does not help to avoid the growing asymmetry in the quality and intensity of the reflection and practice about the subject of the refugees and the migrants, within the developed world (receivers of such people) and the poor world (traditional ejector of the same).

Notes

1. Prior to 1940, the Average Annual Rate of Population Growth in Peru was 1.6 percent. Between 1940 and 1961 went up to 1.8 percent, and between 1961 and 1972 reached the higher level of 2.9 percent. Between 1972 and 1981, the rate fell to 2.7 percent and is presently experiencing a slow decrease in its level. Around 40 percent of the population is less than 15 years old.

2. This historical constant has repeated on April 5, 1992, when President Fujimori of Peru, appealed to the Armed Forces to close the Congress and fire many of the Supreme Court judges, arguing they harassed reforms sought by his Government.

3. De Soto 1988; Matos Mar 1984.

4. For the purposes of this paper, we call *transit countries* all countries located between North of Peru and South of the United States, which are traversed by illegal migrants who travel by land.

5. In some cases those migrants fall into total indigence in the course of its journey, and Peruvian consular officers completely lack resources to aid them or finance their return.

6. Peru is the major producer of coca leaves in the world.

References

Baehr, Peter R. and Tessenyi, Geza, eds. (1991). The New Refugee Hosting Countries: Call for Experience—Space for Innovation. SIM Special N° 11 (SIM).

Comisión Especial del Senado sobre Causas de la Violencia y Alternativas de Pacificación (1989). Violencia y Pacificación (DESCO and ACJ).

Consejo Nacional de Población (1989). Perú: Hechos y Cifras Demográficas, N° 2 (CNP).

De Soto, Hernando (1988). The Other Path. The Invisible Revolution in the Third World (Harper & Row).

Matos Mar, José (1984). Desborde Popular y Crisis del Estado (IEP).

PART THREE

Case Studies in Europe

8

Immigration Regulation: The Cost to Integration

Tomas Hammar

Introduction

In the social science debate about the nature and causes of international migration flows, a great deal of emphasis has been placed on pull and push theories, or theories about the cyclical nature of migration flows and about the importance of chains and networks, or theories about centre and periphery and international migration as a result of the penetration of rich industrial states into developing countries. These theories all seem to forget or underestimate one salient factor. Almost all states do their best to control and regulate immigration. It is these control mechanisms that determine which migration flows are legitimate and which are not. Legitimacy is not established by high abstract principles, but by inducement, control and deterrence mechanisms that are usually established unilaterally, but often bilaterally and multilaterally as well, by both receiving and sending countries. Common sense tells us that flows are being controlled, reduced, turned away or sometimes stimulated and recruited by the states. Sending states sometimes develop policies to determine the direction and composition of emigration. Finally, sometimes cooperative efforts are made by sending and receiving states, even in specific bilateral or multilateral agreements.

In this decade, however, international population movements are growing quickly, in spite of all these control measures. They might, according to all forecasts, take on even greater proportions in the future. The outcome depends to a large extent on the efficiency of the control systems that are now constructed or reinforced. This is true both for the European states, which have already received large immigration during the last decades, and for the classical immigration countries overseas. The questions are everywhere. How can regulation be made more efficient? How can clear signals be given to potential emigrants, signals that immigration has been reduced and is not desired? In other words, recent efforts have concentrated on discouraging and, therefore, delegitimizing most migration using controls and regulations.

In this paper I will discuss the costs of these regulation systems that we already employ or those we are trying to build as walls around our rich, industrial societies. It is important to emphasize, however, that the term "cost" in this discussion does not necessarily mean monetary costs—for instance not only the costs of border police and of examinations of asylum applications. What I refer to instead are all kinds of negative socio-economic and political effects that may be consequences of control mechanisms. These mechanisms not only delegitimize certain types of migration, but have byproducts and costs that spread delegitimization to other aspects of society.

A Fortress Europe

In the beginning of the 1990s, when both national and international bodies discussed the growing immigration pressure from South to North as well as from East to West, Europe began preparing for a new situation. As of January 1, 1993, internal borders will be removed, not only between the twelve countries, but also in relation to the European Free Trade Association (EFTA) countries within the European Economic Sphere (EES).

The dream of free movements of people, never completely forgotten during this century, started some ninety years ago with open borders in Europe and is going to be realized within the EES, but only for citizens of the European member countries. Citizens of countries outside Europe will be controlled, at least as much as they are now. Regulation of new immigration from third countries will have to become more strict and more perfect than before. Will the new Fortress Europe be able to stem the immigration pressure from the rest of the world? To resist this pressure may be an almost hopeless task. A fortress of this kind would perhaps be able to function efficiently only if violence is ruthlessly used by military or paramilitary forces, just as the word "fortress" implies. This is one example of a cost of immigration regulation, which I shall discuss here, a cost that may be heavier than democratic welfare states can afford in the long run.

A number of steps have already been taken in various combinations. External control at the borders, as well as control of all kinds of transportation by air and sea, etc., will be improved. A joint system of visa requirements may be introduced. More efficient and systematic deportations of those denied asylum or residence permits will be attempted. In many states the internal control system, i.e., the control of aliens already inside the borders, is often weak. Employer sanctions to stop illegal immigrants from working are seldom effective. This could perhaps be changed. Several other measures might be used to stop undesired immigration.

All these measures involve costs. I am talking not only about administration and implementation costs, but much more importantly about the negative effects on the controlling states themselves—in other words, new obstacles to international travel, and tensions that may increase between the South and the North, as well as between the East and the West. At the entrance doors a sharp discrimination will be made between citizens of rich industrialized Europe and the rest of the world. This may bring about a corresponding discrimination within European states. Human rights may be violated and the right of asylum may be denied to many who clearly deserve international protection. Families will be divided, and relatives will not be able to visit each other without special permits. It may be so extreme that human lives will be lost and xenophobia and racism will grow. Nevertheless, even if all efforts are made, Fortress Europe will probably not be able to tighten all the holes in its control system. Therefore, illegal immigration will continue to be large, not only in Southern Europe, but throughout the continent.

Integration and Regulation

My focus will not be on the costs of external and internal immigration control, but on the dynamic relation between this control on one side and the integration policy on the other. Hopefully, this will broaden the perspective on the costs of control. There is a close mutual dependence between regulation and integration. Each is affected by the other. However, as both are at the same time dependent also on many other factors, it is often difficult to grasp this interrelationship. I believe this is why the interplay between control and integration is often forgotten or misunderstood.

Regulation of immigration refers to the rules and procedures governing the selection and admission of foreign citizens. It is used by states to determine the size and composition of their immigration flows. Integration policy refers to the conditions that are provided to immigrants already admitted to the country. It is not possible, nor absolutely necessary, to discuss the many problems involved in integration policy. I do not want to

take any specific stand with regard to the issues of pluralism or multiculturalism when using this term. Some readers may find that I use integration
here in about the same way as many authors when they write about
"functional integration," i.e., integration into working life, housing, social
and political life, etc., without discussing ethnic or cultural integration.

All countries that experience immigration and regulate their size and
composition do not pursue an active integration policy. A classical immigration country overseas (for example, the United States), has often taken
for granted that integration is a matter of concern only to the individual
immigrant. No, or very few, special public arrangements have been made
to resocialize immigrants. This is still the policy or rather the nonpolicy with
regard to integration in many states. In others like Canada, however, a more
active integration policy has been developed, especially for the first year of
a newly-landed immigrant.

Guest Workers

During the period of large-scale labour recruitment in Western Europe, i.e.,
up to the early 1970s, integration policies were neglected or little developed
in most immigration countries. Guest-worker countries saw no need for
integration: migrant workers were invited to stay only a limited period and
were then expected to return. Public assistance was to be given, not for
integration, but (if at all) to promote return. The policy of Bavaria in the
Federal Republic of Germany provides a model for expending money to
induce return.

Since most immigrants planned to return after a couple of years, the
official rotation principle corresponded well to the original intentions of the
immigrants. But many who had planned to return, changed their minds and
stayed. The official ideas of rotation and return did not change as easily,
however. They were turned into long-lasting illusions shared by most
people. Policymakers especially found it hard to realize that this guest-worker
policy had been based on unrealistic assumptions.

Today, in the 1990s, employers now and then request short-term import
of migrant workers to fill temporary labour demands. Some economists
even advise them to do so, telling them that this will be a profitable strategy.
They forget that the consequences of such an import are not only of a
short-term economic nature, but that there are also long-term social and
political implications. They have not learned the lessons of the 1960s—that
so-called temporary labour migration in the long run results in a considerable amount of family immigration and permanent settlement.

In the 1970s, the rotation system never functioned as it had been planned.
When the demand for labour was lower in a recession, guest-worker

countries stopped further recruitment, but they did not tell foreign workers already in the country to return, nor did they force them to go back. Instead, they allowed them to stay on for several reasons, including the fact that employers did not want to lose those workers who were already trained for the jobs they did. This was also the time when many foreign workers realized that they did not want to return and decided to bring their families. In fact, after many years away and given the economic conditions in their countries of origin, most of them had no other real choice.

The Gulf states learned this lesson. A system of rotation could work only if ruthless methods were employed. They used such methods at the time of the Gulf War by keeping their guest workers well segregated from the rest of the society. Recruitment had been based on tough contracts that were strictly enforced, and which could be unilaterally terminated by the employer. No family immigration had been allowed. Contract workers were not union members, and their wages were far below the normal standards.

This kind of contract labour is still accepted, not only in some of the Gulf states, but also in many places in Southeast Asia. Even if seasonal workers are allowed in some parts of North America and Europe today, long-term contract labour is completely banned and will hopefully continue to be so in the future. Guest-worker or rotation systems of this kind stand in direct conflict with the normal rules prevailing in the labour markets, and with the interests that trade unions protect. Contract labour systems are too costly in European democratic welfare states, as they violate human dignity, the right to family life, and basic social and political rights. Import of foreign labour can be recommended only to those states in Europe that are ready to accept permanent settlement, i.e., when they give temporary work permits that will include an option to settle as an immigrant.

Illegal Immigration

But the answer may be illegal immigration instead, or more precisely a wide tolerance of the fact that it is a very difficult task to hinder illegal immigrants, and to find and deport those illegals once they have arrived. Several states yield to the interests of some employers who want inexpensive labour and tolerate a large foreign population of illegal immigrants working in the country.

There have been many examples of this both in North America and in Europe during the last twenty years. In some countries, the illegal population has been estimated in the hundreds of thousands; in the United States, at several million. In some countries, where trade unions have reached a high level of organization and exercised a substantial influence on immigration policy, the number of illegal workers has been relatively low. In other states, this number has been low only in some industries where large firms represent a good deal of the production and where most workers are unionized. In sectors with many small enterprises (restaurants, shops, etc.) and where trade unions often are weak, there are greater numbers of illegal immigrants.

The official policy is of course clear: illegal immigration is against the law and should be stopped. However, the enforcement is often missing or extremely inefficient. Employer sanctions are low and the risks of fines are often small. Employers may hope to get some jobs done at a low price. Illegal workers may hope that an amnesty will reach them before they are found and deported. The negative consequences are not always obvious to the individual, but they will sooner or later become obvious to the society. Again they are costs for the receiving society, costs caused by the violation of the principles of the social welfare system. It is not acceptable that illegal immigration results in an unprivileged underclass without residential rights, the right to work, social rights, and the protection of the social security system, but this is what has happened during the last decades and what we fear will happen even more in the near future, depending on what kind of regulations the new Fortress Europe will be able to put in place and monitor.

The Chronological Order:
Immigration Regulation and Integration Policy

Historically, immigration came first, regulation followed and, finally, an integration policy was introduced. We find similar scenarios both during World War I and in the beginning of the 1970s. Before 1914, international population movements were almost completely free from regulation in Europe, with the exception of Russia. At the end of the war, regulation systems were introduced almost everywhere for a number of reasons— national security, wartime shortages of food and housing, but also protection of the national economy, including the labour market, and protection of the nation and the race. The modern nation-states, emerging out of the war economies, continued the immigration control they had started during the war, and for the first time they explicitly included the protection of the domestic labour market in their national interests, especially as deep depressions brought about high unemployment.

Thirty years after World War II, European nation-states, by developing comprehensive social welfare policies, created new social values that they wanted to protect from being diluted or lost as a result of the influx of new immigrants. Social rights, providing basic social security, were granted to all citizens, and sometimes the same social rights were also given to legally settled noncitizens. Over time, because of large labour immigration and long residence periods, this category of noncitizens in several states obtained almost full social rights, which of course can be seen as an indicator of their integration. As a result, if a state decided to admit a group of immigrants, this decision implied that social rights would be extended also to them, or in other words that an increasing number of persons would benefit from pensions, sick allowances, unemployment measures, etc.

For social welfare states of the late twentieth century, immigration control has become indispensable, as large immigration flows might overburden the taxpayers and perhaps damage the welfare system. Regulation and control are today directly tied to the nation-states' welfare policies and the need to know who and how many its beneficiaries are.

Before 1914 and 1973-74, most European countries had a laissez-faire policy. Governments were mainly passive spectators, allowing the market forces to decide the size and direction of migration. During both periods, immigration states first developed a policy of regulating the flow and control of aliens, namely the new aliens acts of 1917-26, and stopping the recruitment of foreign labour in the early 1970s, but there are differences between the two periods to be noted. In the 1970s (but not in the 1920s), regulation was preceded by large-scale immigration, and only in the 1970s was the introduction of regulation immediately followed by the first attempts to develop integration policies. Why these differences?

One answer has already been given. The difference in policy may be explained by the fact that, in the meantime, social welfare systems had been developed in Western Europe. Immigration control was needed to protect these systems. But given such a control, foreign workers and their families informally acquired a new status. They were at least tolerated and tacitly accepted as long-term residents. Many of them already enjoyed some social rights, and the new integration policies soon gave them several others.

In this way, a new category of aliens developed, a category between citizens and aliens, which we can call "denizens." They are noncitizens in a country where they stay and work, but they enjoy full residential and social rights. They are legal long-term, if not permanent, settlers. They are still often called "foreigners," but they deserve another name, for their ties and their rights in the country where they live are much stronger than those of ordinary foreigners living in other countries, visitors or tourists, etc.

However, it is very important to note another interplay between regulation and integration, which was demonstrated in the 1970s. The cessation of recruitment came about, not only because of the oil crisis and the subsequent stagnation of the economy, but also because several immigration countries in Europe, during a ten- to fifteen-year period, had received a large foreign population without being prepared for their integration into the receiving societies. The need for better housing, schooling for the children, family reunification, etc., became increasingly more obvious. Regulation was, in other words, initiated also because of a need to integrate a large number of immigrants.

Policy Decisions and Implementation

Regulation and integration are usually administered by different agencies and organizations. Immigration regulation and aliens control are the tasks of the police and border control, and the responsibility of Ministers of the Interior, Justice or Home Affairs, while integration policy is often a matter of several specialized ministries, like the Ministries of Education, Housing, Social Affairs, etc. Responsibility is also divided on a regional and local level between several administrations, as well as welfare associations and churches.

However, agencies that regulate immigration often hold different views and opinions than agencies dealing with immigrant policy. The staff of the latter are trained differently and their immediate aims are quite different. The regulation side may become too negative because its task is to stop those who try to avoid or even to cheat the control. Those working with integration may become "ombudsmen" for the immigrants, rather than neutral public servants.

Few European countries have tried to combine both sides into a single immigration authority concerned with all aspects of immigration. Sweden has had mostly good results from such an experiment, which started more than twenty years ago, and recently a similar system was also introduced in Norway. There are problems involved in this combination of tasks, but it has stimulated an exchange of experience and viewpoints that has helped to meet the need for oversight, coordination, coherence and planning.

In the 1970s some European states appointed special deputy ministers for immigration. Some of them were responsible for both regulation and integration. Both regulation and integration are subjects of the public debate about immigration policy and also of political decisions. After many years of a low politicization of this policy field, both immigration regulation and integration policy, and, of course, especially ethnic and race relations, have become hotly debated issues that divide the political parties and that are also used by some parties in their political campaigns. Even here in these political debates the two sides are often dealt with as if they were different issues. Their interrelationship is seldom clearly described or analysed.

Political parties or politicians, who give high priority to the values of nation and state, may emphasize regulation in their political campaigns, with the view that the size and composition of immigration flows are matters of national concern, questions of importance for the future of the nation, demographic and economic development, etc. On the other hand, parties and politicians for whom social security, full employment, social rights, etc., are the first priorities, may instead give more weight to the integration of immigrants.

Another political difference should also be mentioned. Regulation locks some noncitizens out of the country. On one hand, it may said that all citizens have a common interest in regulation and control to protect the country against an undesirable mass immigration. On the other hand, some citizens may be interested in integrating immigrants and denizens who are already admitted and settled in the country. These denizens themselves may have a word in the political debate or even, as in some countries, a vote in the political elections. But if it is true that there are relevant differences between the two sides of immigration policy, they are interrelated in the formation of the public opinion, such as xenophobia and racism as a result of restrictive control systems, among other factors. I shall return to this question.

Some Assumptions

In my view the interrelationship between the two sides of any country's immigration policy is already crucial and will be even more so in the future. Even if we do not accept the most threatening scenarios of future mass migration directed toward Europe, most of us foresee a heavy increase in migration pressure from less developed and overpopulated countries in the East and most of all in the South. Europe is therefore building walls to stop and regulate immigration.

I am persuaded that some kind of regulation is indispensable, and that a free or relatively free mass migration would lead to chaos in the rich welfare states, from which no one would benefit, neither the rich within Europe nor the poor outside it. But I do not think that there is a system of regulation that could efficiently stop all undesirable immigration and that would not violate either basic human rights or the principles adhered to by democratic social welfare states. In other words, the costs of regulation will be very high.

There are great differences in the welfare systems of Western Europe. Some countries put more emphasis on individuals' responsibility and ability to solve their own problems, while other countries rely more on public service and collective solidarity. Conservatives have made many reductions in the social welfare systems. Still it is reasonable to maintain that a rich, internally more open European market and union is based on the principles of the social welfare state, and the following assumptions about the costs of regulation are therefore costs that must be paid by such states.

1. A democratic welfare state cannot import guest workers, as this would open a door and damage the control system. Deportations of overstaying temporary workers would meet great difficulties because of the many ties already established by the workers.

2. Such a state had better not import foreign labour when there is a general labour shortage or shortage in a certain sector, as import of labour may lead to longlasting immigration and settlement.

3. Contract work, as it is and has been practised in some parts of the world (the Gulf states, Southeast Asia and previously in Eastern Europe) cannot be employed in Europe as it is not compatible with European labour market standards (wage negotiations, trade unions, same working conditions and wages, etc.).

4. Although legal according to international law, European democratic welfare states cannot enforce decisions to deport large groups of foreign workers who have worked in the country for several years. (A sort of residential right, implicit and established in practise, prevents this.)

5. Given strong migration pressure on its borders, democratic welfare states must regulate immigration to protect the social, economic and political order.

6. No regulation is perfect. Smuggling and holes in the system, etc., will always bring about illegal immigration, which is also very costly because a dual labour market is tolerated, because illegal immigrants often finally get amnesties and settle as legal immigrants with high costs for integration.

7. A perfect or extremely tough regulation requires police, military forces and the use of violence. All this is costly. Such a regulation also has a negative impact on relations between sending and receiving countries (the South and the North, the East and the West).

8. Public opinion in a receiving country is influenced by that country's regulation policy. Strict regulation means discrimination against citizens of some nations (for example, Africa and Asia). This is often interpreted as legitimating discrimination also against denizens who have resided in the host country for a long time. Tough regulation may bring about racism and

xenophobia, and may endanger integration, if countermeasures are not efficiently undertaken by the authorities and opinion leaders.

Regulation and Racism

I would like to address point 8 in more detail. Is there or is there not an interrelation between the present increasingly more restrictive regulation policies, as discussed and implemented by the European states, and the growing negative opinions shown by the polls and the even more open racism? If so, what can we do about it when regulation is a must and racism a hindrance to integration?

This question is most relevant to all European countries today, especially to my own country, Sweden. Although Sweden has been known for its integration policy and its generous refugee policy in the 1980s, both are now under debate. According to opinion polls, the attitudes of Swedes have also undergone negative changes. During 1991-92, a series of ten attempts were made to assassinate anonymous immigrants in the streets of Stockholm.

Racism and xenophobia are growing everywhere in Europe due to many factors, all of which carry some weight. The economic depression is deep and long-lasting; at present unemployment has reached record levels. The demands of the market economy and the need for open competition are strongly emphasized today, much more so than the need for social security. We are developing a society geared more for strong individuals who can fight for their own interests than for those who cannot or do not do this for some reason. Immigrants often suffer as a result, as many of them are not assertive enough, especially during their first years in a new country.

A large increase in the number of asylum seekers may be another explanation for xenophobia and racism. Politicians often maintain that this is indeed the main reason. During the last ten years, the number of asylum seekers has increased five to ten times. Many more would have come, had the European states not employed very strict immigration regulations. According to this argument, it is regulation that has kept racism and hostility against immigrants relatively low.

However, regulation itself may also lead to hostility by drawing a sharp distinction between those aliens who are in the country and those who are outside it, between "us" and "them." Immigration regulation, of course, means that some are locked out, while only citizens or some other privileged, for instance denizens, are welcomed. No one else is admitted to the "club." If this discrimination refers to people from Africa, Asia or Eastern Europe, then this may have a direct impact also on denizens from those same geographic areas who have already settled in European countries, for example, in Italy, Germany or Sweden. Their presence in the country may easily be perceived as a previous mistake, or they may be viewed as nonmembers of the club who have managed to sneak into rich welfare states.

The difference between all those foreigners who are abroad and those few who have been admitted as immigrants is often not understood nor clearly explained by the authorities. This is true especially when immigration has been increasingly restricted and when regulation has been made more strict and efficient everywhere. For instance, when only those asylum seekers who meet the requirements of the Geneva Convention are acknowledged as refugees and de facto refugees are refused asylum, then one can easily conclude that many of those who were previously admitted should also have been refused.

It might be necessary to implement very tough regulations during some periods, but such regulations may legitimate xenophobia and racism. Policymakers and opinion leaders should counter this by making absolutely clear that this policy does not imply that previously accepted immigrants are less welcome, nor can new regulations legitimate racist attitudes or hostilities against immigrants.

Racism may increase in the present period because of the economic depression, large immigration pressure, increasing numbers of asylum seekers, high costs of processing their applications and care for their integration, etc. Racism might increase even more if appropriate measures, such as tough regulations to limit immigration, are not taken. But racism might also grow just because of such regulations if they are perceived as a legitimation of negative attitudes and behaviour. Governments who use restrictive policies must do their utmost to explain their policies, for otherwise a strict policy of regulation is readily interpreted as an approval of intolerance.

Political Dilemmas

We expect a future increase in migration pressure on Europe, a pressure that must be contained in order to protect the welfare systems of the rich industrialized states. This regulation implies high costs, however, and will not be absolutely effective: immigration will continue. Most of it will be illegal immigration, which will be very costly for everyone, including legal and illegal immigrants, as well as for the countries involved.

Regulation policy is, as shown here, closely linked to the integration of immigrants. Britain in the 1970s is just one example of this. Each time Britain laid new restrictions upon immigration, new measures were simultaneously taken to prevent discrimination against immigrants from the New Commonwealth. Today integration policy is mostly neglected, while more and more restrictive regulation policies are being used in Europe. These restrictions are still clearly linked to integration, however. If anything, they have a negative impact on the integration of older generations of immigrants, and they may also cause increasingly negative relations between majority populations and members of ethnic minority groups and their members or, in other words, more racism and xenophobia.

Immigration policy, which has long been almost a nonpolicy, has become highly politicized in emigration countries, but especially in immigration states, and international migration is now for the first time mentioned among the many global issues that cause tensions between the protected rich communities and the South and the East. The immigration debate has become intense in several European countries, and it is not only the right-wing populist parties that, in 1992, attempt to get votes on platforms of more or less explicit xenophobia and racism. Other political parties feel that they cannot allow these extreme parties to monopolize this issue, so they often make similar statements in order not to lose voters.

Immigration policy is complex for politicians, as well as for all of us. It requires long-term perspectives and an international outlook and solidarity, which most politicians seldom can afford to demonstrate in their domestic political competition. Immigration policy also demands a great deal of technical knowledge about the interplay between immigration restriction and control on one hand, and integration policy on the other. The general public must be well informed about different policies and their consequences, scenarios and alternative options.

The recent political debate is, from this point of view, both necessary and most positive. There is a risk, however, that a simplistic demagogy may take over and become the characteristic of this debate. We must counter this risk with information and studies of this most important political issue. International migration and migration policy will probably be for several decades an area where great socio-economic and political costs, as well as basic human values, are at stake. It is an area where solutions must be found, although there are no easy solutions.

References

Appleyard, R.T. *International Migration: Challenge for the Nineties.* Geneva: International Organization for Migration (IOM), 1992.

Castles, S., and G. Kosack. *Immigrant Workers and Class Structure in Western Europe.* London: Oxford University Press, 1973.

Castles, S., W. Booth and T. Wallace. *Here for Good: Western Europe's New Ethnic Minorities.* London: Pluto Press, 1984.

Center for Migration Studies. *International Migration Review* 23, no. 3 (Fall 1989).

Hammar, T., ed. *European Immigration Policy.* Cambridge: Cambridge University Press, 1985.

Hammar, T. *Democracy and the Nation State.* Aldershot: Avebury, 1991.

Kritz, M.M., L.L. Lim and H. Zlotnik, eds. *International Migration Systems: A Global Approach.* New York: Oxford University Press, 1992.

Layton-Henry, Z. *The Political Rights of Migrant Workers in Western Europe.* London: Sage, 1990.

Miller, M.J. *Foreign Workers in Western Europe: An Emerging Political Force.* New York: Praeger, 1981.

Organization for Economic Co-operation and Development (OECD). *The Future of Migration.* Paris: Organization for Economic Co-operation and Development, 1987.

UN Centre for Regional Development. *Regional Development Dialogue* 12, no. 3 (1991).

9

La Situation des Demandeurs d'Asile dans la France d'Aujourd'hui

Frédéric Tiberghien

Les demandeurs d'asile qui se présentent en France suivent différentes filières pour accéder au territoire: ils entrent sous couvert d'un visa d'établissement délivré par les ambassades ou les consulats à l'étranger; ils se présentent spontanément aux frontières et y demandent l'asile; ils pénètrent sur le territoire français sous couvert d'un visa touristique et prolongent irrégulièrement leur séjour avant de solliciter l'asile; ils entrent clandestinement en France et ne forment leur demande d'asile qu'après l'expiration d'un délai variable.

Selon des indications recueillies auprès de spécialistes, mais qui ne sont corroborées par aucune statistique précise, 70% des demandes d'asile adressées auprès de l'O.F.P.R.A. (Office Français de Protection des Réfugiés et Apatrides) le seraient par des clandestins. La question de la situation légale ou illégale des demandeurs d'asile présente ainsi un intérêt pratique évident dans la France de 1992. Après avoir rappelé les statistiques disponibles (I) et le régime juridique applicable à l'entrée et au séjour des demandeurs d'asile sur le territoire français (II), on décrira les mesures récemment prises par les autorités publiques pour contenir les entrées irrégulières de demandeurs d'asile (III). Ces mesures, qui ont commencé à produire un effet certain, n'ont pas dispensé les pouvoirs publics de lancer une grande opération de régularisation des déboutés du droit d'asile (IV). Obéissant à sa propre logique, la jurisprudence a consacré, au même moment, des droits nouveaux, protecteurs des demandeurs d'asile (V).

I-Les Statistiques Disponibles

Les entrées

Les entrées d'étrangers donnent lieu à un certain nombre de comptages, plus ou moins exhaustifs. L'entrée clandestine ne donne évidemment lieu à aucun dénombrement précis. L'O.F.P.R.A, établissement public placé auprès du Ministère des Affaires Étrangères et chargé de se prononcer sur la qualité de réfugié, recense seulement le nombre des demandes d'asile qui lui sont adressées. Ces demandes ont évolué comme suit au cours des dernières années:

	1985	1986	1987	1988	1989	1990	1991
Nombre de demandes d'asile	28.809	26.196	27.568	34.253	61.372	54.717	46.784
Variation	-	9.1%	+5.2%	+24.2%	+79.2%	-10.8%	-14.5%

Source: O.F.P.R.A.

Abstract:

Legal or Illegal Immigration
The Legal Situation of Asylum-Seekers in France Today

This article, written in May 1992, provides an analysis and survey of the evolution of French legislation regarding asylum seekers. In the first section, the author discusses the accuracy of the data concerning immigrant populations in France reported on the basis of those who enter the country, those who leave and those who are refused entry.

The second section canvasses those legal instruments, statutory and administrative (such as decrees and "circulaires") that are relied upon in controlling the entry and sojourn of asylum seekers in France. The author helpfully outlines how the current juridical regime developed and comments on the circumstances surrounding the introduction of various instruments in an effort to add historical context.

In section three particular emphasis is placed on a description of the new legal instruments introduced by authorities, ostensibly in an effort to control illegal entry and fraudulent practices. However, the author concludes that these efforts have had the effect of limiting an asylum seekers ability to enter the territory and of decreasing access to refugee determination procedures. The deterrent measures introduced include an increased reliance on entrance visas, detention at airports in newly created international zones, sanctions against airline and carriers who do not ensure that clients have the appropriate travel documents, and increased vigilance of illegal workers. A recent innovation of organising the return of failed refugee claimants and voluntary repatriation is also discussed.

La population concernée par la demande d'asile est naturellement supérieure à ce chiffre puisque ce dernier n'inclut pas les enfants mineurs: le rapport entre les deux est probablement inférieur à 2.

Les demandes d'asile présentées à l'O.F.P.R.A. sont, pour la plupart, rejetées: le taux d'admission des demandes (nombre de statuts accordés/ nombre de décisions prises par l'O.F.P.R.A.) s'est établi à 15,4% en 1990 et à 19,7% en 1991 et n'a pas cessé de décroître au cours des dernières années. 13.443 personnes en 1990 et 16.112 personnes en 1991 ont ainsi été admises au statut de réfugié. Les personnes dont la demande est rejetée (85% des demandeurs environ) deviennent rapidement des personnes séjournant irrégulièrement en France et sont normalement appelées à faire l'objet d'un arrêté de reconduite à la frontière ou d'une expulsion.

Les sorties

Il n'existe pas de dénombrement exhaustif des sorties d'étrangers: seules des évaluations peuvent être faites sur la base des résultats des recense-

In section four the author addresses the challenge of dealing with an increasingly large population of failed refugee claimants given the settling of the refugee claimant acceptance rate at the 15 to 20 per cent level. Essentially, the author describes how given the events of the summer of 1991, the French authorities were required to respond to an increasingly intransigent human rights advocacy community and public opinion that favoured the introduction of a procedure for reviewing exceptional cases.

In conclusion, Frédéric Tiberghien traces the recent jurisprudence that evolved while the government pursued its regulatory objectives. In sum, it is most apparent that the asylum seekers situation in France has become increasingly complex and the dilemma is aptly described in the following passage:

Between an asylum seeker illegally inside the territory who now has a temporary right to stay, the failed refugee claimant who stays irregularly in France but who cannot be returned to her/his country of origin, the failed refugee claimant whose ability to remain is regularised under the exceptional measures procedures and the asylum seeker who officially presents herself/himself at the border with the risk of being returned, we do not know which is the most desirable situation nor which is the situation that the authorities seek to encourage. However, such a confusing situation cannot last much longer given the risk of further polarizing public opinion and of reinforcing the perception of an increased tendency to reject foreigners indiscriminately.

Abstract by Veronique Lassailly-Jacob and Leanne MacMillan

ments (le dernier a eu lieu en 1990 mais n'est pas encore exploité sur ce point). Il n'est pas davantage possible d'isoler, au sein des sorties, celles qui concernent les demandeurs d'asile ou les réfugiés. On ne dispose donc que d'indications très partielles à leur sujet.

Le nombre d'expulsions d'étrangers a évolué comme suit au cours des années récentes:

	1987	1988	1989	1990
Nombre d'expulsions d'étrangers	1.746	1.235	565	383

Si ce nombre a diminué, le nombre des reconduites à la frontière d'étrangers en situation irrégulière a sensiblement augmenté ainsi qu'il ressort des chiffres ci-dessous:

	1987	1988	1989	1990
Nombre de reconduits à la frontière	15.837	15.665	14.885	18.238

Cette augmentation doit toutefois être relativisée du fait que la majorité des décisions de reconduite à la frontière ne sont pas exécutées (le taux d'exécution s'est réduit de 57,8% en 1987 à 39,4% en 1990). Ce chiffre inclut probablement un nombre important de demandeurs d'asile déboutés.

D'autres sorties concernent les étrangers qui acceptent, d'une manière ou d'une autre, une aide au retour ou à la réinsertion dans leur pays d'origine. Le bénéfice de ces aides a été appliqué aux demandeurs d'asile déboutés, à titre expérimental à partir du 1er janvier 1991, dans cinq départements français. 134 dossiers ont été déposés en quelques mois et 103 personnes étaient reparties en septembre 1991, date à laquelle le système a été étendu (cf ci-dessous).

Il ne faut pas oublier non plus la sortie *juridique* que constitue l'acquisition de la nationalité française. 65.000 étrangers en ont bénéficié en 1990 mais peu d'entre eux doivent être des réfugiés ou demandeurs d'asile.

Les refus d'entrée sur le territoire français

Les statistiques ci-dessus ne donnent aucune indication sur ce qui se passe en amont de l'entrée sur le territoire français. Un demandeur d'asile qui souhaite pénétrer sur le territoire français peut, en effet, le faire de manière clandestine ou officielle et son accès sur le territoire français peut être refusé par les services de la Police de l'Air et des Frontières (PAF). Le nombre de refus d'admission d'étrangers sur le territoire français a évolué comme suit au cours des années récentes, étant rappelé que les chiffres ci-après ne concernent pas uniquement des demandeurs d'asile:

	1986	1987	1988	1989	1990
Refus d'admission sur le territoire	51.436	71.063	66.646	68.020	65.958

Parmi ces refus d'admission, près de 20 % concernent des étrangers ayant franchi irrégulièrement la frontière et ayant été interpellés par la police en zone frontalière. En résumé, les statistiques disponibles ne permettent pas de présenter un tableau statistique précis des entrées légales ou illégales en France des demandeurs d'asile.

II-Le Régime Juridique Applicable à l'Entrée et au Séjour des Demandeurs d'Asile sur le Territoire Français

Ce régime juridique résulte des textes successifs, de valeur différente, qui ont été conçus pour répondre aux circonstances de l'époque.

A) Le premier texte important est le décret du 27 mai 1982 qui avait modifié, en application de l'article 5 de l'ordonnance du 2 novembre 1945, la liste des documents exigés des étrangers pour pouvoir pénétrer sur le territoire français. L'article 12 de ce décret prévoyait en particulier que:

> lorsque l'étranger qui se présente à la frontière demande à bénéficier du droit d'asile, la décision de refus d'entrée en France ne peut être prise que par le Ministre de l'Intérieur, après consultation du Ministre des Relations Extérieures.

Ce décret a été jugé légal par le Conseil d'État (Conseil d'État, Association France Terre d'Asile et autre, 27 septembre 1985, Req. 44.884 et 44.485). Ce texte a institué une règle de compétence qui constitue une garantie importante pour le demandeur d'asile: le refus d'entrée est décidé par le Ministre de l'Intérieur, et non pas par le service de police présent aux frontières, après consultation du Ministre des Affaires Étrangères. En pratique, il n'est pas rare que la consultation du Ministre des Affaires Étrangères se dédouble d'une consultation du HCR (Haut Commissariat des Nations-Unies pour les Réfugiés) ou de son représentant en France. La décision de refus de séjour, compte tenu de sa gravité, fait ainsi l'objet d'une procédure d'examen approfondi par au moins trois autorités: la Police de l'Air et des Frontières, le Ministre des Affaires Étrangères, le Ministre de l'Intérieur.

C'est sur la base juridique de l'article 12 du décret du 27 mai 1982 que des agents de l'O.F.P.R.A. sont également intervenus aux frontières à partir de 1991, afin de garantir la compétence des agents proposant la teneur de l'avis du Ministre des Affaires Étrangères.

B) Le deuxième texte important a été la loi du 17 juillet 1984 instituant un titre unique de séjour et de travail. L'article 15 de cette loi prévoit qu'une carte de résident, d'une validité de 10 ans, est délivrée de plein droit à l'étranger qui a obtenu le statut de réfugié. Cette carte est renouvelée de plein droit en vertu de l'article 16 de cette même loi.

C) Le régime juridique du demandeur d'asile, qui n'a pas fait l'objet d'un refus de séjour lors de son entrée en France et avant qu'il ne soit reconnu réfugié, restait emprunt d'un certain flou. Une circulaire du Premier Ministre en date du 17 mai 1985, publiée au Journal Officiel et adressée aux Commissaires de la République, a clarifié les règles applicables au séjour des demandeurs d'asile tant qu'il n'a pas été statué sur leur demande d'admission au statut de réfugié.

1) Le champ d'application de la circulaire est limité aux étrangers qui sollicitent l'asile en France, c'est-à-dire l'admission et le droit de séjourner sur le territoire, en se prévalant de la Convention de Genève du 18 juillet 1951. Elle ne traite par conséquent pas des conditions d'octroi des titres de séjour aux simples demandeurs d'asile qui ne se réclameraient pas de la Convention de Genève.

2) La circulaire confirme, de manière indiscutable et très opportune, que la reconnaissance de la qualité de réfugié et l'octroi de ce statut sont une prérogative exclusive de l'O.F.P.R.A. et de la Commission des Recours, cette dernière étant, en vertu de la jurisprudence du Conseil d'État (Section, Aldana Barrena, 8 jan. 1982, Rec. Cons. d'État, P.9), placée sur le même plan que l'O.F.P.R.A. en la matière. La procédure de détermination du statut de réfugié fixée par la loi du 25 juillet 1952 se trouve donc indiscutablement confortée.

3) La circulaire consacre la pratique libérale qui veut qu'une personne qui sollicite en France la qualité de réfugié se voit traditionnellement reconnaître un droit temporaire au séjour, jusqu'au moment où il a été statué à titre définitif sur sa demande. Sauf dans l'hypothèse où l'étranger peut faire l'objet d'une réadmission dans un pays tiers (cf. 4-c), elle affirme donc clairement que le droit reconnu à l'examen des prétentions au statut de réfugié fonde un droit au séjour provisoire. A cet effet, elle institue une procédure en deux temps, dont l'objectif est d'accélérer autant que possible la réponse aux demandes de reconnaissance de la qualité de réfugié pour que les intéressés puissent bénéficier au plus vite des droits qui y sont attachés:

a) L'étranger, qui sollicite la reconnaissance de la qualité de réfugié, se voit d'abord accorder une autorisation provisoire de séjour d'un mois *"en vue de démarches auprès de l'O.F.P.R.A.,"* en principe sans aucune condition s'il justifie d'une adresse postale. Le délai d'un mois doit être mis à profit par l'intéressé pour former sa demande d'octroi du statut de réfugié auprès de l'O.F.P.R.A.

b) S'il justifie du certificat de dépôt de sa demande délivré par l'O.F.P.R.A., l'étranger se voit alors délivrer de plein droit, lorsqu'il forme sa demande de première délivrance de carte de séjour, un récépissé portant la mention *"a sollicité l'asile"* et valant autorisation de séjour et de travail pendant trois mois. Ce récépissé est renouvelé automatiquement jusqu'à l'épuisement des voies de recours ouvertes par la procédure de détermination du statut.

c) La circulaire adopte en outre des mécanismes concrets pour permettre le bon fonctionnement du dispositif et décourager les abus. A cette fin, l'O.F.P.R.A., et la Commission des Recours portent à la connaissance des Commissaires de la République les décisions qu'ils prennent. En outre, l'O.F.P.R.A., sur la base de la fiche transmise par la préfecture dès qu'est délivrée l'autorisation provisoire d'un mois, vérifie que l'étranger n'a pas déjà présenté une demande d'admission au statut de réfugié sous une autre identité. Si tel était le cas, l'O.F.P.R.A. avertirait le Commissaire de la République qui, après une procédure d'enquête, s'abstiendrait de délivrer le récépissé valable trois mois.

4) Trois catégories de demandeurs font l'objet d'un traitement particulier au regard du droit au séjour. La circulaire traite ainsi de manière exhaustive l'ensemble des situations susceptibles de se présenter:

a) Les demandeurs d'asile admis avec un visa de long séjour, en particulier les ressortissants d'États du Sud-Est asiatique admis en France dans le cadre de procédures particulières, se voient délivrer un récépissé de demande de carte de séjour d'une validité, renouvelable, de six mois. De même, les étrangers, titulaires d'une carte de séjour en cours de validité, sont laissés en possession de leur carte et ne sont pas soumis à la procédure de droit commun.

b) Les étrangers qui font l'objet de décisions, de procédures ou de poursuites tendant à leur interdire le séjour en France seront traités de manière spécifique. Il ressort clairement de la circulaire que, dans toutes ces situations délicates: la possibilité de former une demande auprès de l'O.F.P.R.A. n'est jamais écartée mais que le gouvernement attend de l'Office une procédure d'instruction accélérée; le pouvoir d'appréciation laissé aux Commissaires de la République ne peut s'exercer que dans un sens favorable aux demandeurs, ce pouvoir d'appréciation étant évoqué au niveau de l'administration centrale dans les cas les plus difficiles.

c) Les étrangers qui proviennent en dernier lieu d'un pays susceptible de leur accorder le bénéfice de la Convention de Genève font également l'objet d'un régime particulier.

La circulaire manifeste ainsi la volonté du gouvernement de contenir autant que possible les flux de réfugiés provenant de pays tiers signataires de la Convention de Genève et susceptibles, comme le prévoit le préambule de la Convention, de partager les charges résultant d'un problème social et humanitaire de portée internationale. Elle n'interdit cependant pas par principe l'accès du territoire français aux intéressés et leur ménage, en toutes circonstances, la possibilité d'y demeurer si la réadmission n'est pas effectivement possible dans un pays tiers. Les objectifs fixés par la Convention de Genève sont donc correctement respectés.

5) Lorsque la procédure de détermination du statut s'achève par l'octroi du statut de réfugié, les Commissaires de la République doivent convoquer dans les meilleurs délais les intéressés en vue de leur délivrer la carte de résident valant titre unique de séjour et de travail ainsi que, sur demande, le titre de voyage prévu par la Convention de Genève. En attendant cette délivrance effective, le récépissé de demande de titre de séjour peut être prorogé de six mois avec indication de la mention _reconnu réfugié_.

6) Lorsque la procédure de détermination du statut s'achève par une décision de rejet, la circulaire prescrit d'assurer le départ effectif des intéressés du territoire français afin de préserver le crédit qui s'attache au statut de réfugié. Les Commissaires de la République sont invités à notifier au besoin les décisions de l'O.F.P.R.A. et de la Commission des Recours et à prescrire le départ du territoire français dans un délai d'un mois. Le récépissé valant autorisation provisoire de séjour est alors retiré au profit d'une autorisation d'une validité de quinze jours au terme de laquelle l'étranger doit justifier des dispositions prises pour organiser son départ. La circulaire ménage des possibilités de prorogation de ce document mais prévoit en définitive, au cas où l'étranger n'a pas quitté le territoire, la saisine du Procureur de la République pour infraction à l'article 15 de l'ordonnance du 2 novembre 1945.

La circulaire réserve enfin le cas des étrangers qui encourraient des risques graves en cas de retour dans le pays d'origine ou le pays de résidence. Elle prévoit dans ce cas que la décision appartient à la direction de la réglementation et du contentieux du Ministère de l'Intérieur. Dans tous les cas, les précautions sont multipliées pour que la sécurité et la dignité de l'étranger soient sauvegardées.

7) La circulaire du 17 mai 1985 s'est substituée à toutes les directives antérieures ayant le même objet. Elle a donc rendu publiques l'ensemble des règles applicables en la matière. Cette volonté de clarification à l'égard de tous était une initiative particulièrement heureuse et de nature à mettre fin aux nombreuses incertitudes qui ont pu régner jusqu'alors.

La circulaire a marqué une consolidation de la politique libérale du gouvernement français à l'égard des réfugiés. Sans aller jusqu'à reconnaître un droit automatique au séjour au profit des demandeurs du statut de réfugié, elle leur permet, en toute hypothèse, de faire examiner à fond leurs prétentions soit par l'O.F.P.R.A., soit par le pays qui a accepté leur réadmission. En contrepartie, elle se montre plus sévère à l'égard des étrangers dont la demande a été définitivement rejetée en rendant effective la reconduite à la frontière.

8) La circulaire du 17 mai 1985 a été largement complétée et amendée par la suite. Plusieurs circulaires sont en effet venues préciser quelques points qui n'avaient pas été initialement traités ou, de manière plus brutale, inverser les dispositions favorables contenues dans la circulaire du 17 mai 1985:

a) Postérieurement à 1985, le Ministre de l'Intérieur a rappelé à plusieurs reprises, par voie de circulaire, le principe selon lequel les demandeurs d'asile déboutés doivent être reconduits à la frontière (circulaire télégraphique no 85-269 du 8 novembre 1985 relative aux demandeurs d'asile; circulaire 87/0029/C du 5 août 1987 relative aux problèmes particuliers posés par l'application de la loi du 9 septembre 1986; circulaire du 5 juin 1990; circulaire 9000176C du 2 août 1990 sur les demandes d'asile présentées par des étranger faisant l'objet ou susceptibles de faire l'objet d'une mesure d'éloignement; circulaire 9100052/C du 11 mars 1991 relative au renforcement de la lutte contre l'immigration irrégulière).

Ces circulaires règlent en particulier les situations suivantes:

- la possibilité d'une régularisation exceptionnelle à titre humanitaire (circulaire du 5 août 1987);
- la possibilité de rester provisoirement sur le territoire français si le retour dans le pays d'origine risque de mettre en danger la vie de l'intéressé;
- la conduite à tenir par les services des préfectures lorsqu'un étranger forme une demande d'asile alors qu'il fait l'objet d'une mesure d'éloignement (arrêté d'expulsion, interdiction temporaire ou définitive du territoire français, arrêté de reconduite à la frontière) ou a été interpellé en situation irrégulière sur le territoire français (circulaire du 2 août 1990);
- le refus de la prorogation de l'autorisation provisoire de séjour lorsqu'un demandeur d'asile débouté forme plusieurs demandes successives d'admission au statut de réfugié sans invoquer des circonstances nouvelles devant l'O.F.P.R.A (circulaire du 11 mars 1991).

b) Les délais d'examen des demandes d'asile formées auprès de l'O.F.P.R.A. puis de la Commission des Recours ayant fortement diminué suite à l'effort de rattrapage mené en 1990 et 1991 grâce au triplement du budget des organismes de détermination du statut de réfugié, le gouvernement français fit part de son intention de supprimer l'autorisation de travail aux demandeurs d'asile. Cette mesure était présentée comme visant à dissuader les demandeurs d'asile de se présenter en France pour bénéficier d'un régime favorable et ne constituant pas un inconvénient grave pour les intéressés dans la mesure où la procédure de détermination du statut dure maintenant, en règle générale, moins de six mois. Dans un avis du 6 juin 1991, la Commission Nationale consultative des droits de l'homme, placée auprès du Premier Ministre, émit un avis défavorable au projet de suppression de l'autorisation de travail et demanda au gouvernement d'abandonner son projet. Malgré cet avis, le Premier Ministre, Madame Edith Cresson, publiait le 26 septembre 1991 une circulaire qui modifiait la circulaire émise par son prédécesseur, Laurent Fabius, le 17 mai 1985 et supprimait la délivrance automatique d'une autorisation de travail aux demandeurs d'asile, sauf pour les demandeurs entrés en France sous couvert d'un visa de long séjour.

9) Peu à peu malmenée, la circulaire du 17 mai 1985, par ailleurs, a fait l'objet d'un débat quant à sa valeur juridique. Pour les uns, signée du Premier Ministre, titulaire du pouvoir réglementaire en vertu de l'article 21 de la constitution, elle présentait un caractère réglementaire et s'imposait à l'administration. Pour les autres, simple circulaire interprétative, elle ne possédait pas un caractère réglementaire et ne pouvait être utilement invoquée par les administrés devant le juge. Ce débat vient d'être tranché récemment par le Conseil d'État dans deux importants arrêts d'Assemblée du 13 décembre 1991, qui seront commentés plus loin. A l'issue de ces arrêts, il est clair que la circulaire du 17 mai 1985 doit être considérée comme dépourvue de valeur réglementaire. Et toute la construction qui visait à organiser par ce biais un quasi *statut* du demandeur d'asile se trouve réduite à néant.

III-De Nouvelles Mesures Dissuasives à l'Égard de la Demande d'Asile

Après un certain nombre d'atermoiements, la politique du gouvernement français est devenue beaucoup moins favorable aux demandeurs d'asile et un tournant a manifestement été pris pendant l'été 1991. Outre les mesures déjà mentionnées ci-dessus, de très nombreuses dispositions sont intervenues pour décourager les demandeurs d'asile de se présenter aux frontières françaises et réprimer plus sévèrement les entrées illégales de demandeurs d'asile.

La délivrance des visas

Après la décision prise en 1986—suite aux attentats terroristes qui ont ensanglanté Paris de rétablir l'exigence du visa pour pénétrer sur le territoire français, des efforts ont été conduits pour rendre plus stricte la délivrance des visas. L'utilisation de l'informatique s'est développée, permettant de mieux contrôler les entrées aux frontières. Par ailleurs, a été institué le 26 juillet 1991 un visa de transit, applicable aux passagers en provenance d'une dizaine de pays pour lesquels des fraudes ont été constatées dans le passé, pour empêcher les intéressés de profiter d'une escale dans un aéroport pour y demander l'asile ou choisir la clandestinité. Cette mesure a été complétée par des contrôles sur la passerelle des avions en vue de prévenir le débarquement des étrangers ayant détruit leurs papiers d'identité durant le vol.

La rétention en zone internationale des aéroports

Afin de lutter contre des demandes jugées abusives d'asile à la frontière et d'effectuer un premier tri parmi les demandeurs, les autorités de police ont pris l'habitude de maintenir pour des durées parfois assez longues (allant jusqu'à quatre ou cinq semaines) en zone internationale des aéroports des étrangers ayant sollicité l'asile. A l'été 1991, il a été décidé de faire intervenir dans ce cadre des agents de l'O.F.P.R.A., connaissant bien la situation dans les pays d'origine et susceptibles de donner un avis éclairé au Ministre de l'Intérieur sur les refus d'admission sur le territoire français (cf plus haut). Les avis émis par les agents de l'O.F.P.R.A. ont été généralement suivis.

Deux difficultés n'ont cependant pas été résolues. La première est relative à la présence d'associations humanitaires en zone internationale des aéroports. Malgré de longues discussions avec les pouvoirs publics, aucune association n'a pu s'y faire admettre, ceux-ci étant très réticents à confier la responsabilité de l'accompagnement dans les aéroports aux associations humanitaires.

La seconde difficulté non résolue concerne le statut de la zone internationale. Mis en cause, par les organisations non gouvernementales (ONG) et par un certain nombre d'étrangers retenus contre leur gré en zone internationale, le Ministre de l'Intérieur n'a eu de cesse de faire voter par le Parlement un texte de loi permettant de couvrir les agissements de ses agents. Un amendement *Marchand* (du nom du Ministre de l'Intérieur), légalisant la rétention de longue durée en zone internationale, a été ainsi passé en force devant le Parlement début 1992. Devant le tollé provoqué par cet amendement, sur la forme autant que sur le fond, le Premier Ministre dut promettre de saisir le Conseil Constitutionnel pour faire vérifier la conformité du texte à la constitution. Par une décision du 25 février 1992, le Conseil Constitutionnel a admis le principe du maintien en zone internationale mais en critiqua les modalités, en particulier la durée excessive de ce maintien (jusqu'à 30 jours). Sitôt connue la décision du Conseil Constitutionnel invalidant l'article 8 de la loi du 26 février 1992, le Ministre de l'Intérieur mit en chantier un nouveau projet de loi sur la zone de transit des ports et aéroports.

Ce projet prévoit un maintien provisoire en zone de transit des ports et aéroports pouvant aller jusqu'à vingt quatre jours ainsi qu'un certain nombre de garanties exigées par le Conseil Constitutionnel (intervention du juge judiciaire avant un délai de quatre jours...). Le 30 mars 1992, saisie par le Premier Ministre, la Commission nationale consultative des droits de l'homme émit un avis nuancé en 5 points sur le projet de loi:

- en cas de demande d'asile à la frontière, l'accès au territoire ne peut être refusé que si la demande est manifestement infondée (terme repris de la décision du Conseil Constitutionnel du 25 février 1992) et il n'appartient pas à l'autorité de police de se livrer à un quelconque autre contrôle;
- le délai maximum de maintien en zone de transit fixé à vingt quatre jours est excessif (un délai de 7 jours paraissant suffisant à la Commission Consultative);
- l'intervention du juge judiciaire n'est pas définie avec une précision suffisante (le contrôle du refus d'admission sur le territoire relevant du juge administratif);
- la loi devrait prévoir une voie de recours effective (au sens de l'article 13 de la Convention européenne de sauvegarde des droits de l'homme) contre les décisions de refus d'admission sur le territoire français, c'est-à-dire un recours suspensif d'exécution devant le tribunal administratif analogue à celui qui est ouvert aux étrangers faisant l'objet d'un arrêté de reconduite à la frontière;
- les associations humanitaires devraient avoir accès à la zone de transit et être habilitées à entrer en contact avec les personnes qui y sont maintenues pour leur apporter l'aide matérielle et juridique qu'elles sollicitent et dont elles ont besoin.

Ce projet de loi devrait normalement être discuté au cours de la prochaine session parlementaire (avril-juin 1992).

Pendant que se préparait ce nouveau projet de loi, une décision du juge judiciaire est venue rajouter un élément de poids à ce débat. En effet, saisi par six demandeurs d'asile qui avaient été retenus dans la zone de transit de l'aéroport de Roissy, le Tribunal de Grande Instance de Paris, par trois jugements du 25 mars 1992, a condamné l'État français à 33.000 francs de dommages et intérêts aux plaignants en estimant qu'ils avaient été victimes d'une voie de fait (atteinte grave à la liberté). Selon le tribunal de grande instance, le maintien en zone de transit:

en raison du degré de contrainte qu'il revêt et de sa durée laquelle n'est fixée par aucun texte et dépend de la seule décision de l'administration, sans le moindre contrôle judiciaire—a pour conséquence d'affecter la liberté individuelle de la personne qui en fait l'objet.

Ce jugement souligne ainsi le vide juridique existant à l'heure actuelle: faute d'une loi définissant l'étendue des pouvoirs de l'administration et l'étendue du contrôle du juge, les demandeurs d'asile sont livrés, en zone de transit des ports et aéroports, à l'arbitraire le plus total des services de police. Ceux-ci pouvant craindre de voir leur responsabilité mise en cause à tout moment, on comprend l'empressement mis, souvent de manière maladroite, par le Ministre de l'Intérieur à trouver une solution, si mauvaise fût-elle.

La question des modalités de l'examen des demandes d'admission sur le territoire français en vue d'y solliciter l'asile reste donc d'une brûlante actualité et n'a pas encore trouvé sa réponse définitive.

Les sanctions infligées aux transporteurs

Afin de limiter les entrées irrégulières de demandeurs d'asile, la France, à l'instar de nombreux autres pays européens, a introduit dans son droit interne des dispositions permettant de sanctionner les transporteurs qui auraient facilité l'entrée d'étrangers non munis des documents nécessaires et de leur imposer le réacheminement des intéressés vers leur pays d'origine.

Pour édicter ces mesures, la France a profité de l'occasion que lui offrait la ratification de la Convention du 19 juin 1990 d'application de l'accord de Schengen du 14 juin 1985 portant suppression graduelle des contrôles aux frontières. Cette Convention imposant aux signataires de prendre un certain nombre de mesures (l'article 26 en particulier en ce qui concerne les sanctions contre les transporteurs), le gouvernement français déposa fin 1991 un projet de loi portant modification de l'ordonnance du 2 novembre 1945 relative aux conditions d'entrée et de séjour des étrangers en France. La loi, adoptée fin janvier 1992 et jugée conforme à la constitution par le Conseil Constitutionnel par une décision du 25 février 1992 à l'exception de l'article 8 déjà mentionné, comporte trois articles spécifiques (articles 3, 4 et 7) qui établissent un système complet de sanctions à l'égard des transporteurs. L'enjeu n'est pas négligeable, les compagnies aériennes acheminant chaque année en France plus de 7.000 personnes dépourvues de documents de voyage ou de visas.

La nouvelle loi met à la charge des transporteurs les frais de garde des passagers non admis entre le moment où le refus d'admission est prononcé et le moment où devient effectif le réacheminement des intéressés (il n'y a pas de prise en charge de la garde durant l'instruction de la demande d'asile).

Une amende administrative d'un montant de 10.000 francs par passager transporté est également prévue. Cette amende peut être contestée devant le juge administratif. Elle n'est pas infligée lorsque l'étranger non ressortissant d'un État de la CEE qui demande l'asile à la frontière française est admis à cet effet sur le territoire français ou lorsque sa demande n'était pas manifestement infondée. Cette dernière notion, que le Conseil Constitutionnel a faite sienne, n'est pas d'une interprétation aisée et donnera lieu, à n'en pas douter, à de sérieuses difficultés d'application par l'administration. Quoiqu'il en soit, ce système d'amendes constituera pour les demandeurs d'asile une dissuasion supplémentaire de chercher refuge en France. *La forteresse Europe* s'édifie ainsi à un rythme soutenu.

Le renforcement de la lutte contre le travail clandestin

Au second semestre 1991, le gouvernement a fait voter par le Parlement un projet de loi accentuant la répression contre les trafics de main-d'oeuvre et le travail clandestin et contre l'organisation de l'entrée et du séjour irrégulier d'étrangers en France. Bien que les mesures ne soient pas dirigées contre les demandeurs d'asile et visent à lutter par tous les moyens contre l'immigration clandestine, elles ne pourront pas ne pas les affecter d'une manière ou d'une autre.

L'organisation du retour au pays d'origine

Une autre innovation de la période récente a consisté à mieux organiser le retour au pays d'origine des étrangers et des demandeurs d'asile déboutés.

1) Une première action expérimentale de rapatriement volontaire a été menée à compter du 1er janvier 1991 dans cinq département français. Les bénéficiaires de cette aide étaient notamment les déboutés d'une demande d'asile postérieurement au 1er janvier 1991 ainsi que les déboutés antérieurs qui s'étaient irrégulièrement maintenus sur le territoire français. L'aide comportait la prise en charge des frais de voyage, une allocation de 1.000 francs par adulte et une assistance administrative. En mai 1991, il fut décidé de prolonger cette expérience et de l'étendre à cinq nouveaux départements. 134 dossiers ont été déposés et 121 acceptés. Ces dossiers ont donné lieu à 103 départs effectifs.

2) L'action expérimentale a été interrompue et remplacée par un programme d'aide à la réinsertion des étrangers invités à quitter le territoire français. Ce programme représente une alternative à la reconduite à la frontière. Les bénéficiaires sont en effet les étrangers qui ont fait l'objet

d'une décision de refus de délivrance ou de renouvellement d'un titre de séjour ou d'une décision définitive de rejet de l'O.F.P.R.A. ou de la Commission de Recours des réfugiés et qui sont invités à quitter le territoire français dans le délai d'un mois sous peine de faire l'objet d'un arrêté de reconduite à la frontière ou de poursuites judiciaires pour séjour irrégulier. Les demandeurs d'asile déboutés, qui n'auront pas pu bénéficier de la régularisation exceptionnelle prévue par la circulaire du 23 juillet 1991, figurent parmi les premiers bénéficiaires de ce programme. La demande de réinsertion aidée doit être spontanée et autonome; elle doit être déposée dans le délai d'un mois suivant l'invitation à quitter le territoire français auprès de l'Office des Migrations Internationales (O.M.I.).

L'aide comporte, d'après les règles fixées par la circulaire du Ministre de l'Intérieur et du Ministre des Affaires Sociales en date du 14 août 1991:

- un entretien permettant de dresser un diagnostic professionnel et familial;
- la prise en charge des frais de voyage pour l'intéressé et sa famille;
- l'attribution d'une allocation de 1.000 francs à chaque membre majeur de la famille repartant;
- une assistance administrative en France pour organiser le départ (vente de mobilier, recouvrement de créances ou de cautions, clôture des comptes bancaires...).

Le départ doit intervenir dans le délai d'un mois suivant l'adhésion au programme. Mis en application à compter du 1er septembre 1991, le programme est encore trop récent pour qu'il soit possible d'en dresser le bilan. Fin février 1992, 907 candidatures avaient été reçues à l'O.M.I., 821 ont été acceptées, se traduisant par 659 départs.

3) En complément de ces programmes d'aide à la réinsertion, des mesures ont été prises pour reconduire effectivement à la frontière les délinquants de nationalité étrangère. Une circulaire du Garde des Sceaux en date du 23 octobre 1991 adressée aux membres du parquet donne à ceux-ci des consignes très précises pour que des poursuites pénales soient engagées à l'encontre des demandeurs d'asile qui, entrés irrégulièrement en France, auraient commis d'autres infractions de nature criminelle ou correctionnelle. Ces dispositions sont notamment applicables aux étrangers en situation irrégulière qui forment tardivement une demande d'asile (un délai supérieur à deux mois après l'entrée en France est considéré comme tardif), sans faire état de circonstances particulières pour justifier cette tardiveté. Dans un tel cas, le préfet pourra prendre un arrêté de reconduite à la frontière même si son exécution est suspendue jusqu'à la décision de l'O.F.P.R.A.

Des consignes sont également données pour poursuivre systématique-
ment les demandeurs d'asile qui forment plusieurs demandes sous des
identités distinctes ou produisent de faux documents pour tenter d'établir
leur prétendue qualité de réfugié. D'ailleurs, une circulaire antérieure du 16
juillet 1991, prise par le Ministre de l'Intérieur et relative aux suites à donner
aux demandes d'asile multiples recommandait déjà de prendre un arrêté de
reconduite à la frontière à l'égard des fraudeurs et d'engager à leur encontre
des poursuites pénales.

Comme on peut le constater, la plupart des mesures ci-dessus, qui
s'inspirent de la volonté de lutter contre un détournement de la procédure
de l'asile et contre la fraude, se traduisent plus ou moins par une restriction
des possibilités d'accès à la procédure. Et le résultat recherché est probablement en passe d'être atteint: le nombre des demandes adressées à l'O.F.P.R.A
diminue depuis deux ans.

IV-La Régularisation de la Situation des Déboutés

A la suite du renforcement considérable des moyens matériels et humains
des organismes de détermination du statut, le stock des dossiers en instance
a rapidement décru. Le taux d'admission au statut de réfugié s'étant par
ailleurs stabilisé entre 15 et 20 %, le problème des *déboutés* du droit d'asile
s'est récemment posé avec une acuité grandissante: d'une part au sujet des
nouvelles demandes faisant l'objet d'un rejet rapide (et pour lesquelles la
reconduite à la frontière devrait être l'issue normale), d'autre part pour les
demandeurs d'asile dont le dossier avait mis plusieurs années avant d'être
examiné.

Un mouvement assez déterminé de soutien aux déboutés s'étant dessiné
pendant l'été 1991 dans l'opinion publique française (grèves de la faim,
manifestations de soutien en province...), le gouvernement français désigna
un médiateur et, à l'issue d'un rapide examen de la situation, décida
d'ouvrir une procédure de régularisation exceptionnelle pour une partie
des intéressés.

L'opération s'est traduite par l'édiction de plusieurs circulaires portant
des dates rapprochées, qui témoignent de l'évolution rapide de la position
du gouvernement:

- une circulaire du Garde des Sceaux en date du 18 juin 1991,
  faisant suite aux instructions du Ministre de l'Intérieur du 31
  mai 1991 suspendant la prise ou la mise à exécution de décisions
  d'éloignement du territoire des étrangers entrés en France avant
  le 1er janvier 1990, ordonnant au parquet de suspendre les
  poursuites pénales à l'encontre des étrangers réunissant les

conditions qu'elle précise et de différer l'exécution des décisions judiciaires d'éloignement prononcées à l'encontre des intéressés;

- une lettre conjointe du Ministre des Affaires Sociales et du Ministre de l'Intérieur en date du 16 juillet 1991, adressée aux préfets, prévoyant une mesure exceptionnelle de régularisation en faveur des demandeurs d'asile déboutés dont la durée de procédure a été égale ou supérieure à trois années et dont le dossier de demande d'asile a été déposé avant le 1er janvier 1989, sous réserve qu'ils n'aient pas troublé l'ordre public;

- une circulaire conjointe du Ministre de l'Intérieur et du Ministre des Affaires Sociales en date du 23 juillet 1991 décrivant les opérations de régularisation concernant les demandeurs d'asile déboutés;

- une nouvelle circulaire des mêmes Ministres en date du 25 septembre 1991 complétant les directives données par la circulaire du 23 juillet 1991.

La procédure d'admission exceptionnelle au séjour et au travail s'adresse aux personnes entrées en France avant le 1er janvier 1989 (l'autorisation provisoire de séjour *"en vue de démarches auprès de l'O.F.P.R.A."* fait foi de la date d'entrée) et à l'égard desquelles la durée de la procédure d'examen de la demande d'asile a excédé trois ans ou deux ans en cas d'attaches familiales en France. Il est à noter que les demandeurs d'asile exclus du bénéfice de la Convention de Genève en application de son article 1er F, ne peuvent pas bénéficier de cette mesure exceptionnelle. Les personnes susceptibles d'être régularisées doivent faire la preuve de leur insertion professionnelle, cette dernière étant normalement établie par la production de bulletins de salaire et d'un contrat de travail d'une durée minimale d'un an.

Les demandes de régularisation devaient être adressées aux préfectures avant le 30 novembre 1991, dernier délai. En cas de régularisation, les intéressés sont mis en possession d'un récépissé de demande de séjour, dans l'attente de la délivrance du titre définitif. En cas de rejet de la demande de régularisation, le débouté est normalement invité à quitter le territoire français et fait l'objet d'un arrêté de reconduite à la frontière s'il n'a pas déféré sous un mois à l'invitation à quitter le territoire. 51.356 demandes de régularisation ont été déposées avant le 30 novembre 1991. Ces demandes ont donné lieu aux décisions suivantes, sachant qu'il restait encore 13.467 dossiers en instance fin février 1992: 8.323 irrecevabilités, 11.191 admissions, 18.375 rejets.

Le nombre des demandes adressées aux préfectures fin 1991 atteste de l'importance quantitative du nombre des déboutés en situation irrégulière à cette date. Une partie des intéressés ayant sans doute préféré rester dans la clandestinité, on peut penser que le nombre réel des déboutés en situation irrégulière était probablement supérieur à celui des déboutés qui ont accepté les risques de la procédure de régularisation. Le nombre de déboutés en situation irrégulière serait d'environ 120.000 aujourd'hui. Cette opération, d'un genre et d'une portée totalement nouveaux, a été justifiée par des considérations humanitaires tirées de l'insertion professionnelle des intéressés. En réalité, le gouvernement ne pouvait pas admettre officiellement que la procédure d'examen des demandes d'asile avait été plus ou moins bâclée pendant la période de résorption des stocks en attente de décision et a été conduit à choisir une voie qui ne remettrait en cause ni les décisions négatives de l'O.F.P.R.A., ni l'autorité de la clause jugée par la Commission des Recours. Après la régularisation exceptionnelle d'un peu plus de 100.000 étrangers en 1982, l'opération de régularisation menée en 1992 en faveur des déboutés confirme s'il en était besoin la difficulté d'un verrouillage efficace des frontières et la nécessité, à intervalles plus ou moins éloignés, de ramener dans la légalité une fraction de ceux qui sont entrés illégalement sur le territoire français.

V-L'Évolution Récente de la Jurisprudence

Pendant que le gouvernement durcissait les textes et lançait une vaste opération de régularisation exceptionnelle, il revenait au juge de se montrer plus souple sur quelques points fondamentaux.

1) En premier lieu, le Conseil d'État a jugé par deux décisions d'Assemblée, rendues conformément aux conclusions de son Commissaire du Gouvernement, que les étrangers faisant l'objet d'une mesure d'éloignement du territoire français pourraient désormais se prévaloir des stipulations de l'article 8 de la Convention européenne de sauvegarde des droits de l'homme (Conseil d'État, Assemblée, Belacen, 19 avril 1991 ; Mme Babas, 19 avril 1991 ; L'Actualité Juridique Droit Administration, 1991 p.551, note F. Julien Laferrière ; Les Petites Affiches, 8 juillet 1991, note M. Reydellet). Selon cet article 8:

> 1. Toute personne a droit au respect de sa vie privée et familiale, de son domicile et de sa correspondance; 2. Il ne peut y avoir ingérence d'une autorité publique dans l'exercice de ce droit que pour autant que cette ingérence est prévue par la loi et qu'elle constitue une mesure qui, dans une société démocratique, est nécessaire à la sécurité nationale, à la sûreté publique, au bien-être économique du pays, à la défense de l'ordre et à la prévention des infractions pénales, à la protection de la santé ou de la morale, ou à la protection des droits et libertés d'autrui.

Il s'agit en l'occurrence d'un renversement de jurisprudence, le Conseil d'État ayant antérieurement jugé qu'un étranger ne pouvait utilement se prévaloir de cet article pour contester un arrêté d'expulsion (Conseil d'État, Touami ben Abdeslem, Rec. Lebon, tables p.820; JurisClasseur Périodique, 1981, II, 19613, note Pacteau). En opérant ce renversement de jurisprudence, le Conseil d'État français s'aligne sur la jurisprudence de la Commission européenne des droits de l'homme qui faisait, depuis plus de vingt ans, le lien entre l'expulsion et le droit à une vie familiale. Il offre aussi une protection complémentaire aux étrangers qui peuvent désormais contester les mesures d'éloignement sur le fondement de la loi interne (ordonnance du 2 novembre 1945) et sur celui de la Convention européenne des droits de l'homme. Le second fondement est intéressant dans la mesure où il conduit le Conseil d'État à exercer un contrôle de proportionnalité sur la décision qui lui est déférée et non pas simplement un contrôle minimum, qui est le contrôle généralement exercé par le juge administratif sur les mesures de haute police.

La solution adoptée par le Conseil d'État vaut pour les arrêtés d'expulsion (qui interdisent le retour en France tant qu'ils n'ont pas été rapportés) comme pour les décisions de reconduite à la frontière (qui n'interdisent pas à l'étranger de se présenter de nouveau à la frontière muni des documents nécessaires à son entrée en France). L'atteinte à la vie familiale est cependant beaucoup plus difficile à justifier dans le cas d'une reconduite à la frontière *"eu égard aux effets d'une mesure de reconduite à la frontière"* comme le souligne le Conseil d'État dans l'affaire Mme Babas (déjà mentionné précédemment). Cependant, la jurisprudence ultérieure confirme que l'article 8 de la Convention peut fonder une annulation effective d'un arrêté de reconduite à la frontière (L'Actualité Juridique Droit Administration, 1991, p.695, chronique générale de jurisprudence). Cette nouvelle protection ouverte aux étrangers et aux demandeurs d'asile par l'article 8 de la Convention européenne des droits de l'homme s'ajoute aux protections reconnues par une jurisprudence encore récente:

- lorsque l'administration décide d'expulser un étranger à qui la qualité de réfugié a été refusée, elle ne peut pas expulser cet étranger sur les frontières d'un pays où sa vie ou sa liberté seraient mises en danger (Conseil d'État, Assemblée Buayi, 6 novembre 1987, Documentation Réfugié no 25, chronique F. Tiberghien);
- lorsque l'administration décide de reconduire un étranger à la frontière, elle doit apprécier si la mesure envisagée n'est pas de nature à comporter pour la situation personnelle et familiale de l'intéressé des conséquences d'une exceptionnelle gravité (Conseil d'État, Assemblée, Préfet du Doubs C/Mme Olmos Quintero et Imambaccus, Rec. Lebon p. 184 et 182, A.J.D.A 1190, p. 709, chronique de jurisprudence administrative française).

L'intérêt majeur des arrêts d'Assemblée du 19 avril 1991 réside cependant ailleurs pour les demandeurs d'asile ou les déboutés du droit d'asile. En effet, la Convention européenne de sauvegarde des droits de l'homme comporte également un article 3 ainsi rédigé *"Nul ne peut être soumis à la torture ni à des peines ou traitements inhumains ou dégradants."* Si l'article 8 de la Convention européenne peut être invoqué par les étrangers victimes d'une mesure d'éloignement prise par l'administration, n'en va-t-il pas de même pour l'article 3 de la même Convention ?

Dans ces conditions, cet article ne peut-il pas être invoqué par les déboutés du droit d'asile pour éviter un renvoi dans leur pays d'origine ? Si le Conseil d'État n'a pas encore eu l'occasion de trancher ce point, le Ministre de l'Intérieur l'a fait dans une circulaire no 91.232.C du 25 octobre 1991 qui décrit les conséquences à tirer de la jurisprudence du Conseil d'État du 19 avril 1991 quant à l'éloignement des étrangers. Selon le Ministre de l'Intérieur, le respect des prescriptions de l'article 3:

> s'impose à l'autorité administrative lorsqu'elle envisage de mettre à exécution une mesure d'éloignement prise à l'encontre d'un étranger, à destination d'un pays déterminé... Le respect de l'article 3 de la Convention européenne s'impose même lorsque l'étranger concerné n'a pas le statut de réfugié et n'est donc pas protégé par l'article 33 de la Convention de Genève du 28 juillet 1991 qui prohibe le renvoi des réfugiés vers les frontières du pays où ils craignent pour leur vie ou leurs libertés.

La circulaire invite donc les préfets à prendre toutes garanties à cet égard et fixe les règles d'information préalable de l'étranger susceptible d'être reconduit à la frontière. On le constate au rappel de ces quelques arrêts d'Assemblée du Conseil d'État: c'est essentiellement par la voie jurisprudentielle, au moment où la loi et les pratiques administratives se durcissent, que se fixent les garanties applicables aux demandeurs d'asile.

2) En deuxième lieu, le Conseil d'État vient de consacrer par deux nouveaux arrêts d'Assemblée du 13 décembre 1991 (NKodia et Préfet de l'Hérault C/Dakoury) le droit pour un demandeur d'asile à se maintenir sur le territoire français jusqu'à l'épuisement de la procédure de détermination du statut de réfugié, c'est-à-dire jusqu'à l'intervention de la décision de la Commission des Recours des réfugiés. Se fondant sur les stipulations de l'article 31-2 de la Convention de Genève, le Conseil d'État juge que:

> ces dispositions impliquent nécessairement que l'étranger qui sollicite la reconnaissance de la qualité de réfugié soit autorisé à demeurer provisoirement sur le territoire jusqu'à ce qu'il ait été statué sur sa demande.

C'est la seconde fois que le Conseil d'État se fonde sur la Convention de Genève pour *"découvrir"* un principe général du droit (Conseil d'État, Assemblée, Bereciartua Echarri, Documentation Réfugiés no 37, p 1, chronique F. Tiberghien).

Ce principe se traduit par une avancée importante pour les demandeurs d'asile, y compris ceux qui sont entrés clandestinement en France: les intéressés bénéficient désormais d'un véritable droit au séjour provisoire jusqu'à ce qu'il soit statué sur leur demande de reconnaissance de la qualité de réfugié. Le paradoxe de cette importante décision d'Assemblée est que le Conseil d'État, en fondant sa décision sur un principe général du droit, a écarté par là-même l'application de la circulaire déjà mentionnée du Premier Ministre en date du 17 mai 1985 qui fixait les droits des demandeurs d'asile pendant la durée de la procédure.

Suivant son commissaire du gouvernement, le Conseil d'État a implicitement jugé que cette circulaire était illégale à un double titre et dépourvue de tout caractère réglementaire. La contrepartie de cette décision d'Assemblée est ainsi d'accroître la précarité de la situation juridique des demandeurs d'asile sur tous les points qui étaient réglés par la circulaire.

Il est encore trop tôt pour tirer toutes les conséquences des arrêts d'Assemblée du 13 décembre 1991: le principe du droit au séjour provisoire pour les demandeurs d'asile comporte-t-il le droit d'entrée sur le territoire français et l'accès au séjour provisoire pour tous les demandeurs d'asile qui se présentent à la frontière ? La réponse est apparemment négative et l'on a vu plus haut que le décret du 27 mai 1982 et l'amendement *"Marchand"* de début 1992 permettent précisément à la police de l'air et des frontières d'opérer, en amont de l'entrée sur le territoire, un véritable tri parmi les candidats à l'asile: les uns sont autorisés à entrer sur le territoire français pour y demander l'asile, les autres se voient refuser cet accès.

La solution dégagée par le Conseil d'État n'est, quoi qu'il en soit, pas très satisfaisante pour les pouvoirs publics car elle confère une véritable prime à la clandestinité: l'étranger qui entre clandestinement en France pour y demander l'asile bénéficie d'un droit au séjour provisoire tandis que celui qui arrive officiellement par un port ou un aéroport risque de se faire refouler aux frontières par la police...

L'arrêt du Conseil d'État pose par ailleurs une autre question, analogue à celle qui a été soulevée au sujet de la Convention européenne des droits de l'homme: à partir du moment où le Conseil d'État se fonde sur l'article 31-2 de la Convention de Genève pour reconnaître un droit provisoire au séjour en faveur des demandeurs d'asile, n'est-ce-pas du même coup l'ensemble de la Convention de Genève qui leur devient applicable?

Au total, on ne peut manquer de relever un autre paradoxe dans l'évolution récente de la législation et de la jurisprudence: alors que les textes les plus récents, européens (Convention de Schengen, etc...) et nationaux, se font plus restrictifs à l'égard des demandeurs d'asile, la Commission européenne des droits de l'Homme et le Conseil d'État exploitent à fond les virtualités, à l'époque insoupçonnées, des Conventions adoptées bien avant le traité de Rome de 1957 pour tenter de contrecarrer les tendances qui poussent inexorablement en direction d'une Europe *forteresse* à l'égard des étrangers et demandeurs d'asile.

Conclusion

Comme on peut le constater à la lueur des éléments rappelés ci-dessus, la situation des demandeurs d'asile est, depuis quelques années, devenue extrêmement complexe et fluctuante en France. Après avoir tenté de définir au début des années 1980 un statut juridique pour le demandeur d'asile et de limiter la pression des demandeurs d'asile aux frontières, le gouvernement à dû faire face à la croissance du nombre des clandestins et des déboutés du droit d'asile et intégrer les conséquences de la libre circulation des personnes à l'intérieur de la CEE à partir de 1993. Le cadre juridique précédemment élaboré s'est vite avéré insuffisant et craque de toutes parts. Les textes se succèdent et se superposent, la jurisprudence tente vaille que vaille de combler leurs lacunes ou d'atténuer leurs excès; plus personne ne maîtrise vraiment la matière et une grande confusion s'est instaurée.

Si les chiffres les plus récents laissent penser que la pression des demandeurs d'asile aux frontières diminue, les catégories anciennes reposant sur une distinction entre immigrants légaux et illégaux et sur une différence de traitement juridique entre ces deux situations, perdent de leur pertinence et de leur clarté. Entre le demandeur d'asile clandestin qui a désormais un droit provisoire au séjour, le débouté du droit d'asile qui séjourne irrégulièrement en France mais ne peut pas être renvoyé vers son pays d'origine, le débouté dont la situation au regard du séjour est régularisée à titre exceptionnel et le demandeur d'asile qui se présente officiellement aux frontières avec le risque d'être refoulé, on ne sait pas quelle est la situation la plus enviable ni celle que les pouvoirs publics cherchent à encourager. Une telle situation de confusion ne pourra pas durer longtemps, au risque d'indisposer profondément l'opinion publique et de renforcer une tendance évidente au rejet indistinct de l'étranger.

Frédéric Tiberghien is French. Graduated in Economic Science, Political Science and Philosophy, he is also a former student of the famous "Ecole Nationale d'Administration" of Paris. Maître des Requêtes au Conseil d'Etat, he is currently Président Directeur Général de l'Entreprise Générale de Télécommunications, Paris, France. He is a member of the administrative council of France Terre d'Asile, President of the association "Documentation Réfugiés" and vice-president of the UNHCR French Committee. He published a book in 1984 entitled "La protection des réfugiés en France" (Ed. Economica et Presses Universitaires d'Aix en Provence, second edition in 1988). He is also a co-editor of "Les réfugiés dans le monde," La documentation Française, Problèmes politiques et sociaux, no 699, 1993.

PART FOUR

Case Studies in Australia and the United States

10

New Issues in Migration: Case Study—Australia

Lois Foster

Introduction

Australia is recognized internationally as an immigrant-receiving country and a substantial haven for refugees. This is significant on at least two grounds. First, Australia is one of only a small number of countries that have official proactive policies for population building by means of permanent settlement of immigrants and refugees, who then are entitled to citizenship status.[1] Second, a high proportion of immigrants and refugees, relative to the Australian population, continue to be absorbed annually (approximately 55,000 and 172,000 each year in the past decade).[2] This number is dwarfed by the movement into and out of Australia by foreign-born temporary entrants and temporary movements of Australian residents for holiday, education and work-related travel, which totalled in excess of nine million in 1991.[3]

By 1991, about 22 percent of the Australian population was born overseas,[4] a direct and intended legacy of the postwar immigration program. An unintended consequence has been the high level of ethnic diversification—immigrants and refugees have come from more than one hundred countries and speak about eighty different languages. That this is "a good thing" is the conventional wisdom, crystallized in the words of Kalantzis et al.,[5] "one of the world's most homogeneous societies, culturally insular and racist, has been peacefully transformed into one of the most diverse." Aboriginal Australians may not accept this interpretation so readily.

The genesis of white Australia has been at the expense of the indigenous Aboriginal population. They were ruthlessly pushed aside, their lands seized without compensation and their numbers and culture decimated.[6] Nonetheless, the late twentieth century has seen not only a persistence of the Aboriginal presence against all odds but also a revival in Aboriginal identity among urban Aborigines and the politicization of the debate over rights for tribal and urban Aboriginal people. The issue of recognition of indigenous people by some formal structure of reconciliation was placed on the national agenda by the federal Labor government under R.J. Hawke in 1988, although as yet no resolution has been achieved. The Aboriginal perspective, usually ignored by white Australia, is indifferent if not hostile to policies of continued immigration and multiculturalism.

Legal immigration has played a salient role in the building of the Australian nation and has been actively encouraged throughout most of its history. Indeed, more than six million people have migrated to Australia since British settlement in 1788.[7] Almost without a break, a planned government-controlled immigration program has been maintained and legitimated by (admittedly fluctuating) support from the major political parties, business, unions and the Australian people.[8] The ideology promoted by successive Australian governments has as a central motif the idea that immigration is a process leading to permanent residence and hence citizenship.[9] This stance has been reflected in legally- and legislatively-based policies, regulations and programs for immigration and settlement with the cooperation of the voluntary nongovernment sector, including the churches, welfare and service agencies and with, to some commentators,[10] the co-option of ethnic communities themselves, particularly those from non-English-speaking backgrounds. Australian governments have set themselves firmly against guest-worker programs of the European kind, although temporary migration is a legitimate element of immigration policy.[11]

That many immigrants have followed a different agenda is evidenced by resistance to assimilation in Australian society,[12] the preservation of languages and cultures different from the dominant anglophone forms;[13] considerable return migration, even to the present day,[14] and a reluctance to take out Australian citizenship.[15] The first two aspects have been of continuing concern to governments and have been addressed by human rights, multiculturalism and language policies.[16] A concerted drive on citizenship was conducted in 1989 as an aftermath of the 1988 Bicentenary. As well, there has been a steady reduction in the qualifying period and criteria (for example, level of English-language competence) for citizenship to encourage applications. On the other hand, little official attention has been paid to emigration, although, as Moore[17] explains, additional inducements have entailed allowing long-term residents with citizenship status to return to countries of origin for periods up to three years without incurring any penalty. After prolonged absence from Australia, those without citizenship risk having to reapply to migrate. In general, except during wartime, Australian governments do not control the permanent departure of residents.

Until relatively recently, the issue of illegal immigration has not attracted serious attention or concern. Australia's lack of shared territorial borders, location in a less populous hemisphere and strict entry procedures (including a virtually universal visa system, provision for deportation of unauthorized entrants and prohibited noncitizens, and offshore application for migration) have made it difficult for the undocumented to even reach Australia. In the past, few avenues for asylum seekers, apart from Ministerial discretion, were available. As a consequence, illegal immigrants have tended to be "overstayers" on student and tourist visas rather than bona fide asylum seekers, although this situation has begun to change in the 1990s. In economically buoyant times, illegal immigrants have melted into the Australian workforce and society in general. In many cases, bureaucrats and employers, who are looking for docile workers, have turned a blind eye to illegal immigrants.

The remainder of the paper surveys the political and legal norms, domestic and international, regarding immigration to Australia. The case study will be organized by reviewing major trends and issues. Although it is necessary to span the entire post-World War II period to identify the roots of the present situation, the aim is not to provide extensive detail but to analyse and explain key features of the Australian experience. The radical amendments to the Migration Act 1958, proposed in 1989 and continued since that time, mark the most recent turning-point in Australia's immigration history. The final section examines the validity of the idea of legal and illegal discrimination in the Australian context and, in so doing, identifies some new issues in migration for this country.

Immigration and Australia: Trends and Issues

From the inception of white Australia, immigration has been a central mechanism for populating this vast continent. Government intervention, either by the colonial power (England) or by successive Australian governments after Federation in 1901, established the legislative and bureaucratic infrastructure to regulate legal migrant flows in and out of Australia and to define and deal with illegal migration. The bulk of Australia's immigration history has been marked by exclusionist and exclusivist policies.[18] That is, overt and covert negative discrimination on the grounds of race, ethnicity, gender, religion, political affiliation and nationality have all been practised. It was not until 1973 under the Whitlam Labor government that a truly nondiscriminatory policy was introduced.

The key feature of the modest immigration program undertaken in the twentieth century, up until the cessation of all immigration from 1939 to 1947, was its discrimination against non-Caucasians. By this means, the population's British origin component was kept artificially high and the population grew only slowly to a level of about seven million at the cessation of hostilities in 1945. It was inevitable in the aftermath of war that immigration would become a boom industry, necessitating an expanded bureaucracy and a Migration Act more in tune with the times. The crisis of near-invasion and losses in the male population engendered a new drive for legal immigration. The government's population and immigration advisory committees supported an expansion in the population, identifying immigration as the only means of direct population control open to government.

The initiation of a federal Department of Immigration in the early postwar period signalled a quantum leap in the structuring and control of migration, which has persisted unchanged except for increasing complexity, to the present.[19] Apart from the specialized Department and Ministry for Immigration, a highly sophisticated network of advisory bodies, official inquiries and public consultations have been the devices used by governments to shape immigration (and, by default, population) policy since the late 1940s.[20] Public opinion has played only a limited role. Social and economic factors in Australia and in countries of emigration have been of crucial importance in determining the nature of actual population movements into and out of Australia.[21] In particular, trends in the movement of international labour and capital have been highly significant in determining which countries are, or have been, exporters or importers of surplus labour.[22]

Moore[23] points out that certain basic principles have always underlain the immigration program, for example, Australia's right to boost its population by migration, whether by economic migrants or refugees. Others have been added and made more explicit in recent times. These have included and given support to concepts such as national sovereignty, nondiscrimination, primacy of Australian social morals and laws, individual (not community) migration, permanent settlers (not guest workers) and social cohesion. The specific objectives of the program have been of the following kind: social, especially to achieve family reunion; economic, to contribute to national development; population, to augment population growth by natural increase; and humanitarian, fulfilling international commitments regarding refugees.[24]

The increase in numbers after the inception of the large-scale postwar immigration program in 1947 was predictable. By 1991, the Australian population had reached in excess of seventeen million, in large part due to immigration and its subsequent effects on natural increase.[25] The ethnic heterogeneity of the subsequent inflow was less predictable or even intended. Notwithstanding, the Migration Act of 1958 (only the second to be put in place since the White Australia Policy of 1901 and remarkably similar to it;[26] took some account of the increased multicultural pressures; for example, it removed the dictation test, which had been one of the ways of discriminating against applicants whose first language was not English. Nonetheless, it still retained an exclusivist element by providing social service benefits to British immigrants, but not to immigrants of other national origins. Through failure to maintain high targets of British immigrants, even as early as the 1950s and into the 1970s, successive governments were forced to enter into migration agreements with a variety of European and other countries to facilitate population movement.[27] Conditions of these agreements provided a range of incentives, including financial support for travel, dedicated job opportunities, subsidized housing and so on; all of them designed to encourage healthy adults of working age and their families to migrate to Australia. The competition with other immigrant-receiving countries, such as Canada and the United States, is generally understood to have rendered these measures palatable, even though it meant welcoming "culturally different" migrant flows.

The gendered nature of immigration policy was simply taken for granted. It was reflected in the definitions of masculinity and feminity projected about "desirable" immigrants. For example, publicity (or propaganda) directed to potential immigrants and to the Australian public was filled with images of men as "the workers"; emphasis being placed more on health, physical strength and good attitudes to work rather than necessarily on skills. Women were perceived in the traditional role of "breeders, nurturers and carers"[28] and their movement to Australia was most often associated with males in their role as spouse, fiancée, daughter or other dependent. The only other times when women migrants as women were actively sought were to redress the population imbalance (an excess of male migrants of non-English-speaking background) and make up deficits in labour force numbers in service work, particularly domestic service.[29] It is only very recently by means of the 1991 Women's Issues Plan[30] that the Department of Immigration has signalled its desire to stimulate the flow of women as Principal Applicants.

The move to a nondiscriminatory policy was probably the single most significant change in the years up to 1989. Indeed, it has had major implications for the composition of the annual immigration targets. This is not to say that controversy over composition has disappeared, but it has meant that legal barriers to discrimination are at least in place. In spite of this, Australia's Asian-Pacific neighbours (including Indonesia, Malaysia,

Fiji, China, Vietnam and Japan) continue to claim racism in Australia's immigration policies and in her treatment of refugees.

The issue of numbers is the other persistent problem. Probably the key factor influencing targeted and actual immigration levels is the state of the economy in Australia and in countries of origin. Other and more contentious elements have entered public and government discourse on immigration in the past decade. These include arguments over ecologically sustainable development, concentrations of immigrants in cities and anxiety over challenges to social cohesion.[31]

If economic immigrants have not always been viewed positively by the Australian public, how do refugees fare? Most Australians would probably agree that "refugee migration is something special: in its causes, its character, and the obligations it imposes."[32] Refugee migrants move for different reasons and the element of choice is much reduced if not absent altogether. The concerns are for the well-being of the individual, not for those of either the sending or receiving society; the justification based on humanitarian values and acceptance of international obligations (for example, arising under the 1951 United Nations Convention and definition of a refugee, the 1967 Protocol, the Convention relating to the Status of Stateless Persons, the Universal Declaration of Human Rights, the International Covenant on Civil and Political Rights, the Convention on the Political Rights of Women, the Declaration of the Rights of the Child and the International Convention on the Elimination of All Forms of Racial Discrimination) rather than the economic, cultural or political values commonly applied in the selection and admission of other kinds of immigrants.

Since 1945, Australia has accepted more than 500,000 refugees and displaced persons, about 10 percent of the inflow of immigrants for that period. These refugees have come from more than forty countries in Europe, Africa, Asia and the Middle East, Central and South America. The Department of Foreign Affairs and Trade[33] suggests that in per capita terms, Australia has taken more refugees and displaced persons than any other country. Of a proposed immigrant intake of about 120,000 for 1991-92, the numbers of refugees are expected to reach 12,000. In addition to admitting refugees on a long-term basis, Australia provides foreign aid to agencies such as the United Nations High Commissioner for Refugees (UNHCR) and special grants directly to countries in special circumstances such as war, famine or flood in which their populations are subjected to dislocation.

Australia selects refugees for resettlement from overseas. It works in liaison with international agencies and forums, including UNHCR. The Australian government has taken such steps as endorsing the Comprehensive Plan of Action (CPA), proposed by the international community of the Asian region, with the objective of developing a humane and effective mechanism for dealing with the many movements of populations from country to country in that region.[34] It also supports efforts to afford special protection of refugee women and children and has a dedicated domestic program to assist the needs of the refugee women and girls accepted into Australia.

Nonetheless, because of the expansion of the postwar economy (even given Australia's predilection for a pattern of alternating economic boom and bust), the large-scale sponsored immigration program, with its costs and benefits, was not strongly challenged until the 1980s. A combination of increasing recession, so-called racist attacks on the particular multicultural nature of Australia's population,[35] the coming together of environmental conservationists, supporters of low population growth and anti-immigrationists,[36] the rending of the bipartisan approach of the major political parties and continued pressure for gender equity from the women's movement, all combined to raise the temperature of the immigration debate. With the imminence (and inherently problematic definition) of the 1988 Bicentenary "celebration," the federal Labor government announced the first national inquiry into immigration in 1987, conducted by the Committee to Advise on Australia's Immigration Policies (CAAIP) and chaired by Dr. Stephen FitzGerald. The CAAIP (also known as the FitzGerald) Report was published in 1988. It displeased the government, partly because it entered into critical discussion of the policy of multiculturalism and on the alleged excessive influence of certain peak ethnic organizations, which the government said was going beyond the inquiry's terms of reference. Thus, it was not until 1989 that a substantial overhaul of the 1958 Migration Act was achieved.

Since 1989 certain issues have become highlighted in the wide-ranging discussion over immigration. Of particular note are the following: tensions over the implementation of the CAAIP Report and the functioning of the 1989 Amendments, with the associated voluminous and highly complex Regulations; increased numbers of asylum seekers, anxiety over the level of immigration in a time of severe recession; questioning of the costs and benefits of temporary entrants, such as tourists and students; the innovative recommendation by a government advisory body to subsume immigration policy within an overall population policy and renewed calls for declaring Australia a republic, which, as a consequence, would be more highly integrated with the Asian region. These matters can only be sketched here and none receives systematic and individual attention.

The CAAIP Report recommended a high-level program. It identified four main migration categories: family, independent and concessional (requiring points testing), skilled and business, and refugee and humanitarian. (A de facto additional category arises out of the special relationship between Australia and New Zealand, which enables New Zealand citizens to enter Australia freely, that is, without applying for a visa.) The targets set for the categories were to favour skill over other attributes. Thus, the policy the CAAIP Committee advocated sharpening the economic focus of immigration, which was consonant with the prevailing economic rationalist push by Australian governments. This roused the displeasure of the powerful ethnic lobby. In the end, the federal government accepted, only with modifications, the recommendations of its own inquiry. The matter of the overall target and the balance among the categories is becoming increasingly contested in the run up to the 1993 federal election.

Even more controversial has been the provision for detailed regulations that have removed many of the previous wide discretionary powers of the Minister. This also has upset the ethnic lobby. In particular, their disapproval with what they see as tightening restrictions on immigration to the detriment of the family reunion program was a factor in the 1990 federal election campaign. Rumours still circulate of deals between a major national ethnic organization and the then-prime minister involving a trade-off between softening the immigration regulations in return for support from ethnic voters. Supporters of this interpretation suggest that the installation of a new Immigration Minister and Secretary (Permanent Head) of the federal Immigration Department immediately after the election was more than a happy coincidence.

Another consequence of the selective implementation of the CAAIP Report has been the entry of a new player in the immigration debate. This is the Bureau of Immigration Research (BIR), part of the federal Department of Immigration, Local Government and Ethnic Affairs (DILGEA). While the actual impact of the BIR can be debated (some critics have dismissed it as merely the propaganda machine of the Immigration Department), its potential and symbolic significance is considerable. Through its charter to sponsor research into immigration and population matters and to raise public awareness of such matters via its national outlook conferences and publications, the BIR provides an authoritative grounding for advice to the government and simultaneously boosts the legitimacy of policy with the electorate. One development that emerged directly out of BIR's First National Immigration Outlook Conference held in November 1990 was the announcement by the Prime Minister of an inquiry by the National Population Council to examine the issue of whether Australia needs a population policy in addition to specific immigration, settlement and multiculturalism policies.

The report from this inquiry, entitled *Population Issues and Australia's Future*,[37] was released in December 1991. The aim of the inquiry was "to provide a report on the major issues which flow from the increase in

Australia's population, as a result of net migration and natural increase" and to give "attention to the population issue from the perspective of the impact on Australia's economy, environment, human service delivery, infrastructure, social equity and international obligations."[38] Among the findings and recommendations of this inquiry were the following:

- support for a population policy which does not specify any long-term optimum population number but adopts a precautionary approach in accord with ecologically sustainable development principles, includes pro-active and responsive components, and has immigration as the core (pp.ix-x);

- support for Australia's involvement in a multi-lateral review of mass population movements and an active research program into factors influencing population such as illegal migration, economic and other implications of temporary movement to Australia, and causes and consequences of emigration from Australia (pp.xi-xiii); and

- support for a responsible international policy to address root causes of global population movements, given that immigration is an ineffective and inappropriate tool to reduce mass population pressures and for an enhanced Australian foreign aid program (p.xx).

If these ideas were accepted by government, fundamental changes in many of Australia's domestic and international policies and relationships would be inevitable.

There are, of course, many policies in Australia that affect immigration indirectly and are additional to an immigration policy. These constitute a highly comprehensive system of settlement services for legal immigrants. In the forefront are the initial English-language training and information programs for adult and child migrants, which are provided at government expense. Others include accommodation, postarrival health checks and counselling, small repayable loans to refugees, social security and health benefits, access to the Commonwealth Employment Services, and recognition of trades and professional qualifications. Only very recently has BIR-sponsored research[39] been able to show that the costs of some of these policies are largely balanced by the resources generated by migrants through actual transfers of funds, wages, taxes, goods and services produced, savings of education costs for those fully or partly educated overseas, etc. Even with this new evidence, the media frequently report claims about the alleged costs of immigration to support the call for reduced immigration intakes. A full-blown population policy might lead to a more integrated view of optimizing scarce resources and away from the ready scapegoating of immigrants that occurs now.

The government also received a report on refugees in 1991. It was prepared by the National Population Council's Refugee Steering Committee and contained a "comprehensive analysis of refugee issues with the objective of providing a basis for future policy formulations in this area."[40] This report identified the diverse responses Australia makes to refugee and refugee-like movements internationally. These are diplomatic initiatives, development aid and provision of resettlement places, in that order of priority. Emphasis was placed on Australia continuing to support and work with regional and global international agencies to take preemptive action wherever possible and to coordinate and include nongovernment organizations as part of a structured approach to refugee, asylum seeker and other refugee-like flows. The clear message in the report is that Australia must maintain a controlled and structured program with respect to spontaneous and mass population movements.

To illustrate from current arrangements, Australia updated its refugee and humanitarian policy in 1991, providing for admission of people accepted under traditional refugee and humanitarian criteria, as well as those who do not meet those criteria, for example, people in countries experiencing severe ethnic unrest or civil war.[41] Priorities in the admission of external refugees are established by ranking applicants in terms of most desirable categories. These are: the presence of family already in Australia, close ties with Australia, and humanitarian claims and resettlement potential. Citizens or permanent residents of Australia aged 18 years and over can nominate people to be considered for admission on refugee and humanitarian grounds. The Australian government bears the costs associated with moving refugees from their location to Australia and supplies initial support, such as accommodation on arrival. The government also encourages the voluntary sector, such as churches and other community groups, to resettle refugees under the Community Refugee Settlement Scheme (CRSS), which receives government funding.[42]

Another issue is the potential for temporary residents, having quite readily gained access by means of a visitor's visa for instance, to change their status to permanent settlers. This was the subject of a Joint Standing Committee on Migration Regulations Report.[43] This report documented the great increase in such applications for change of status, more than a fourfold increase from about 8,000 in 1980-81 to about 36,000 in 1989-90. These additional entrants have the potential to distort quotas in categories as well as the overall number of immigrants accepted in any year. Recently, a tough stand has been taken on change-of-status applicants. Measures include stricter time-lines for meeting documentation requirements, increased fees to accompany applications and wide publicity about penalties where change of status is refused.

Opportunities are available to onshore persons with valid entry documents and illegal migrants to apply for refugee status. The process for dealing with these is on a case-by-case basis and has three components. The first is primary assessment and decision; the second, review of negative assessments; and finally, a humanitarian safety net under which the relevant Minister may use discretion to grant entry because of compelling considerations. In this latter event, the individual is one who has been determined not to be a refugee by the earlier two stages.

The suggestions regarding increased and diversified foreign aid and regional and global cooperation in the NPC Report[44] may render some of these arrangements for refugees, asylum seekers and other illegals obsolete. As the full implementation of the NPC Report is unlikely in the short term, however, current pressures for managing illegal immigrants cannot be ignored. One illustration is the case of the Chinese students. In 1989, following unrest in China, the federal government announced that PRC nationals in Australia, in the main for English-language training, would be permitted to stay for as long as four years. This was a landmark decision for a number of reasons. To allow approximately 20,000 nationals from one country to stay, to apply for change of status, to receive services normally not available to temporary entrants and, in the event of permanent residence being granted, to have the right to sponsor other relatives resulting in chain migration, appeared paradoxical to many in the light of Australia's previous experience and official management of asylum seekers.

The most well-known cases of asylum seekers have been the Southeast Asian boat people. Earlier arrivals by this means in the late 1970s were generally given refugee status and allowed to stay. The official response to later arrivals, for example, groups of alleged Cambodians and Chinese in the 1990s, has been different, with extensive investigations, detention and deportation. Compassion fatigue may be part of the explanation for the altered approach, but it is also thought to be a reaction to the unusual approach adopted towards the Chinese students and the subsequent displeasure of the Chinese government. This one event has magnified concerns over more conventional and regulated refugee migration as well as spontaneous asylum seekers.

Illegal migration has now assumed a high profile in Australia. One indicator of official interest was signalled by the release of a federal parliamentary report on illegal immigrants[45] as part of a stringent review of the new Migration Regulations. The data contained in that report suggested that the illegal population stood at about 90,000 at April 30, 1990 (excluding the PRC cases). As Australia now has an annual temporary entry of overseas residents of more than four million, the proportion of overstayers becoming illegal immigrants is relatively small and much of the problem is perceived to be a result of force of circumstances rather than deliberate deception. Even so, apart from this being a breach of the supposedly tight control Australia keeps on the official immigration program, as visitors and students represent the bulk of the overstayers, the general public is quick to criticize this behaviour in terms of "jumping the immigration queue."[46] Some commentators are worried also that the conditions of illegality encourage the abuse of civil rights of overstayers, especially by employers. Most overstayers eventually leave voluntarily, but there is machinery in place to detect and deport illegal immigrants. Deportations at best, however, result in only a couple of thousand leaving the country annually.

Illegality arising from deliberate intention, on the other hand, has resulted in modifications to existing legislation and/or regulations. For example, late in 1991, legislative amendments passed through Parliament to curtail marriage rackets. The targets are agents, lawyers and individuals applying for permanent residence on the basis of contrived or pretended relationships (marriages, de facto relationships or interdependency relationships).[47] The penalties envisaged include jail, fines and cancellation of entry permits, which could result in arrest, detention and deportation. Other amendments were introduced to reduce hardship for overseas-born women who enter Australia sponsored by Australian men. In the case of breakdown of such relationships (often as a result of domestic violence) before the women have obtained permanent residence, there has been a fear of deportation.[48]

Conclusion: Immigration Futures—
Australia vs the Rest of the World

With the backgound to the case study outlined, what can we conclude about Australia and immigration in the future? The sporting analogy alluded to in the title of this final section is deliberate. Of the countries in the southern hemisphere, Australia is the only site of considerable legal immigration, both economic immigrants and refugees. Applications for permanent settlement to Australia come from almost every country in the world and temporary entrants cover a similarly wide spectrum. On the basis of numbers alone, there must be a competition for entry.

Prior to 1973, the competition was biased against those from certain racial and ethnic backgrounds. This was an obvious case of racial (or negative) discrimination. Of course, Australia was not alone in this. With the international precedents set particularly by the United Nations, however, such discrimination has been widely considered illegal. Since that time, the bias has been transformed to other attributes, generally relating to education and skill levels. If we accept that to discriminate is to make or constitute a difference in or between persons or things, that is, to differentiate, then selection of immigrants on education/skill grounds still constitutes discrimination. The Australian government would argue that such discrimination is legal. As only a few among many can be chosen, Australia has defined her immigration categories and the attributes by which individuals are allocated to them in ways that allow her to select preferred settlers. For example, "family" is defined narrowly so that the extended families common in many cultures are not admitted under the family reunion category, free of the constraints of a preset points level. Similarly, education and skills are generally defined according to Australian conditions (and also, some would argue, on patriarchal criteria), although there is now more willingness to recognize overseas qualifications and to define skills in terms of competencies rather than merely paper qualifications.

Australia bases its legal discrimination on the fact that political, legal and administrative structures and processes are involved in the decisions over immigration policy. Allegations of unfairness arise when applicants disagree with the ways they have been defined by Australian authorities. This occurs offshore, for example, when potential immigrants fail to achieve the required point score, have skills not in demand in Australia or fail health checks or when refugees are screened out of contention because they are perceived to be economic migrants. It occurs onshore when asylum seekers and illegals fail to obtain change of status, for example, because the grounds of close relationship to an Australian citizen or permanent resident are seen to be bogus or their status as a refugee cannot be proven to the satisfaction of the Australian authorities.

Challenges to the current legal/illegal dichotomy may arise in the future. Suggested scenarios include the following.

Internal pressures for modification by Australia of its immigration policies

(a) As the controversy over immigration appears to be endemic in this country, immigration targets may be drastically revised down or up. Anti-immigrationists might suggest that all in-migration should be stopped except for the refugee and humanitarian category or that the intake in all categories be reduced. This reduces the field of legal discrimination. To achieve this may actually encourage illegal discrimination. Proimmigrationists might greatly increase the field of legal discrimination by increasing the number of legal categories or lifting quotas on existing categories; thus, illegal discrimination would have little force. Either of these possibilities is likely to intensify the ethnic divisions in Australian society and put even more pressure on the legitimacy of multiculturalism as the best policy to manage a polyethnic state.

(b) The latest advice to the Australian government from its advisory body, the National Population Council,[49] attempts to insulate the decision making over numbers and composition of the migrant intake from the politicization occurring with the clash of pro- and anti-immigration pressure groups and the tensions voiced among ethnic groups. For example, large-scale public demonstrations have been held in some major cities recently by Greek-Australians protesting against the possible recognition by the Australian government of an independent Macedonia following the conflict in Yugoslavia. The report's intent has been to move discussion to a more rational weighing up of evidence, grounded in research on the one hand and in a less parochial perspective on the other. That is, the politicians and bureaucrats are asked to take into account social, economic and ecological impacts, the prevention and containment of abuses (in areas such as illegal immigrants, spouse-derived entry, change-of-status, asylum seekers), and the need to upgrade postarrival provisions. They are expected to view settler arrival not in isolation, but also against a backdrop of globalization.[50] Although the appeal here is to greater rationality, the approach might also be interpreted as conservative. That is, it does not fundamentally question the continuance of immigration as a tool for population building (a central rationale in Australia's position), and argues for a continuation of the status quo, even the maintenance of a steady state. This could be a more comfortable path for decision makers to tread.

(c) Rather than the politics and pragmatics of the numbers game, there may be some profound change in ideology so that the moral dimension of immigration comes to the fore. This is explained by Jayasuriya[51] in the following terms:

> With the emergence of new patterns of international migration, the fashioning of Australian immigration policy needs to be more outward-looking. It ought not to be based purely upon any self-centred philosophy focussed on national sovereignty and selfish economic grounds or ecological rationale. A humane and democratic society will be cognizant of the moral and value considerations, grounded in a larger view of humanity, that move us beyond the narrow boundaries of the nation state.

That is, there should be greater emphasis on the normative in policymaking over immigration. Rather than focusing on Australia's right to control who enters, a balance should be struck between equal interests. The greatest pressures for population movements to Australia are those arising from the desire for family reunification and for the resettlement of refugees. If equal weight is given to these interests as well as to Australia's interests, families and refugees are the groups who should constitute the bulk of immigrants in the future. Given Australia's regional location, this must mean a significant Asianization of this country, which is in line with pronouncements made recently by Prime Minister Keating in foreshadowing Australia's transformation to a republic. The federal election planned for 1993 is probably the litmus test for this scenario.

External Forces and Their Capacity to Affect Australia

Castles[52] paints a picture in which population movements and the internationalization of the economy, culture and language, combined with the tensions that arise in nations with large and diverse populations, may lead to the demise of the nation-state. He suggests that this process has proceeded apace in the case of Australia, given that Australia as a nation can no longer be defined by its ethnicity or by exclusion. On the negative side, this has led to greater contradictions as racist and nationalist sentiments mobilize against what is seen as the influx of "others." On the positive side, the Australian state has been reasonably effective in managing its heterogeneous civil society and maintaining social control. External agents have been particularly influential in bringing about the demise of institutionalized racial discrimination in the official immigration policy. Notwithstanding, there is a vociferous lobby against the official multiculturalism policy, which applies a continuing pressure on Australian governments, and the multicultural industry created to support the policy. The dissension over multiculturalism is readily conflated with the immigration debate. However, continued ethnic diversification through migration and mobility in Australian society may, in the long term, neutralize the impact of antimulticulturalism attitudes and behaviours, for example, racial violence.

Because of this dynamic situation, the end result cannot be predicted with any certainty. It may be that Boyd and Taylor's warning about Canada will be relevant to the Australian context. They state that the likelihood of massive "visible, growing, and increasingly spontaneous"[53] illegal migration might tip the balance against crisis management and in favour of action, such as radical isolationism. This may be less of an issue for Australia, but there are already critics of government immigration policy who claim that the program is out of control. For example, they adduce as "evidence" the government's inability to predict and control chain migration (and especially from Third World countries,[54] or claim that the government is soft on undocumented arrivals, such as the boat people or overstayers (especially from Pacific islander nations, Australia having resisted calls from the governments of some of these countries for access of their nationals to guest-worker migration to Australia).

Optimists might take comfort from the fact that even problems such as these may act as a spur, as Castles[55] indicates, to innovative thinking to devise "new forms of social identification and political legitimacy." This is especially true in the case of Australia with a history of policy formulation for immigration having to resolve tensions between "competing policy goals and the dynamic pluralist interaction of mobilised interests."[56]

Notes

1. The other recognized immigrant-receiving countries include the United States, Canada, New Zealand and, with special conditions, Israel.

2. Jupp, *The Australian People*; BIR, *Australia's Population Trends and Prospects*. In 1981, net migration totalled 121,785; the lowest figure for the decade was 54,766 in 1983 and the highest was 171,700 in 1988 (BIR, *Australia's Population Trends and Prospects*, 3). The accompanying table indicates the outcomes of the migration program by categories for 1990-91 and the suggested levels in the years to 1993.

Migration Outcomes and Planning Levels

	Program Outcome			Planning Levels	
	1990-91			1991-92	1992-93
	'000			'000	'000
Family	R	VI	Total		
Preferential	8.2	30.6	38.8	37.0	38.0
Concessional	-	22.5	22.5	19.0	21.0
Family subtotal	8.2	53.1	61.3	56.0	59.0
Skilled					
Employer nomin. (a)	1.7	5.8	7.5	7.0	9.0
Bus.Migration	-	7.0	7.0	5.0	5.0
Spec. talents	0.1	0.1	0.1	0.5	0.5
Independents	0.4	34.7	35.1	30.0	32.0
Skilleed subtotal	2.2	47.6	49.8	42.5	46.5
Spec. Eligib.	0.8	0.5	1.2	0.5	0.5
Refugees, Humanitarian and Special Assistance					
Refugees and Global Special					
Humanitarian	1.5	9.8	11.3(c)	5.7	
Special Assist.ance	-	-	-	6.3	
	1.5	9.8	11.3	12.0	12.0(d)
Total Program	12.7	111.0	123.6	111.0	118.0

Note: (I) The program outcome is the number of visas issued and people granted permanent residence in Australia after arrival. There is currently no eligibility for Grant of Resident Status (GORS)/Permanent Entry Permit After Entry (PEPAE) under the Concessional Family and Independent categories. GORS figures for 1990-91 include those granted resident status under PEPAE.

(II) R = Resident; VI = Visa Issue

(a) Includes Labour Agreements

(b) Includes estimated onshore residence approvals of 9,000 per year for Preferential Family and 2,000 per year for Skill, and estimated onshore residence approvals for Refugees and Global Special Humanitarian declining over the period (processing will involve only four-year Temporary Entry Permits for onshore humanitarian cases).

(c) Includes a 1,000 contingency reserve, which was activated and used during the year.

(d) To be reviewed annually.

Source: Adapted from DILGEA's *Review '91 Annual Report 1990-91*, 27.

Currently, the consultations by the Minister of Immigration, Gerry Hand, are ongoing prior to his submission of the actual 1992-93 target to Cabinet in April 1992. A news item in a large metropolitan daily (*The Melbourne Age*, March 2, 1992, 16) commented that the Minister's submission might recommend a target lower than the suggested 118,000 because of the arguments over whether migrants are taking work from Australian-born job seekers in the current situation of high unemployment (in excess of 10 percent) and sought-after places in the overcrowded tertiary education sector (more than 50,000 qualified graduates failed to find places in colleges and universities in Australia in 1992).

3. These figures are gathered from the Arrivals and Departures Cards completed by all travellers into and out of Australia and are collated and published regularly by the Australian Bureau of Statistics (ABS). The figure of 9,211,200 for all movements into and out of Australia was quoted in ABS, *Overseas Arrivals and Departures Australia*, 1.

4. ABS, *Overseas Arrivals and Departures Australia*, 8.

5. Kalantzis et al., *Cultures of Schooling*, 2.

6. McConnochie et al., *Race and Racism in Australia*; Reynolds, *Frontier*; Yarwood and Knowling, *Race Relations in Australia*.

7. Foster et al., *Discrimination Against Immigrant Workers in Australia*, 22.

8. Birrell and Birrell, *An Issue of People*.

9. Betts, *Ideology and Immigration*.

10. Cf. Jakubowicz, "State and Ethnicity"; Jakubowicz et al., *Ethnicity, Class and Social Welfare in Australia*.

11. Details of the immigration program, for example, as reported in the Annual Reports of the Department of Immigration or in documents prepared by the

Department for wide distribution, such as *At A Glance* (DILGEA 1991), a concise description of the immigration program (published so far only in 1990 and 1991), make these points clear.

12. The concept of immigrant resistance has been canvassed by a number of Australian academics working in the area of immigration including Castles, Kalantzis, Cope, De Lepervanche, Martin, Jakubowicz and Bottomley. Some of their writings are noted in the References list.

13. Lo Bianco, *National Policy on Languages*.

14. NPC, *Population Report 9 Emigration*.

15. BIR, *Australian Citizenship Statistical Report No. 1*.

16. Australia has an abundance of federal and state bodies (for example the Federal Human Rights and Equal Opportunity Commission, the Office of the Status of Women and the National Office of Overseas Skills Recognition and the State Commissioners for Equal Opportunity and Anti-Discrimination Boards), legislation and associated regulations (for example, the Human Rights and Equal Opportunity Commission Act 1986, the Racial Discrimination Act 1975, the Sex Discrimination Act 1984, the Affirmative Action Act 1986, the Privacy Act 1988, and Racial Vilification Acts to be found only in New South Wales 1989 and Western Australia 1990) to protect the rights of its citizens and permanent residents. It is also a signatory to many international conventions including the Universal Declaration of Human Rights, the International Covenant on Civil and Political Rights, the Convention on the Elimination of All Forms of Discrimination Against Women, ILO Convention 111 concerning Discrimination in Respect of Employment and Occupation and ILO Convention 156, Workers with Family Responsibilities. The National Agenda on multiculturalism (OMA 1989) aims to manage the consequences of ethnic and racial pluralism in the interests of the individual and the society as a whole and has three dimensions: cultural identity, social justice and economic efficiency. The national languages policy (Lo Bianco 1987) affirms English as Australia's official language and supports the maintenance of languages other then English, including Aboriginal languages.

17. Moore, "Australia," 7.

18. Foster and Stockley, *Australian Multiculturalism*.

19. DILGEA, *Review '91 Annual Report 1990-91*, 1-9.

20. Details of earlier structures can be found in the publication *Australia and Immigration 1788 to 1988* (DILGEA 1988). Some idea of the complexity can be gained from the current structure of DILGEA. The substantive divisions of the Department are migration and citizenship, refugees and international, settlement and ethnic affairs, including the Adult Migrant English Program, temporary entry, compliance and systems, which manages student, tourist and other short-term entrants, as well as effecting the removal of persons who have no legal right to stay in Australia. Other associated structures are the Bureau of Immigration Research, the National Accreditation Authority for Interpreters and Translators, the Immigration Review Tribunal (providing the final tier of

merit review of certain decisions under the Migration Act) and the National Population Council, which advises on economic and social development through appropriate population policies. More information can be obtained from DILGEA Annual Reports.

21. Collins, *Migrant Hands in a Distant Land*.

22. Abella, "Recent Trends in Asian Labor Migration: A Review of Major Issues"; Castles, *Global Workforce, New Racism and the Declining Nation State*; Castles et al., *Here for Good*; Ethier, "International Trade and Labour Migration"; Lever-Tracy and Quinlan, *A Divided Working Class*; Richmond, *Immigration and Ethnic Conflict*.

23. Moore, "Australia," 7-9.

24. CAAIP, *Understanding Immigration*, 27-28.

25. NPC, *Population Issues and Australia's Future: Environment, Economy and Society A Discussion Paper*, 33.

26. For details, see DILGEA, *Australia and Immigration 1788 to 1988*.

27. Ibid.

28. Bottomley et al., *Intersexions: Gender/Class/Culture/Ethnicity*; De Lepervanche, "Breeders for Australia."

29. Kunek, "Greek Female Migration in the Post World War II Period in Australia."

30. DILGEA, *Women's Issues Plan*.

31. Although immigration has been a constant factor in Australia's population growth and generally accepted as such, a subtext of anti-immigration feeling allied with racism has never been far from the surface of public opinion. In general, however, government immigration policy in terms of size and composition of migrant flows has been in advance of public opinion. As we moved into the 1980s, the debate over immigration became more strident, echoing earlier feelings, but it has also altered in some ways, becoming more complex. There is no space to trace the details of the elements of the debate, but the results of government inquiries, such as the Australian Population and Immigration Council (1977); Galbally (1978), Jupp (1986), FitzGerald (1988) and National Population Council 1991 Reports and the analyses of academic commentators, including Appleyard (1983); Birrell (1990); Birrell et al. (1984); Collins, *The FitzGerald Report* (1988); Day and Rowland (1988); Hawkins (1989); Jupp (1989); Rivett (1988); Shergold (1984) are useful sources.

32. Day, "Australia's Obligations to Refugees," 370.

33. DFAT, "Refugees and Displaced Persons," 4.

34. NPC, *Refugee Review*, 159.

35. The most highly publicized attacks on the concept of multiculturalism and its perceived link to immigration policy were the so-called Blainey debates of 1984, 1987 and 1988. They were named after Professor Geoffrey Blainey, whose public lecture to a community group in 1984 was seized upon by the media, activating an immense outpouring of comments that were subsequently revived in later years with different triggers. The essence of the original Blainey

argument was that immigration policy was running ahead of public opinion and that the government would do well to heed the silent majority of 'old' Australians who wished to see a reduction in Asian immigration. For detailed discussion, see Milne and Shergold (1984) and Cope et al. (1991).

36. Cf. Smith, *Population, Immigration and the Limits to Australia's Growth*.

37. NPC, *Population Issues and Australia's Future: Environment, Economy and Society Final Report*.

38. Ibid., vi.

39. These studies include: *Immigrants and the Social Security System* (Whiteford 1991); *Immigration and the Australian Economy* (Foster and Baker 1991); *Migrant Unemployment and Labour Market Programs* (McAllister and Jones 1991); *Settlement Needs of Newly Arrived Ethnic Groups* (Jupp et al. 1991). All of the studies have been published by the Australian Government Publishing Service (AGPS) in Canberra.

40. NPC, *Refugee Review*, foreword.

41. This has facilitated special consideration onshore of Yugoslav, Sri Lankan, and Lebanese nationals, among others, enabling many of them to convert temporary visitor visas to extended stay visas or even to achieve permanent residence status.

42. DFAT, "Refugees and Displaced Persons," 5.

43. Joint Standing Committee Parliament of Australia, *First Report on Migration Regulations*.

44. NPC, *Refugee Review*.

45. Joint Standing Committee Parliament of Australia, *First Report on Migration Regulations*.

46. Australia receives in excess of one million applications for immigration each year. Obviously only a very small proportion succeed; hence, the necessity for strict criteria based on categories and set targets.

47. IARC, "New Penalties for `Pretended Relationships'," 8.

48. DILGEA, *Folk Law*, 3.

49. NPC, *Population Issues and Australia's Future: Environment, Economy and Society Final Report*; NPC, *Refugee Review*.

50. See also Withers, "Immigration and Australia's Development," 16-17.

51. Jayasuriya, "The Moral Dimension of Immigration: A Neglected Issue," 3.

52. Castles, *Global Workforce, New Racism and the Declining Nation State*, 20-21.

53. Boyd and Taylor, "Canada," 47.

54. Birrell, *The Chains That Bind*.

55. Castles, *Global Workforce, New Racism and the Declining Nation State*, 21.

56. Parkin and Hardcastle, "Immigration Policy," 315.

References

Abella, Manolo. "Recent Trends in Asian Labor Migration A Review of Major Issues." In *Asian Migrant* 4, no. 3 (1991):72-77.

Appleyard, Reginald. *International Migration in East Asia and Australasia: Trends and Consequences*. Perth: University of Western Australia, 1983.

Australian Bureau of Statistics (ABS). *Overseas Arrivals and Departures Australia*. (Cat. No. 3402.0) Canberra: ABS, December Quarter, 1991.

_____. *Immigration Policies and Australia's Population: A Green Paper*. Canberra: Australian Government Publishing Service, 1977.

Betts, Katherine. *Ideology and Immigration: Australia 1976 to 1987*. Melbourne: Melbourne University Press, 1988.

Birrell, Robert. *The Chains That Bind: Family Reunion Migration to Australia in the 1980s*. Canberra: Australian Population and Immigration Council, 1990.

Birrell, Robert, and Tanya Birrell. *An Issue of People*. 2d ed. Melbourne: Longman Cheshire, 1987.

Birrell, Robert, David Hill and John Nevill. *Populate and Perish? The Stresses of Population Growth in Australia*. Sydney and Melbourne: Fontana with Australian Conservation Foundation, 1984.

Bottomley, Gillian, Marie De Lepervanche and Jeannie Martin. *Intersexions: Gender/Class/Culture/Ethnicity*. Sydney: Allen and Unwin, 1991.

Boyd, Monica and Taylor, Chris. "Canada." In *Handbook on International Migration*, edited by W. Serow et al., 37-47. New York: Greenwood Press, 1990.

Bureau of Immigration Research (BIR). *Australian Citizenship Statistical Report No. 1*. Canberra: Australian Government Publishing Service, 1990.

_____. *Australia's Population Trends and Prospects*. Canberra: Australian Government Publishing Service, 1990.

Castles, Stephen. *Global Workforce, New Racism and the Declining Nation State Occasional Paper no. 23*. Wollongong: Centre for Multicultural Studies University of Wollongong, 1990.

Castles, Stephen et al. *Here for Good: Western Europe's New Ethnic Minorities*. London: Pluto Press, 1984.

Collins, Jock. *Migrant Hands in a Distant Land: Australia's Post-War Immigration*. Sydney: Pluto Press, 1988.

_____. "The FitzGerald Report: One Step Forward, Many Steps Backwards." In *Migration Action* 10, no. 2 (1988):2-7.

Cope, Bill, Stephen Castles and Mary Kalantzis. *Immigration, Ethnic Conflicts and Social Cohesion*. Canberra: Australian Government Publishing Service, 1991.

Day, Lincoln. "Australia's Obligations to Refugees." In *Population, Immigration and the Limits to Australia's Growth*, edited by J. Smith, 370-379. Adelaide: The Flinders Press, 1991.

Day, Lincoln, and David Rowland, eds. *How Many More Australians? The Resource and Environmental Conflicts*. Melbourne: Longman Cheshire, 1988.

De Lepervanche, Marie. "Breeders for Australia: A National Identity for Women?" In *Australian Journal of Social Issues* 24, no. 3 (1989):163-182.

Department of Foreign Affairs and Trade (DFAT)."Refugees and Displaced Persons." In *Backgrounder* 2, no. 19 (1991):4-5.

Department of Immigration, Local Government and Ethnic Affairs (DILGEA). *Australia and Immigration 1788 to 1988*. Canberra: Australian Government Publishing Service, 1988.

_____. *At A Glance*. Canberra: Australian Government Publishing Service, 1991.

_____. *Folk Law*. Canberra: DILGEA, 1991.

_____. *Review '91 Annual Report 1990-91*. Canberra: Australian Government Publishing Service, 1991.

_____. *Women's Issues Plan*. Canberra: Australian Government Publishing Service, 1991.

Ethier, William. "International Trade and Labour Migration." In *American Economic Review* 75, no. 4 (September 1985):691-707.

FitzGerald, Stephen. *Immigration: A Commitment to Australia—report of the Committee to Advise on Australia's Immigration Policies* Canberra: Australian Government Publishing Service, 1988.

Foster, Lois and David Stockley. *Australian Multiculturalism : A Documentary History and Critique*. Clevedon and Philadelphia: Multilingual Matters, 1988.

Foster, Lois, Anthony Marshall and Lynne Williams. *Discrimination Against Immigrant Workers in Australia*. Canberra: Australian Government Publishing Service, 1991.

Galbally, Frank. *Review of Post-Arrival Programmes and Services to Migrants*. Canberra: Australian Government Publishing Service, 1978.

Hawkins, Freda. *Critical Years in Immigration: Canada and Australia Compared*. Kensington: University of New South Wales Press, 1989.

Immigration Advice and Rights Centre (IARC). "New Penalties for `Pretended Relationships'." In *Immigration News* No. 27 (1991):8.

Jakubowicz, Andrew. "State and Ethnicity: Multiculturalism as Ideology." In *Australian and New Zealand Journal of Sociology* 17, no. 3 (1981):4-13.

Jakubowicz, Andrew, Michael Morrissey and Joanne Palser. *Ethnicity, Class and Social Welfare in Australia*. Sydney: University of New South Wales Social Research Centre, 1984.

Jayasuriya, Laksiri. "The Moral Dimension of Immigration: A Neglected Issue." In *Migration Monitor* No. 21-22 (1991):3-5.

Joint Standing Committee Parliament of Australia. *First Report on Migration Regulations Illegal Entrants in Australia—Balancing Control and Compassion*. (Tabled September 11, 1990).

_____. *Second Report on Migration Regulations Change of Status—Marriage and de facto Relationships.* (Tabled May 16, 1991).

Jupp, James. *Don't Settle For Less: Report of the Committee for Stage I of the Review of Migrant and Multicultural Programs and Services.* Canberra: Australian Government Publishing Service, 1986.

Jupp, James, ed. *The Australian People.* Sydney: Angus and Robertson, 1988.

_____. *The Challenge of Diversity: Policy Options for a Multicultural Australia.* Canberra: Australian Government Publishing Service, 1989.

Kalantzis, Mary, Bill Cope, Greg Noble and Scott Poynting. *Cultures of Schooling: Pedagogies for Cultural Difference and Social Access.* London: Falmer Press, 1990.

Kunek, Srebrenka. "Greek Female Migration in the Post World War II Period in Australia." In *Australian Studies* No.2 (1989):36-58.

Lever-Tracy, Constance and Michael Quinlan. *A Divided Working Class.* London: Routledge, 1988.

Lo Bianco, Jo. *National Policy on Languages.* Canberra: Australian Government Publishing Service, 1987.

McConnochie, Keith, David Hollinsworth and Jan Pettman. *Race and Racism in Australia.* Reprint. Wentworth Falls, NSW: Social Science Press, 1989.

Milne, Frances, and Peter Shergold, eds. *The Great Immigration Debate.* Sydney: Federation of Ethnic Communities' Councils of Australia (FECCA), 1984.

Moore, Ronald. "Australia." In *Handbook on International Migration,* edited by W. Serow et al., 7-24. New York: Greenwood Press, 1990.

National Population Council (NPC). *Population Report 9 Emigration.* Canberra: Australian Government Publishing Service, 1990.

_____. *Population Issues and Australia's Future : Environment, Economy and Society— A Discussion Paper.* Canberra: Australian Government Publishing Service, 1991.

_____. *Population Issues and Australia's Future : Environment, Economy and Society— Final Report.* Canberra: Australian Government Publishing Service, 1991.

_____. *Refugee Review.* Canberra: Australian Government Publishing Service, 1991.

Office of Multicultural Affairs, (OMA) Department of Prime Minister and Cabinet. *National Agenda for a Multicultural Australia ... Sharing Our Future.* Canberra: Australian Government Publishing Service, 1989.

Parkin, Andrew, and Leonie Hardcastle. "Immigration Policy." In *Hawke and Australian Public Policy Consensus and Restructuring,* edited by C. Jennett and R. Stewart, 315-338. South Melbourne: Macmillan, 1990.

Reynolds, Henry. *Frontier: Aborigines, Settlers and Land.* Sydney: Allen and Unwin, 1987.

Richmond, Anthony. *Immigration and Ethnic Conflict.* New York: St Martins Press, 1988.

Rivett, Ken. "The New Case for Immigration." In *Australian Quarterly* 60 (1988):275-284.

Secretariat to the Committee to Advise on Australia'sImmigration Policies. *Understanding Immigration*. Canberra: Australian Government Publishing Service, 1987.

Serow, William, Charles Nam, David Sly and Robert Weller, eds. *Handbook on International Migration*. New York: Greenwood Press, 1990.

Shergold, Peter. "Australian Immigration Since 1973." In *The Great Immigration Debate*, edited by Frances Milne and Peter Shergold, 14-28. Sydney: Federation of Ethnic Communities' Councils of Australia, 1984.

Smith, Joseph. *Population, Immigration and the Limits to Australia's Growth*. Adelaide: The Flinders Press, 1991.

Withers, Glenn. "Immigration and Australia's Development." In *Growth 39 The Costs and Benefits of Immigration*, edited by J. Nevile, 11-17. Melbourne: Committee for the Economic Development of Australia (CEDA) Study, 1991.

Yarwood, A.T., and Michael Knowling. *Race Relations in Australia: A History*. Australia: Methuen, 1982.

11

United States Immigration Policy: The Conflict Between Human Rights and Perceptions of National Identity and Self-Interest

Arthur C. Helton

The United States regards itself as a nation that welcomes immigrants. Its immigration policy, however, has not always been so benign, and has been shaped by many complex and sometimes contradictory factors. In general, humanitarian concerns call for policies that would allow a relatively large number of persons to immigrate. However, economic and political considerations have played a major role in constraining immigration admissions in the U.S. Race has been a factor leading to restrictive immigration policies for certain groups. Foreign policy concerns have also been crucial in determining admissions policies, particularly for refugees.

This chapter begins by briefly discussing the historical background of U.S. immigration policy. It will consider the importance of race and labour market considerations in shaping policy. The paper will then discuss the treatment of refugees within the United States.

Next, current immigration and refugee provisions will be explored, focusing on the provisions involving family-based and business-related immigration, the provisions that purport to diversify migration, refugee protection, employment controls and miscellaneous provisions involving issues of social policy. Finally, the paper will consider international human rights law and whether current United States immigration policy complies with these universal principles.

Race as a Factor in the Formulation of Immigration Policy

The Chinese Exclusion Case

The mid-nineteenth century was marked by tremendous westward expansion in the United States, which in turn had a significant impact on immigration. Specifically, the California gold rush resulted in a large increase in Chinese immigration, particularly as Chinese workers were sought for the construction of the transcontinental railroad. These labourers worked for far lower wages and under worse conditions than did their American counterparts.[1]

In 1868 the United States and China entered into the Burlingame Treaty.[2] Under this agreement, citizens of the United States and China who were visiting or residing in the other country were guaranteed "the same privileges, immunities and exemptions . . . as may be enjoyed by the citizens or subjects of the most favoured nation." An outcry arose throughout the West against the Chinese. This antialien sentiment was, at least in part, a product of economic and social concerns. The country was experiencing drought and depression, which fuelled resentment against foreigners who were seen as taking American jobs. The reaction against the Chinese caused many people to fear that integrating a large number of Chinese into the American population would not be possible without serious social unrest.

By the middle of the 1870s, the nativist sentiment in California began to have an impact on national politics. For example, anti-Chinese sentiments were reflected in the supplemental treaty of 1880 between China and the United States. This agreement allowed the United States to limit Chinese immigration to protect and to further the national interests of the United States. However, the treaty did not give the United States the right to prohibit immigration completely.[3]

This did not prevent the United States from imposing tightened controls on movement to and from the country. In the 1880s Congress passed the Chinese exclusion laws, restricting entry to and exit from the United States by Chinese immigrants. The 1882 and 1884 legislation established a "certificate of identity," which was required for reentry by Chinese labourers into the United States after a trip abroad. Finally, in 1888 Congress passed a law that prohibited any reentry to the United States by Chinese labourers, even if they obtained a certificate of identity prior to their departure from the United States. The legislation further provided that no more certificates would be issued. These provisions left many Chinese labourers, who were residents of the United States, stranded in China. It also made it impossible for Chinese immigrants in the United States even to visit China.

The exclusionary legislation was unsuccessfully challenged in *The Chinese Exclusion Case*.[4] That case involved Chae Chan Ping, a resident of the United States since 1875, who visited China in 1887. He obtained a certificate of identity prior to his departure. When he attempted to return to the United States after passage of the 1888 legislation, he was refused entry into the country. He brought suit, claiming that the legislation violated the Constitution and the terms of the Burlingame and 1880 treaties. A unanimous Supreme Court rejected his challenge. The Court held that the Act of 1888 was valid, even though it contravened the treaties. Furthermore, it held that the government had the power to exclude aliens, including those seeking reentry, from the country as an inherent attribute of sovereignty and without regard to equal protection and due process limitations under the Bill of Rights. The Chinese Exclusion Act was not repealed until 1943.[5]

Discrimination against Asian immigrants was prevalent in United States immigration policy through the middle of the twentieth century. The Immigration Act of 1917 instituted an Asiatic Barred Zone, refusing entry for persons of "Oriental" heritage. The Japanese were exempt from this exclusion only because of a so-called "gentleman's agreement" between the United States and Japan, under which Japan agreed to restrict the number of Japanese-issued passports for the United States. The subsequent 1924 Immigration Act effectively excluded Asians, including Japanese. While the 1952 Act ended the complete exclusion of Asian immigrants,[6] it established quotas for Chinese and all persons indigenous to a fixed Asia-Pacific triangle.

The National Origins Quota System

Race and similar characteristics continued to shape U.S. immigration policy in the twentieth century. By the end of the nineteenth century, policymakers still had little confidence that a large number of immigrants could be incorporated into society without great upheaval. Some of the reasons for this apprehension included the growth of cities and industrialization, the Catholic and Jewish religions of most of the new immigrants, and the apparent determination of many immigrants from Southern and Eastern Europe to maintain their traditions.

The fear of a large increase in immigration following World War I pressured Congress into adopting additional restrictive measures. In 1924 Congress passed the National Origins Act.[7] This legislation was designed to maintain the ethnic and racial status quo of the United States. The Act imposed a limit on the number of immigrants based solely upon their national origins, lowering the annual quota for immigrants to approximately 150,000. Allocations within that quota were provided for each country outside of the Western Hemisphere. These allocations were based upon the proportion of persons of each nationality already in the United States in 1920.

Under the national origins quota system, the annual quota allotment was never fully utilized. Approximately two-thirds of the annual quota for immigration were reserved for countries for which there was not a great demand for immigration by their nationals, such as Great Britain, Germany and Ireland. At the same time, the number of visas allotted to other countries—such as Italy, Greece, China and the Philippines—did not meet the demand for immigration. Thus, under this system, as much as one-third of the annual quota was not used.

The Immigration and Nationality Act of 1952 continued this system basically without change.[8] In 1965 the Act was amended to eliminate nationality quotas.[9] Annual visa allotments were to be distributed without discrimination. Immediate relatives and certain special immigrants remained exempt from the numerical limitation. The amendment imposed a worldwide ceiling of 170,000 Eastern Hemisphere immigrants. Subsequent legislative developments universalized this nondiscriminatory approach.

African Refugee Admissions

The U.S. experience with African refugee admissions suggests that the racial considerations that have traditionally informed United States immigration policy are equally important to its refugee policy. The Refugee Act of 1980 was intended to promote fairness in refugee admissions policy, particularly by ensuring that objective criteria and regular procedures are used to determine which refugees will be admitted into the United States.[10] The Refugee Act provides U.S. authorities with the discretion to set annual refugee admissions ceilings; from 1980 to the present, over a million refugees have been admitted on that basis.

However, only 2 percent of the refugees admitted under the Act have come from Africa—the continent with the largest number of refugees in the world. As a specific example, of the 112,811 refugees who were admitted to the United States from places of first asylum in 1991, a mere 4,424 were from Africa. Those select few were chosen for essentially political reasons: 3,948 (89 percent) of them were from Communist Ethiopia. This reflects an ideological predilection that has all too frequently dominated United States refugee policy in the past.[11]

The Treatment of Haitian Asylum Seekers

The influence of racial considerations in American immigration policy today is reflected as well in the situation of Haitian asylum seekers and their treatment by U.S. authorities. In 1981, in response to the prospect of large numbers of Haitians entering the country illegally, the United States began a program to intercept vessels on the high seas carrying undocumented aliens.[12] The Executive stated that illegal immigration had become "a serious national problem detrimental to the interests of the United States." Haitian migration was viewed as especially problematic—even though Haitians constituted only 2 percent of illegal aliens within the United States in 1981 when the interdiction program was established.

In late 1981 U.S. Coast Guard vessels began to stop and board suspicious vessels bound for the United States to determine whether undocumented aliens were on board. Any undocumented aliens found were to be returned to their country of origin. A specific interdiction agreement between the United States and Haiti authorized the Coast Guard to take such measures concerning Haitian nationals. Once the Coast Guard found undocumented Haitians aboard a vessel, they were transferred to a patrol vessel for questioning. After interviewing the passengers briefly at sea, Immigration and Naturalization Service (INS) interviewers determined whether any of the asylum seekers had a reasonable fear of returning to Haiti.[13] As of 1990, only six of the 21,461 Haitians intercepted under this program were brought to the United States to request asylum.

Since the ouster of President Jean-Bertrand Aristide in September 1991, the number of Haitian boat people fleeing to the United States has increased dramatically. Over 10,000 of the estimated 35,000 boat people who have fled have been identified by U.S. authorities as having claims worthy of full consideration in the in-land asylum procedure. The United States government recently responded to the influx by intercepting boats on the high seas and returning the Haitians on board directly to Haiti, without the benefit of any kind of hearing on their claims of persecution. Genuine refugees will undoubtedly be repatriated in clear violation of international law.[14]

Diversity Visas under the 1990 Act

The Immigration Act of 1990,[15] *inter alia*, provides for the allocation of 55,000 "diversity" visas, to be distributed to those nationalities that have been adversely affected by allotments under previous immigration laws. These visas will be allotted on a first-come, first-served basis, with each eligible country receiving a fixed number of visas. The 55,000 visas will not be available until October 1, 1994. During the period 1991-94, 40,000 transition diversity visas will be available annually.

The 1990 legislation sets out a detailed methodology for allocating the diversity visas—dividing them between "high admissions" and "low admissions" regions and countries—and the allocation system is likely to provide very few visas to South America, Mexico and Asia. More visas should go to Africa (East Africa, in particular) and Europe. Some have criticized the program as a return to the "national origins" quota system, which was biased in favour of Northern and Western Europeans. In fact, lobbying by Irish immigrant groups was crucial to the enactment of the diversity provision, and immigrants from Ireland received a guaranteed set-aside of the available transitional visas under the program.

Labour Market Impact as a Policy Factor

The American labour market has undeniably influenced United States immigration policy. In periods of labour shortages, the United States is receptive to foreign workers. However, when unemployment is high, stricter controls are placed on foreign workers.

The Mexican Braceros Program

During World War II, the United States experienced a serious agricultural labour shortage. Because of this need, the U.S. entered into an agreement with Mexico in 1942, allowing Mexican workers to work temporarily in American agriculture. Between four and five million Mexicans were employed under the Braceros Program until it ended in 1964.[16]

The United States was willing to accept a large number of Mexican migrants during labour shortages, but that willingness dissipated when those shortages ended. For example, following World War II, nativist sentiments were often directed towards Mexicans and Latin Americans. Moreover, Mexicans admitted under the Braceros program were victimized by civil rights violations, and their presence in the country was thought to depress wages in the Southwest. The Braceros Program expired in 1964 and was not renewed.

Business-Related Immigration and Mechanisms to Protect American Labour from Displacement

Immigration laws have provided for the admission of needed skilled and unskilled workers, and have also sought to protect American labour from displacement by these foreign workers. Business needs have favoured admissions, while political considerations have inspired solicitude for the interests of native workers. A sometimes contradictory immigration policy has resulted.

In 1885 the Contract Labor Law[17] was passed in response to employers transporting cheap labour from abroad. This law made it unlawful to import aliens under contract to perform any type of services or labour within the United States.

By 1952, there was widespread belief that foreign workers were necessary to fill the gaps in the American labour pool. Furthermore, the National Labor Relations Act and the Fair Labor Standards Act were perceived to offer sufficient protection against abuses by employers in their use of foreign labour.

The Immigration and Nationality Act of 1952 essentially presumed that foreign workers with offers of employment were admissible into the United States, unless American workers would suffer disadvantage; the Act thus gave the Secretary of State the power to block the entry of aliens who would perform skilled or unskilled labour if American workers would be displaced or if their wages or working conditions would be adversely affected. This law was amended in 1965 after intensive lobbying by the American Federation of Labor-Congress of Industrial Organization. After this amendment, the law presumed that foreign workers were not needed; the alien and his intended employer were to bear the burden of obtaining an individualized certification from the Department of Labor assuring them that there would be no such displacement or adverse impact.

Under a provision continued in current law, an alien is prohibited from entering the country to perform skilled or unskilled labour, unless the Secretary of Labor certifies that the alien will not displace a U.S. worker or adversely affect the wages and working conditions of similarly employed individuals in the United States. An alien is eligible for employment only if there are not sufficient American workers who are "able, willing, qualified ... and available at the time of application for a visa and admission...." Only then will labour certification be granted.

Refugees

Foreign Policy as an Incentive to Admission

Foreign policy considerations have long influenced which refugees are admitted to the United States. Such considerations are explicitly permitted by statute in annual consultations between the Executive Branch and Congress to establish overseas admissions schemes each year. They have also impermissibly influenced asylum adjudications. Specifically, in implementing the Refugee Act of 1980, the immigration authorities were required to seek advisory opinions in individual cases from the Department of State's Bureau of Human Rights and Humanitarian Affairs (BHRHA). Such opinions, to which an adjudicator may give "significant weight,"[18] are often distorted by foreign policy considerations. In practice, conclusory pronouncements by the State Department have frequently promoted ideological bias in asylum adjudications.

Immigration Enforcement Considerations

United States asylum policy has all too often reflected immigration enforcement priorities. One example is detention policy in the United States for arriving unadmitted aliens. In 1981, the INS began systematically detaining all Haitians entering the United States, until they underwent a hearing and status determination. This was a fundamental change from the prior policy, under which only those aliens who were determined to be likely to abscond or to pose a threat to national security were detained. Although the policy initially mandated only the detention of Haitians, a decision by a federal court judge resulted in INS extending the policy in 1982 to all arriving undocumented asylum seekers. That policy remained in effect until 1992.

The detention policy has caused extreme hardship to innocent asylum seekers. Detention was prolonged, frequently for over a year; detainees had limited access to outside communication and were held in remote locations, making access to counsel impracticable. The policy actually punished those "oppressed of other nations" whom Congress sought to welcome with the Refugee Act of 1980, which codified the right to apply for asylum. Yet, the policy has remained largely impervious to judicial challenge out of undue deference to the Executive Branch's prerogative to control immigration.[19]

On April 27, 1991, the INS Commissioner issued a memorandum establishing an eighteen-month pilot release program in four locations—New York, Miami, Los Angeles and San Francisco—and involving 200 arriving aliens. In those cities, aliens at ports of entry were detained only as long as it took to establish their identities and to ascertain that their claims appeared substantial and that they were not inadmissible on other grounds. The resulting detention periods were relatively brief. The success of that pilot program led the INS to expand the release program nationally and to make it permanent on April 20, 1992.

Current Arrangements in General

Under the Immigration Act of 1990, visas are to be distributed within three broad categories: family, employment and diversity. For each of fiscal years 1992-94, 465,000 visas will be allocated to persons who fall within one of the five "relative" categories. That number will increase to 480,000 in 1995 and thereafter. Employment-related visas number 140,000 under the 1990 Act. Forty thousand transition diversity visas are allocated for 1992-94, and, as of the fiscal year 1995 (beginning October 1, 1994), 55,000 diversity visas will be available. The number of visas granted will total 700,000 for the fiscal years 1992-94, but, after the expiration of certain transitional provisions, will decrease to 675,000 in 1995 and thereafter.

Current Arrangements in Family-Based Immigration

The 1990 Immigration Act made a number of changes in family-based immigration. First, it created five classifications for family-based immigration: immediate relatives and four different preference categories of increasingly distant degrees of family relations. Second, it set aside 465,000 visas to be allocated to family members. The 465,000 visas are distributed according to the four "preference" classifications. The number of family member visas is reduced by the number of immediate relative visas that were issued the year previously; there is, however, a floor of 226,000 visas for other relatives. The 1990 Act defines "immediate relatives" as spouses, minor children of U.S. citizens and parents of U.S. citizens over 21; and certain widows and widowers of U.S. citizens. An unlimited number of visas can be issued to immediate relatives.

The 1990 Act grants first preference status to unmarried children of U.S. citizens. Second preference status is given to the spouses, minor children and unmarried sons and daughters of permanent resident aliens. Third preference status is given to married sons and daughters of U.S. citizens. The fourth preference encompasses brothers and sisters of adult U.S. citizens. With no limit on the numbers of visas to immediate relatives, and with 465,000 visas allocated to other relatives, family-based immigration is significant. The total number of immigrants may exceed 700,000 (675,000 beginning in 1995) if the number of immediate relative applications increases.

The 1990 Act places per-country limitations on immigration. Each country is limited to 7 percent of 366,000 or 25,620 visas. Also, 75 percent of the spouses and minor children of permanent residents are exempt from the per-country limit. The 1990 Act also has a special provision for Hong Kong, according to which 10,000 visas will be granted for the fiscal years 1991-93, with an increase to 25,620 after 1993.

Business-Related Immigration

Skills-Oriented Criteria

The 1990 Act increases the number of visas available for employment-related immigration from 54,000 to 140,000, organized into five preference groups.[20] About forty thousand visas, as well as all unused special immigrant and investor visas, are allocated annually for first preference "priority workers." This category—which is similar to a category in the 1952 Act—encompasses persons with extraordinary ability in science, arts, business, education or athletics, outstanding professors and researchers, and multinational executives and managers.

The second preference group is allocated about 40,000 visas, plus any unused visas from the first preference category. This group includes professionals with advanced degrees and persons of exceptional ability in the arts, sciences or business.

The third preference group receives about 40,000 visas and any unused visas from the first and second preference groups. This group includes skilled workers with two or more years of training, who are generally professionals (no advanced degree requirement) and other workers, including unskilled labour.

About ten thousand additional visas are allocated to the fourth preference group for "Special Immigrants," including religious workers. Any unused visas are transferred to the first preference group and spill down to the second and third preference groups. The fifth preference group, which includes investors, is allocated about 10,000 visas. Again, any unused visas from the fifth group are transferred to the first preference group and, from there, potentially to the second and third groups.

The 1990 Act requires that all employers seeking labour certification for an alien give notice of such application to the union's bargaining representative or, if there is no such representative, to all employees at the facility. Furthermore, any person, even if he or she is not an applicant for the position in question, may comment formally to the Department of Labor during the certification process.

Investor Provisions and Economic Development Policy

To promote foreign investment in the United States, the Immigration Act of 1990 allocates 10,000 visas to persons entering the United States to engage in a new commercial venture. An alien must have invested at least $1 million in the commercial enterprise to qualify for these visas. Furthermore, the venture must benefit the U.S. economy and must create full-time employment for at least ten U.S. citizens or lawful residents, not including the immigrant or his or her spouse or children.

The "employment creation" immigrant status was intended by Congress to encourage investment in rural areas and in areas with a high unemployment rate. Three thousand of the 10,000 visas are specifically reserved for persons establishing new commercial ventures in these areas. In order to qualify for these visas, the investment in these targeted areas may be less than $1 million (but not less than $500,000). Furthermore, the Attorney General is authorized to increase the necessary investment from $1 million to $3 million for investments in metropolitan areas with low unemployment rates.

Immigration Enforcement Through Employment Controls

Denial of employment authorization is the principal enforcement technique contemplated under the 1986 Immigration Reform and Control Act.[21] Specifically, persons with no legal status in the United States authorizing work are barred from employment. In the past, this legal disability did not stop employers from hiring undocumented aliens, and the fact that they were not legally allowed to be in or to work in the country created conditions ripe for their exploitation. The 1986 law provided for sanctions on those employers who hire unauthorized workers. The penalties are initially civil fines, but can become criminal penalties for repeat offenders.

Under the statute, it is unlawful for an employer to "knowingly" hire, recruit or refer for hire aliens who lack work authorization. The employer must examine a job applicant's documentation of his or her identity and permission to work. The employer must retain a form attesting to having made the proper verification. In this way, the employer can avoid exposure to sanctions. If the employer believed that an employee could legally be hired—for example, if false documents were presented—his or her good faith is a complete defence to sanction. Some have argued that a reliable identifying card or system will be necessary to enforce employer sanctions fully. Civil libertarians, however, have resisted the notion as an unwarranted infringement on personal privacy.

Employer sanctions have been criticized for encouraging unlawful discrimination. Employers may be reluctant to hire individuals who look or sound foreign, for example, if they look or sound Hispanic, for fear of being subject to sanctions. The law does, however, include an antidiscrimination provision, stating that it is an "unfair immigration-related practice" to discriminate against an individual because of national origin or against a citizen or prospective citizen because of his or her citizenship status. In practice, such discrimination has proven difficult to eradicate, although several employer and worker educational activities are currently underway.

Social Policy

Social objectives, in addition to political and economic considerations, have sometimes animated the formulation of immigration policy in the United

States. Early objections to immigration, for example, were based on concerns about maintaining American culture and traditions. Recently, other issues have become the focus of intense debate. The issue is almost always whether individuals who possess a particular trait should be permitted to immigrate to the United States, or whether their possession of that trait renders them undesirable for admission or subject to expulsion.

One such trait is the possession of prohibited political beliefs. When Congress passed the McCarran-Walter Act in 1952[22] over President Truman's veto, it specifically designated Communist ideology as such a trait: those aliens who were Communists or anarchists were barred from admission to the United States. Specifically, the 1952 Act permitted government authorities to deny visas or immigration status to aliens who were considered to jeopardize the public interest or national security, or who proposed to engage in activities that advocated certain proscribed doctrines.

By 1990, the U.S. State Department had compiled a list of about 345,000 individuals who were denied visas to the United States on ideological grounds; two-thirds of the people on that list have been added since 1980.[23] Those on the list were often not aware that they were ineligible to receive a visa until after the application was made and denied. Frequently, the denials were unjustified. The ideological exclusion provisions were criticized both for penalizing prospective entrants for purely political views and for denying United States citizens the opportunity to hear those views expressed. These exclusion provisions of the McCarran-Walter Act were repealed in most respects in 1990. Substituted in their place were provisions to deny admission to an applicant whose entry could adversely affect U.S. foreign policy objectives, and to disqualify for immigrant visas those who had been members of certain proscribed organizations, subject to limited waiver opportunities.

Another controversial trait is testing positive for the HIV virus. The need to contain the spread of AIDS is the stated rationale for the exclusion. Critics contended that the real animus was directed at the carriers—often Haitians or homosexual men—rather than at the disease.

Currently, U.S. immigration law allows for exclusion of aliens determined by the Secretary of Health and Human Services (HHS) to have a "communicable disease of public health significance," subject to limited waivers. Aliens who carry diseases that would pose such a risk can be excluded. HHS is responsible for determining which diseases meet the newly-promulgated standard, and HIV is currently so defined. The contentious issue is not whether HIV is communicable (as it obviously is), but rather whether its possession by an individual seeking entry would pose a risk "of public health significance." The Department of Health and Human Services recommended that HIV not be a ground of exclusion. But the ground was retained as a concession to the political right wing, which organized a massive letter-writing campaign to oppose HHS's proposal.

Refugees

Refugees can gain status in the United States in one of two ways: they can either be determined a refugee and be admitted from abroad, or they can apply for and be granted asylum once in the United States. Both procedures lead to permanent resident status. The 1980 Refugee Act gives U.S. officials the power to establish annual ceilings for overseas admissions. Political biases are integral to the design of the system. When the president, in consultation with Congress, establishes the ceilings for refugee admissions, he or she is supposed to consider "foreign policy" in determining which refugees are of "special humanitarian concern" to the United States. This designation paves the way for the application of political and geographical standards. Overseas refugees admissions thus reflect political and ethnic biases. The vast majority of refugees admitted from abroad over the past decade have been those fleeing Communism in Eastern Europe, the Soviet Union and Indochina.

Once an asylum seeker arrives at the United States border, he or she is exempt from admissions ceilings. Here, he or she can apply for asylum, irrespective of his or her immigration status. The protection claim can be made affirmatively to the Immigration and Naturalization Service, or raised as a defence to removal in immigration court proceedings. Final asylum rules issued in 1990 created a professional corps of adjudicators who are to be assisted by a documentation centre on conditions in the country of origin. Adequate resources will be required, of course, for effective implementation in order to achieve the insulation from foreign policy and immigration enforcement considerations contemplated in the issuance of the 1990 rules.

The Import of Human Rights Law

General provisions of international human rights law constitute constraints on a government's immigration policy and refugee protection arrangements. Specific human rights precepts can thus be considered to apply to U.S. policy and practice in these areas.

Among the most fundamental tenets of international human rights law is the prohibition of invidious discrimination. The 1948 Universal Declaration of Human Rights[24] provides in Article 2 that all persons are entitled to protection of their fundamental human rights "without distinction of any kind, such as race, colour, sex, language, religion, political or other opinion,

national or social origin, property, birth or other status." Among these
fundamental entitlements are the right to recognition as a person before the
law (Article 6), equal protection under the law (Article 7), an effective
judicial remedy (Article 8), not to be subjected to arbitrary detention (Article
9), a fair hearing (Article 10), freedom from arbitrary interference with
privacy and the family (Article 12), freedom of movement (Article 13),
freedom to seek and enjoy asylum (Article 14), freedom of thought and
conscience (Article 18), freedom of opinion and expression (Article 19), and
freedom of peaceful assembly and association (Article 20). These broad
principles are codified in the International Covenant on Civil and Political
Rights,[25] to which the U.S. became a party in 1992. Beyond these universal
principles, international refugee law—the 1951 Convention relating to the
Status of Refugees and its 1967 Protocol[26] (to which the U.S. became a party
in 1968)—provides specific protection for refugees (Article 1), including
nonreturn to places of persecution (Article 33) and avoidance of unnecessary detention (Article 31).

The humanitarian justifications for U.S. immigration and refugee policy—
family unity and protection from persecution—find specific support under
human rights law. Other justifications, such as labour market needs or
economic development, are not directly related to civil and political rights.
Certain immigration objectives and initiatives, however, contravene human rights provisions, including the doctrine under which certain aliens
who have not effected a technical immigration law "entry" into the U.S.[27] are
deprived of constitutional equal protection or due process of law. Addition-
ally, measures subjecting asylum seekers to arbitrary or unnecessary detention and summary return procedures (like those used with Haitian boat
people) infringe on universal standards. A rights perspective would also
condemn a violation of associational or privacy freedoms in admissions
criteria.

Invidious discrimination in the formulation of immigration policy obviously offends general human rights principles. Also, the infusion of
nonhumanitarian foreign and immigration policy in refugee reception and
status determination may specifically violate international refugee law.
Application of human rights law in the formulation of immigration and
refugee law can thus identify which factors are impermissible for purposes
of policy making, and, conversely, which factors should be promoted in the
policy process.

Conclusion

A complex combination of factors have influenced the formulation of U.S.
immigration and refugee policy. Principal among the factors are race,

labour market impact and foreign policy. When measured against universal human rights law and principles, certain factors are violative and should be eliminated. Others are not incompatible with human rights, including labour market impact or foreign policy objectives, at least where they are not used as pretexts to diminish humanitarian considerations. Still other factors, including family unity and protection from persecution, are explicitly recognized in international law and should be enhanced.

Specifically, admissions criteria based explicitly or implicitly on invidious racial discrimination or political affiliation violate human rights principles and should be eliminated. Of course, difficulties may arise in proving official motive in instances where provisions are explicitly neutral but result from implicit racial motivations. The legal fiction that diminishes the right of an unadmitted alien to be a person before the law should be abolished. On the other hand, respect for family life would favour enhancing affirmative admissions arrangements to promote family unity and prohibit measures that would infringe impermissibly on personal privacy, including the moral judgements that were implicit in retaining HIV as an exclusion ground.

Fundamentally, then, any conflict between human rights and perceptions of national identity and self-interest must focus on the quality and substance of those perceptions. Some are neutral and unremarkable. Other assertions of self-interest are in reality concealed expressions of bigotry and prejudice, which are erroneously equated with national identity. Such considerations are in clear conflict with the values of a society established on principles of fundamental human rights. They should be excluded from the policy process.

Notes

1. Aleinikoff and Martin, "Immigration: Process and Policy."
2. July 29, 1868, United States-China, 16 Stat. 739, T.S. No. 48.
3. Nov. 17, 1880, United States-China, 22 Stat. 826, T.S. No. 49. According to Article I of this treaty, the United States could "regulate, limit or suspend such coming or residence, but not prohibit it."
4. *Chae Chan Ping v. United States*, 130 U.S. 581 (1889).
5. Gordon and Mailman, "Immigration Law and Procedure," 12-18.
6. The Immigration and Nationality Act of 1952, Pub. L. No. 82-414, 66 Stat. 163, secs. 201(a) and 202(b), 8 U.S.C. §§1151(a) and 1152(b).
7. Immigration Act of 1924, Act of May 26, 1924, 43 Stat. 153.
8. Note 4, *supra*.

9. The Immigration and Nationality Act, sec. 202(a), 8 U.S.C. §1152(a), as amended by sec. 2, Act of Oct. 3, 1965, Pub. L. No. 89-236, 79 Stat. 911.

10. Helton, "Political Asylum Under the 1980 Refugee Act: An Unfulfilled Promise," 243.

11. This general pattern appears to be repeating in 1992. As of the end of February, 51,585 refugees were admitted into the United States, but only 1,503 (about 2.9 percent) were from Africa; of these Africans, 1,102 (73 percent) were from Ethiopia.

12. Lawyers Committee for Human Rights, "Refugee Refoulement: The Forced Return of Haitians Under the U.S.-Haitian Interdiction Agreement," 10.

13. According to the New York Protocol of 1967 which incorporates the pertinent provisions of the 1951 United Nations Convention relating to the Status of Refugees, a "refugee" is a person who "owing to a well-founded fear of persecution for reasons of race, religion, nationality, membership in a particular social group or political opinion, is outside the country of his nationality and is unable or, owing to such fear, unwilling to avail himself of the protection of that country." 19 U.S.T. 6223, T.I.A.S. No 6577, 606 U.N.T.S. 267.

14. Article 33 of the Protocol, to which the United States is a party, *supra* note 13, prohibits the "return" of refugees in "any manner whatsoever" to a place of possible persecution.

15. Immigration Act of 1990, Act of Nov. 29, 1990, Pub.L. No. 101-649, 104 Stat. 4978.

16. The literal translation of "bracero" is "one who works with his arms."

17. The Contract Labor Law of 1885, Act of Feb. 26, 1885, Ch. 164, 23 Stat. 332.

18. *In re Salim*, Interim Dec. No. 2922 (BIA 1982).

19. Helton, "The Mandate of U.S. Courts to Protect Aliens and Refugees Under International Human Rights Law," 2339-341.

20. Section 302(b)(2) of the Miscellaneous and Technical Immigration and Naturalization Amendments, Pub. L. No. 102-232, amended the five employment-based preferences, redefining the fixed numbers as percentages. Thus, in a year in which the worldwide ceiling is 140,000, the first three preference groups would receive 40,040 (instead of 40,000) (28.6 percent) and the last two preference groups would receive 9,940 (instead of 10,000) (7.1 percent). The amendment ensures appropriate allocation in any year in which the worldwide allocation exceeds 140,000, as it would if family-sponsored visas go unused in a previous year.

21. Immigration Reform and Control Act of 1986, Pub. L. No. 99-603, 100 Stat. 3359.

22. Note 4, *supra*, sec. 212 (a), 8 U.S.C. Sec. 1182 (a).

23. Lawyers Committee for Human Rights, "The Alien Blacklist: A Dangerous Legacy of the McCarthy Era," 6.

24. G.A. res 217 A (III), 10 Dec. 1948.

25. G.A. res 2200 A (XXI), 16 Dec. 1966.

26. Note 9, *supra*.

27. *See* The Association of the Bar of the City of New York, The Committee on Civil Rights, "The Right to Recognition as a Person Before the Law: The Case for Abolishing the Immigration Law Entry Doctrine," 46 The Record 304 (1991).

References

Aleinikoff, Thomas A., and David A. Martin. *Immigration Process and Policy.* 2d ed. St. Paul, Minnesota: West Publishing Co., 1991.

Carliner, David, Lucas Guttentag, Arthur C. Helton, and Wade J. Henderson. *The Rights of Aliens.* Carbondale, Illinois: Southern Illinois University Press, 1990.

Gordon, Charles, and Stanley Mailman. *Immigration Law and Procedure.* New York: Matthew Bender & Co., 1991.

Helton, Arthur C. "Political Asylum Under the 1980 Refugee Act: An Unfulfilled Promise." In *University of Michigan Journal of Law Reform* 17 (Winter 1984) 17:243.

_____. "The Mandate of U.S. Courts to Protect Aliens and Refugees Under International Human Rights Law." In *The Yale Law Journal* 100 (1991):2335.

Lawyers Committee for Human Rights. "Refugee Refoulement: The Forced Return of Haitians Under the U.S.-Haitian Interdiction Agreement." New York: Lawyers Committee for Human Rights, 1990.

_____. "The Alien Blacklist: A Dangerous Legacy of the McCarthy Era." New York: Lawyers Committee for Human Rights, 1990.

Contributors

Howard Adelman is Professor of Philosophy and Director of the Centre for Refugee Studies at York University. He was also a founder of the Refugee Documentation Project (a research centre on refugees), Operation Lifeline (the organization that led in organizing Canadian private sponsorship of Indochinese refugees), as well as *Refuge*, Canada's periodical on refugees.

Rainer Bauböck is Assistant Professor at the Institute for Advanced Studies, Department of Political Science. He has published books and articles on the political status of minorities, on labour migration, social policy issues and the domestic labour debate. His main theoretical interest is in politics and the policies of migration, ethnicity and nationalism. He is currently writing a book on transnational citizenship.

A. Essuman-Johnson is Lecturer in Political Science at the University of Ghana at Legon. He is currently studying the refugee problem in West Africa. His research covers international politics and the political economy of African development.

Grant Farr is the Vice Provost for International Education at Portland State University and Director of the Middle East Studies Centre. He has worked for a number of years with Afghan refugees and has published a number of works on this subject. He has travelled and lived extensively in Pakistan, Iran and Afghanistan.

Lois Foster is a Reader in Sociology at La Trobe University in Melbourne, Australia, and is currently seconded as a social research consultant to the federal Bureau of Immigration Research.

Tomas Hammar is affiliated with the Centre for Research in International Migration and Ethnic Relations at Stockholm University.

Arthur C. Helton is a lawyer and Director of the Refugee Project of the Lawyers Committee for Human Rights. He is also chairperson of the Advisory Committee to the New York State Inter-Agency Task Force on Immigration Affairs and an Adjunct Professor of Law at the New York University School of Law, where he teaches immigration and refugee law.

Gaim Kibreab is Associate Professor at Uppsala University in Sweden. He studied law at Haile Selassie University in Ethiopia. His research is on African refugees in relations to development problems. He has written several books and articles on the subject, and is currently studying the environmental impact of refugee settlements in the Sudan.

Lawrence Lam is Assistant Professor of Sociology at York University and Associate Director (Education) at the Centre for Refugee Studies. He has written numerous journal articles, book chapters and reports, including a forthcoming book on Vietnamese boat people in Hong Kong. His expertise is in refugee studies, international migration and Chinese minorities in Canada.

Oscar Schiappa-Pietra is a lawyer and consultant to the Inter-American Institute of Human Rights, President of the National Commission for Displaced Population in Peru, Professor at San Marcos Law School and former advisor to the Prime Minister of Peru.

Frédéric Tiberghien is a graduate in Economic and Political Science and Philosophy. Maître des Requêtes au Conseil d'Etat, he is currently Président Directeur Général de l'Entreprise Générale de Télécommunications, Paris, France. He is a member of the administrative council of "France Terre d'Asile", President of the association "Documentation Réfugiés" and vice-president of the UNHCR French Committee. He published a book entitled "La protection des réfugiés en France" and is also a co-editor of "Les réfugiés dans le monde."

Index